Empty Beds

Empty Beds

Indian Student Health at Sherman Institute, 1902-1922

Jean A. Keller

Michigan State University Press • *East Lansing*

Michigan State University Press
East Lansing, Michigan 48823–5245
Printed and bound in the United States of America.

08   07   06   05   04   03   02   1   2   3   4   5   6   7   8   9   10

LIBRARY OF CONGRESS CATALOGING-IN-PUBLICATION DATA
Keller, Jean A., 1953–
Empty beds : Indian student health at Sherman Institute, 1902–1922 / Jean A. Keller.
p. cm. — Native American series
Includes bibliographical references and index.
ISBN 0-87013-633-x (cloth : alk. paper) – ISBN 0-87013-650-x (paper : alk. paper)
1. Sherman Institute (Riverside, Calif.) 2. Indians of North America—Health and hygiene—
California—History. 3. School health services—California—History. Indian students—Health and
hygiene—California—History. 4. Off-reservation boarding schools—California—History.
5. School Health Services—History—California. 6. History of Medicine, 20th Cent.—California.
7. Indians, North American—education—California. I. Title. II. Series.
RA448 .5 .I5K45 2002
362.1'089'97079497—dc21
20-02014206

Book and cover design by Sharp Des!gns, Lansing, MI

Visit Michigan State University Press on the World Wide Web at: *www.msupress.msu.edu*

Dedication

THIS BOOK IS DEDICATED TO MY HUSBAND, BRUCE, AND TO MY DAUGHTER and son, Sloane and Jackson, for their never-ending support and encouragement. My accomplishment is their accomplishment. Years of bringing books and papers everywhere we went did not dull their enthusiasm for my work, and after all this time, they still love to hear my stories about the children of Sherman Institute. This book is also dedicated to my mother, Judy Duff, who raised me to believe I could do anything and when I doubted, taught me the value of a "carrot." Her wisdom kept me going.

To Lori Sisquoc (Fort Sill Apache/Cahuilla), curator of the Sherman Indian Museum and my friend, I offer gratitude and deepest thanks. Without the unlimited access Lori provided to archival records of Sherman Institute, I could not have conducted my research. Lori's intelligence and insight enriched the research, and her companionship made it a truly enjoyable experience.

Last, but certainly not least, I dedicate this book to Cliff Trafzer (Wyandot), my friend and mentor. He saw something in me that I did not see in myself and took the time to teach me what to look for. With his trust and encouragement, I developed the confidence necessary to complete this book the way it needed to be done.

Contents

Figures

Tables

Abbreviations Used in Notes

ARBIC	Annual Report of the Board of Indian Commissioners
ARCIA	Annual Report of the Commissioner of Indian Affairs
ARSI	Annual Report of the Secretary of the Interior
BIA	Records of the Bureau of Indian Affairs (National Archives, Record Group 75)
CIA	Commissioner of Indian Affairs
CSF	Classified Student Files
LPB	Letterpress Book
LR	Letters Received (Records of the Superintendent)
LS	Letters Sent (Records of the Superintendent)
NA	National Archives
PSWR	Pacific Southwest Region (Laguna Niguel, California)
SI	Records of Sherman Institute (National Archives, Pacific Southwest Region, Record Group 75)
SIMA	Sherman Indian Museum Archives
TR	Telegrams Received (Records of the Superintendent)
TS	Telegrams Sent (Records of the Superintendent)

Preface

ONE HUNDRED YEARS AFTER THE ESTABLISHMENT OF THE SHERMAN INSTI-
tute in Riverside, California, only a single original building remains.
Once the school's administration building, it now houses the Sherman
Indian Museum, a place rich in Native American culture, both past and
present. Near the back of the museum lies "The Vault." It is a small, cool,
and dark room, secured by a heavy metal door, designed to provide a safe
place for things of importance. On the shelves lining the vault's walls sit
stacks of old student registers, letterpress books, yearbooks, cherished
artifacts, and boxes containing thousands of loose documents. All these
are things of importance, in that they provide tangible evidence of
Sherman Institute's history and of the lives of students attending the
school for the past hundred years. Though documents relating to
Sherman Institute are also found at the National Archives in Laguna
Niguel, California, it is in the vault at the Sherman Indian Museum that
the heart of the school's history lies.

The documents at the Sherman Indian Museum remain as they were
when placed in the vault as long ago as 1902. Tissue pages of letterpress
books remain stuck together by ink not completely dried when closed;
loose documents are packaged in brown paper and tied with red ribbon.
Lori Sisquoc (Fort Sill Apache/Cahuilla), curator of the Sherman Institute
Museum, and I opened these records with care and wonder, cognizant
of the incredible fact that we were the first to peruse these records of

history since they were created lifetimes ago. In exploring these precious resources, we looked for clues to student life and health at Sherman Institute, of children separated from their families, sometimes never to return home. As mothers, we viewed this journey of discovery with reverence and, ultimately, with love for the children whose lives we came to know. The children listed in Sherman Institute documents were not simply names, but other mothers' children. This perspective shaped research and writing, as important issues of student health, sickness, and death were explored.

Student health at nonreservation Indian boarding schools in the United States was not always considered an important issue. Beginning with the establishment of Carlisle Indian School in 1879, nonreservation boarding schools earned a deserved reputation of being unhealthy environments for Indian children. This was largely the result of an educational orientation that placed more emphasis on expeditiously assimilating as many Indian children as possible than on insuring that the educational and living environments into which the children were placed were worthy of their lives. Little thought was given to the health of Indian children sent to the schools. However, as student morbidity and mortality at the schools escalated precipitously, Indian Office officials came to realize that student health was a necessary prerequisite for education. Further, the presence of sick and dying Indian children proved catastrophic for public relations, particularly as Indian parents refused to send their children to nonreservation boarding schools because of the perception that such places would be detrimental to their children's health. Unhealthy living conditions at nonreservation boarding schools threatened to seriously impact the efficaciousness of the assimilation program so aggressively pursued by the U.S. government.

By the time of Sherman Institute's establishment in 1901, an increasing recognition of the important role student health played in Indian education had begun to emerge throughout the country, in large part due to the actions of Progressive Era reformers. This recognition led to Indian Office policy changes intended to prevent continuing student morbidity and mortality at nonreservation boarding schools. The policies incorporated an array of preventive measures, including physical plant design, sanitation, education, and medical care. However, funding constraints and a lackadaisical attitude among many superintendents resulted in only limited improvements to the living environment and student health at nonreservation boarding schools.

This was not the case at Sherman Institute. Priority attention given to student health by the school's superintendents and medical personnel resulted in Sherman Institute maintaining a healthy living environment for students throughout the research period—1902 to 1922. Epidemics, accidents, and illnesses occurred throughout this period, many of which resulted in students' deaths. Yet, compared to the morbidity and mortality at other nonreservation boarding schools, among reservation populations, and within the white community, Sherman Institute students faired very well. Strict compliance with Indian Office preventive health policies and implementation of school-specific health practices resulted in a relatively healthy student population at Sherman Institute during the research period.

Nonreservation boarding schools have been the subject of many works by noted scholars such as David Adams, Brenda Child, Michael Coleman, K. Tsianina Lomawaima, Scott Riney, and Robert Trennert. Each of these studies provided an important comparative context within which to view Sherman Institute. Work by these scholars offered invaluable data regarding the political and administrative aspects of other nonreservation boarding schools, thus facilitating an understanding of the machinations involved in running Sherman Institute. This proved to be of particular benefit, since scholarly studies of Sherman Institute have never before been conducted. Unfortunately, published research on nonreservation boarding schools has given student health issues only cursory consideration. The reasons for this are varied, but probably have a great deal to do both with the complexity of the issue and with the availability, or lack thereof, of complete medical records. Works by the referenced scholars were intended to offer an overview of the subject institutions, rather than a comprehensive study of a single aspect of them.

In her dissertation, "Fighting the Scourge: American Indian Morbidity and Federal Indian Policy, 1897–1928," Diane Therese Putney offered a brilliant study of health issues at nonreservation boarding schools in terms of federal policy. Without the use of Putney's research, it would not have been possible to study student health at Sherman Institute in a meaningful context. Her work allowed a far deeper understanding of the many facets of Indian student health at nonreservation boarding schools than would have been possible utilizing only the available documents housed at the Sherman Indian Museum and the National Archives.

Without the dedicated assistance of Lori Sisquoc at the Sherman Indian Museum and Paul Wormser at the National Archives in Laguna Niguel, research for this book would probably have taken years longer and not been nearly as thorough. Lori allowed unlimited access to the thousands of documents housed in the museum vault and aided in the journey of discovery, sharing both triumphs and defeats. Of greater importance, she provided insight into Native American culture and traditions that had a profound influence on my interpretation of the data contained within the documents. Lori continually reminded me that the documents contained only one version of the truth. Paul suggested avenues of research previously not considered and brought out box after box of archival documents, with nary a complaint. When information seemed conflicting or perplexing, he served as a sounding board for my musings. Even when staff was shorthanded and time a critical factor, Paul insured that hundreds of documents were copied and delivered into my hands.

Finally, reviews of this manuscript by Cliff Trafzer, Monte Kugel, and Roger Ransom, all of the Department of History, University of California, Riverside, proved particularly beneficial in defining the focus of salient issues, heeding the Native voice, and remembering that documents provide only data. Understanding the health issues of Indian students at Sherman Institute required much more than simply compiling data, but instead, remembering that each name and each action was that of an individual who acted in the context of time and culture.

———

Introduction

RESEARCH FOR THIS BOOK BEGAN WITH THE THESIS THAT NONRESERVATION boarding schools operated as death factories for Indian children. I did not base this thesis on knowledge, but on perception. Prior research on Native American disease and epidemiology in the nineteenth century and cursory information about the living environments at nonreservation boarding schools convinced me that such places would be natural breeding grounds for diseases of all types. Numerous secondary references to multiple deaths resulting from epidemics, and boarding school cemeteries filled with Indian children, reinforced this perception. I was quite sure that research into student health at Sherman Institute would support my thesis. Since Sherman Institute had been in existence almost one hundred years, and student health seemed to be a significant issue in nonreservation boarding schools, I also believed I would find an abundance of information pertaining to both. None of these assumptions proved to be true.

Sherman Institute formally opened its doors on 9 September 1902 in Riverside, California. It continues to operate today as Sherman Indian High School, one of only four remaining nonreservation boarding schools in the United States. The school began as Perris Indian School, located in Perris, California, approximately twenty miles south of Riverside. Perris Indian School opened in 1892 with an initial student population of 8, expanding to 350 by the time Sherman Institute opened in 1902.

Although almost the entire student population and staff moved en masse from Perris Indian School to Sherman Institute, some of the younger students and a matron remained at the Perris school until 1904, with Harwood Hall serving as superintendent for both schools.

Hall had been instrumental in lobbying for the closure of Perris Indian School and the establishment of Sherman Institute. He based his arguments for closure primarily on the issue of unhealthy living conditions due to an inadequate supply of water. Conversely, he based his arguments for establishing a new school on the healthy environment of Riverside, its abundant water supply, and the civilizing influence of Riverside's genteel citizens on the school's Indian students. Despite the fact that in 1901 there existed a growing consensus against nonreservation boarding schools as proper venues of education for Indians, Congress approved funding for the construction of Sherman Institute, and the following year it opened as one of the flagship schools in the Indian School Service.

Research revealed that with the exception of a few undergraduate essay papers on the history of Sherman Institute, nothing had ever been written about either Perris Indian School or Sherman Institute, in spite of the fact that they had a combined tenure of over one hundred years. That Riverside is a university town with three institutions of higher learning within its corporate boundaries and several more in adjacent towns added to the incredulity that scholarly discourses on Sherman Institute did not exist. Consequently, before conducting research on student health at Sherman Institute, it became necessary to research the school itself, as well as Perris Indian School, in order to provide a context into which to place the issue of health. From this research emerged comprehensive histories of both schools that will be future publishing endeavors.

Although research revealed an abundance of information regarding various issues at Sherman Institute, such as politics, economics, curriculum, religion, and the outing program, the sole focus of this book is student health. Each of these elements in some way touches the issue of health, but in this book they are dealt with insofar as they add necessary perspective, and are not used as theoretical or analytical adjuncts. So too,

neither the history of Indian education in the United States nor the particularly heinous invention of nonreservation boarding schools are
included. These are topics worthy of study in their own right, and they
have, in fact, been written about numerous times by other scholars. This
book is thus finely focused on student health at Sherman Institute
between the years of 1902 and 1922.

As career Indian School Service bureaucrats, Sherman Institute
superintendents Harwood Hall (1902–9) and Frank Conser (1909–22)
documented every transaction at the school, no matter how small.
Consequently, there currently exist literally thousands of primary source
documents detailing the minutiae of life during the twenty-year research
period. This material is housed at the Sherman Indian Museum and the
Pacific Southwest Region National Archives in Laguna Niguel, California.
Since health had become an important issue by the time Sherman
Institute opened, a considerable portion of these documents deal with
health issues at the school.

The primary source documents include letterpress books, loose documents, and student files. Most of the documents represent correspondence between the commissioner of Indian affairs and school
superintendents. The remainder includes payment vouchers; requests for
authorization; personnel reports; supply orders; and correspondence
between superintendents and reservation teachers, supervisors, students,
and parents. Student case files include enrollment applications, physical
health certifications, curriculum and grades, letters, and in some cases,
detailed hospital records. Unfortunately, however, students' voices are
sorely lacking from the available primary source material.

Only a very few letters from students, and no letters to students from
family members, remain in the existing archival collections. In large part,
this is due to the Sherman Institute superintendents' practice of allowing students to retain private correspondence. They encouraged students
to write letters to their families at least on a monthly basis, and when
return letters arrived, they gave them directly to the students. These letters remained in the students' personal belongings and presumably were
taken with them when the students returned home.

Understanding that the lack of Native voices impacted the depth of research, I endeavored to obtain information from the descendants of Sherman Institute students. Letters were sent to the tribal councils of every Southern California tribe and reservation from which students came to Sherman Institute between 1902 and 1922. The letters apprised council members of the research I was conducting, offered to share any information regarding students from their tribe or reservation, and asked if any tribal member who had memories, stories, letters, photographs, and so on from students would be willing to share them with me, even if they did not want them included in the book. Only Morongo Reservation responded, enthusiastically posting my query on the reservation cable television station. Unfortunately, there were no respondents. An alumni oral history project planned for the centennial celebration of Sherman Institute in October 2001 will hopefully add the missing Native voices to the research, although they will regrettably not be included in this book.

Following completion of the primary source research, I endeavored to place information obtained for Sherman Institute in a comparative context. How did student health at Sherman Institute compare with that of other nonreservation boarding schools, of reservation populations, and of the white community?

The quest for comparative health data from nonreservation boarding schools of the era proved frustrating. While a number of books have been written about Indian education in the nineteenth and twentieth centuries, those that both focus on nonreservation boarding schools and encompass the years between 1902 and 1922 are limited to six. Unfortunately, few of these books provide more than a cursory, qualitative discussion of student health, and none offer quantitative data regarding morbidity and mortality.

The most comprehensive discussion of student health at a nonreservation boarding school during the research period is found in Scott Riney's *The Rapid City Indian School, 1898–1933*. In "Providing for the Children," Riney devotes several pages to health issues at the school, including medical care, preventive measures, epidemics, tuberculosis, and trachoma.[1]

However, because the school did not keep accurate records of illnesses and deaths, detailed information is not available for comparative purposes. Riney found far more information on the preventive health procedures implemented at Rapid City, and many of these are the same as those found at Sherman Institute, potentially offering important comparative opportunities. Yet, without the accompanying morbidity and mortality statistics, such comparisons lack depth and relevance.

While Michael Coleman covers health issues at all schools in only six pages and offers no quantitative or procedural data with which to compare Sherman Institute, in *American Indian Children at School, 1850–1930*, he offers invaluable insight into student attitudes toward disease. Coleman notes that students "generally did not blame the schools for the sickness which struck them or kin or schoolmates."[2] In Coleman's research, he found that Native American narrators often specifically noted the concern and dedication of teachers and medical staff during health crises. The few Sherman Institute student letters pertaining to health communicate the same sentiment. Students did not blame the school or medical staff for their illnesses, but thanked them for the care given. Students sent home because of illness often wrote to Sherman Institute superintendents, asking to be allowed to return to school.[3]

K. Tsianina Lomawaima's *They Called It Prairie Light* offers wonderful insight into Chilocco Indian School from the students' perspective, but unfortunately, the book focuses on the 1920s and 1930s. Only four pages summarize the lives of "The First Students," and only one sentence mentions health matters, clearly limiting the comparative value of the work with this study of Sherman Institute.[4]

At eight pages, Robert A. Trennert Jr.'s discussion of health in *The Phoenix Indian School: Forced Assimilation in Arizona, 1892–1935*, exceeds that of any other secondary source on nonreservation boarding schools.[5] However, this discussion has as its dual focus trachoma and tuberculosis, with little more than one paragraph devoted to all other illnesses and epidemics. While tuberculosis and trachoma clearly represented the most important threats to Indian student health at both Phoenix Indian School and Sherman Institute, Trennert offers no comparative quantitative data.

Boarding School Seasons by Brenda J. Child offers a unique look at nonreservation boarding school life through the eyes of children at Flandreau Indian School and Haskell Institute between 1900 and 1940.[6] Child devotes an entire chapter to "Illness and Death," but unfortunately provides little specific information that could be utilized on a comparative basis with Sherman Institute. Much of her narrative is in relation to the Meriam report of 1928, occurring after the end of the Sherman Institute research period.[7]

Finally, David Wallace Adams offers "Coping with Disease and Death," encompassing eleven pages within *Education for Extinction: American Indians and the Boarding School Experience, 1875–1928.*[8] Although providing a succinct summary of health in nonreservation boarding schools during the research period, accompanied by enlightening excerpts from student letters, Adams provides no details regarding disease at specific boarding schools, quantitative or otherwise.

Based on the above summaries of existing secondary works on health at nonreservation boarding schools between 1902 and 1922, it is obvious that this book is unique. In addition to providing the only scholarly discourse on Sherman Institute, it offers the only study of student health at nonreservation boarding schools during the early twentieth century. The comprehensive data provided here relating to student health at Sherman Institute, both qualitative and quantitative, will enable future researchers of student health at other nonreservation boarding schools to compare their health data with that of at least one school.

This book is organized topically, with the chronological progression of each topic contained within the relevant chapter. Although each chapter deals with a particular student health issue at Sherman Institute between 1902 and 1922, the organizational orientation of the book is based on two main concepts: prevention and results. This orientation facilitates analysis of the efficacy of health policies designed by the Indian Office and Sherman Institute superintendents to prevent student morbidity and mortality. In other words, what was done to prevent student illness and death at Sherman Institute, and did it work?

The first three chapters—"Design for Living," "Prevention," and "Medical Care"—discuss the preventive health policies and practices implemented at Sherman Institute between 1902 and 1922. As one of the last nonreservation boarding schools built in the United States, Sherman Institute benefited from lessons learned through tragic mistakes at established schools. By the beginning of the twentieth century, the Indian Office recognized student health as being important, and within a few years, health emerged as the most critical issue in Indian education. This recognition resulted in the creation of numerous preventive health policies and programs that were integrated into everything from Sherman Institute's design to its curriculum. Further, school superintendents Harwood Hall (1902–9) and Frank Conser (1909–22) were both seasoned Indian school administrators who, as dedicated bureaucrats, strictly complied with Indian Office policy. They also brought to Sherman Institute health policies and practices that in their experience at other boarding schools had been successful in maintaining and improving student health. The combination of compliance with Indian Office health policies and the implementation of school-specific health practices created an environment at Sherman Institute intended to maintain a healthy student population.

The last four chapters deal with the results of the preventive health programs discussed in the first three chapters. "Morbidity and Mortality" serves as an overview of student illness and death at Sherman Institute, with data presented in statistical form. This format facilitates various comparisons and establishes a context for the remaining three chapters.

"Epidemics, Accidents, and Illnesses" deals with every cause for morbidity or mortality except tuberculosis and trachoma. The chapter is comprised of a series of stories about the epidemics, accidents, and illnesses that adversely impacted the health of students at Sherman Institute. The intended purpose of the chapter is to put a human face on health, to acknowledge the children who came to school who were sick or hurt and who sometimes died before seeing their families again.

The last two chapters of this book, "Tuberculosis: Policy and Practice," and "Sore Eyes," focus entirely on the two diseases responsible for the highest morbidity and mortality rates at Sherman Institute between 1902 and 1922. The combined impact of these diseases on student health at Sherman Institute and at every other nonreservation boarding school in the United States was complex and devastating. Yet the tragic results wrought by these diseases upon Indian children ultimately caused the Indian Office to take aggressive action in improving the living environment at nonreservation boarding schools.

The results of research conducted on student health at Sherman Institute between 1902 and 1922 did not support my original thesis. Sherman Institute did not operate as a death factory for Indian children, but in fact provided a healthy living environment for them. This is not to say that separating children from their parents for the purpose of assimilation is healthy, or that eliminating traditional lifeways for the sake of "civilization" is healthy. Neither of these actions, both integral to the nonreservation boarding school concept, constitutes a healthy living environment for Indian children, or any others, for that matter.

To say that Sherman Institute provided a healthy living environment is also not to say that the number of children who became sick and died, either at the school or upon returning home, was reasonable. For every parent of a dying child, even one death is too many. Yet, compared to that of populations at other nonreservation boarding schools and on reservations, or even to that of twenty-first-century elementary school children, the student health record at Sherman Institute fared well. In considering tuberculosis, for example, children at Sherman Institute had significantly lower morbidity and mortality rates than did Indians living on reservations.

The relatively good health of Sherman Institute students between 1902 and 1922 resulted from a number of factors. The school existed at a time when the Indian Office had prioritized student health and was attempting to stem the rising tide of morbidity and mortality by enacting various preventive health policies and programs. The location of the school in a temperate climate with abundant water, good farmland, and a supportive community contributed greatly to the healthy living environment. Sherman Institute had two experienced superintendents who put a premium on student health, for a number of reasons. As such, they not only diligently complied with Indian Office health policies but also implemented practices learned from experience that succeeded in maintaining and improving student health. The school physicians, despite providing only part-time medical care, were highly qualified professionals, each at the top of the medical field in Riverside. The doctors brought a high level of medical expertise to the school, as well as stability, with Dr. Parker serving as school physician for seven years and Dr. Roblee for twenty-eight years.

Research results indicating Sherman Institute maintained a healthy student population came from thousands of archival documents. In many ways, they are all that exist to tell the story of student health between 1902 and 1922. Few student narratives in the form of letters remain, and children who attended Sherman Institute during this period are now gone. Their voices are silent. However, in some ways, their voices live on and tell us that Sherman Institute did have healthy children. Countless students from that period sent their children to the school, and those children sent their own, when the time came. Records held at the Sherman Indian Museum tell of multiple generations of Sherman Institute students, beginning with children in the first class and continuing to the present. On the museum website and at annual alumni days, memories of the school are shared: "Sherman Institute was consistently one of dad's topics. He had wonderful experiences there and remembers all of his old classmates."[9] Obviously, not every student had such pleasant memories of boarding school, but the point remains that, in general, students at Sherman Institute had enough positive experiences there to want to send their children and grandchildren to the school. If it were an unhealthy place, a death factory, it is highly unlikely that students would send their own children to Sherman Institute. So, in some ways, the Native voice remains.

CHAPTER 1

Design for Living

AS ONE OF THE LAST NONRESERVATION BOARDING SCHOOLS BUILT IN THE United States, Sherman Institute benefited from lessons learned regarding student health at established schools. The lessons touched many aspects of life at the school, but perhaps nowhere more than in Sherman Institute's physical plant. From the initial design process to final construction, providing a healthy environment for students remained a primary consideration. Once established, strict sanitation practices helped keep Sherman Institute students healthy.

Early nonreservation Indian boarding schools gave little consideration to the issue of student health and even less to the impact their physical plants had on health. Since rapid assimilation of Indian youth into white society formed the core of nonreservation boarding schools' existence, the gathering of children into the schools' folds received priority attention. Only after the government removed children from their reservation homes and ensconced them within the boarding schools could the promised assimilation begin. The U.S. government had a muted urgency to accomplish this task. Unfortunately, this urgency translated into establishing most nonreservation boarding schools wherever vacant buildings already existed—usually abandoned Army barracks—instead of constructing schools to serve the intended purpose. The buildings used by the Indian Office for Indian schools were universally ill-fitted for the housing and education of young children and youth, with cramped dormitories, inadequate lighting and heating, and little sanitation.[1] Yet the physical plants of schools often received scant attention because of the prevailing opinion that anything the schools offered was better than reservation living conditions.

Disease and death became increasingly common occurrences among the children living at nonreservation boarding schools, and as a result, student health emerged as a critical issue. At first, Indian Office officials blamed the students' elevated morbidity and mortality on their perceived inherent physical weakness.[2] Upon further investigation, officials realized that the substandard facilities at most schools had a significant adverse impact on student health. Thus, in addressing this issue at nonreservation boarding schools, dealing with problems in a school's physical plant became the first line of defense against students' illness and death. Government officials, themselves products of the Progressive Era, believed that humans could methodically alleviate the tangible problems they saw causing Indian morbidity and mortality at every school. By the time the U.S. Senate approved funding for Sherman Institute in 1900, matters of school design and physical plant adequacy had reached the same level of importance as curriculum. In the following years, the health of school children became the Indian Office's key priority, and government officials recognized the role school facilities played in students' illnesses and deaths. The new focus on student health had a profound effect on the physical and mental well-being of students living at Sherman Institute during the first two decades of the twentieth century.

As early as 1891, the Indian Office acknowledged the importance of maintaining student health at the nonreservation boarding schools, as well as the need for improving school facilities in order to accomplish this goal.[3] However, not until 1895 did the Indian Office establish actual guidelines for physical plant improvements. After inspecting schools throughout the country and taking note of their obvious deficiencies, Superintendent of Indian Schools William Hailmann issued a lengthy circular on hygiene to all agents and school superintendents. The circular explained practical ways to make inexpensive modifications in school buildings to improve heating, lighting, ventilation, and the general sanitary condition of the school. Hailmann stipulated that three hundred cubic feet of air space and forty square feet of floor space be allotted to each student, equating roughly to the amount of space occupied by a single bed, plus a minimal amount of space around its perimeter. These air and floor space requirements served to reinforce another of Hailmann's orders that each student be issued a single bed, ending the common practice at nonreservation boarding schools of placing two or three children in a single bed. The circular further mandated the use of water closets (flush toilets) instead of vaults and cesspools (outhouses), though it provided no mechanism for the funding of replacements.[4] Superintendent Hailmann intended that inspecting officials would enforce compliance with the various measures set forth in the hygiene circular, thus improving sanitary conditions at the schools, and ultimately lowering student morbidity and mortality rates.

The Indian Office rarely enforced Hailmann's directives, however, despite the support of Commissioner of Indian Affairs Daniel Browning, for two main reasons: lack of knowledge and lack of funding. An imperfect understanding of disease mechanisms and the role played by improper sanitary conditions at school facilities, coupled with a chronic shortage of available resources for making the stipulated changes, crippled Hailmann's intended program.

In July 1897, Secretary of the Interior Cornelius N. Bliss appointed William J. McConnell to a four-year term as Indian inspector, with the hope that he would provide improvement in conditions at the Indian schools. After touring Indian schools for six months and finding facilities to be generally deplorable, McConnell made two recommendations that he felt were necessary to improve conditions and student health at boarding schools. First McConnell recommended that the Indian Office hire a specialized medical director, "an up-to-date physician familiar with modern ideas of sanitary regulations," to instruct school superintendents and physicians on sanitary matters and implement his directives.[5] He also suggested that the Indian Office create a position for a sanitary engineer, who could study plans for both new and old buildings and make specific recommendations to promote hygienic conditions.[6] Superintendent

Hailmann endorsed both recommendations, but because Commissioner William Jones, who had just assumed office, was opposed to both, McConnell's proposals did not come to fruition. In defending his opposition to hiring a sanitary engineer to direct physical plant improvements, Jones assured Secretary Bliss that Indian Office architects had already carefully designed all new school buildings along the "best lines of modern school architecture and sanitary science, so far as funds would permit," and that he was spending all the money he could to improve sanitary conditions at the schools.[7] Jones failed to mention the dangerous condition of old school buildings, the penurious amount of available funding for sanitary improvements, and the fact that even new schools were seriously overcrowded due to his aggressive enrollment policies.

In an attempt to curtail rising student morbidity and mortality, particularly from tuberculosis and other "filth" diseases, Indian Office regulations became somewhat more sophisticated than Hailmann's 1895 directives. By the beginning of the twentieth century, the Indian Office provided detailed guidelines regarding ventilation, temperature, and sanitation at nonreservation boarding schools. These regulations acknowledged the direct connection between a school plant and student health and, true to Progressive Era ideology, were theoretically based upon prevailing medical science doctrines regarding disease transmission. Unfortunately, medical science was changing so rapidly at the turn of the century that it was difficult for anyone but an "up-to-date" medical professional to comprehend the nuances and ramifications of these changes. Due to Jones's refusal to hire a medical director, the Indian Office was not blessed with such a professional. Instead, individuals with an incomplete understanding of current medical science developed school health regulations, and as a result, information was often incorrect and regulations ineffective.

A telling example of this dissemination of incorrect information may be found in the 1901 *Course of Study for the Indian Schools of the United States,* in which the importance of ventilation in combating disease transmission is discussed:

The most fertile cause of contamination in schools is the breathing of children in rooms inadequately supplied with air. The breathing process involves the using up of oxygen and giving off of carbon dioxid [*sic*], and small quantities of organic matter, which is undergoing decomposition, reduce the quantity of oxygen below a certain limit, and the air becomes unfit for breathing purposes and evil effects follow.[8]

In discussing the causes of disease, the *Course of Study* stated that in poorly ventilated dormitories and playgrounds, where many children meet, "the bad effects result from the decomposing organic matters given off from the lungs, which act as poisons, having been thrown off from the lungs because they are unfit for use." When the decomposing organic materials were taken back into the body, the report stated, "they interfere with normal processes."[9]

Regulations designed to counteract the "contaminated air" specified that windows in classrooms be "lowered a little from the top and raised from the bottom ever so little," and that air be kept moist, with a temperature of sixty-eight degrees. Furthermore, regulations from the Indian Office suggested that at least once during each classroom session, all doors and windows should be opened. The *Course of Study* instructed employees to warm dormitories for children to undress and retire, but not to keep them warm throughout the night. An additional requirement stipulated that every individual needed a minimum of ninety-eight cubic feet of air in each direction.[10]

Although seemingly based on scientific fact, the description of contamination by "decomposing organic matters given off from the lungs" actually reflects a hybridization of two opposing theories of disease causation: the miasmatic and the contagion or "germ" theories.[11] Though the advent of bacteriology largely discounted the miasmatic theory as early as 1880, the Indian Office incorporated this concept into its official regulations as late as 1901. The stress placed on good ventilation and pure air as "the great natural disinfectant, antiseptic, and purifier" clearly benefited student health, but the rationale for these requirements was dated, incorrect, and in some cases harmful. The lack of up-to-date medical information thus resulted in continued morbidity and mortality at the nonreservation boarding schools throughout the country. Further, inadequate funding to effect change and a general lack of enforcement limited compliance with official regulations to those schools whose superintendents prioritized student health at any cost.

Sherman Institute was one of the last nonreservation boarding schools built in the United States. That it was built at all is interesting, considering the fact that by 1900 the country was already moving away from nonreservation boarding schools. Nevertheless, as a result of relentless political lobbying by local businessmen and community leaders, and despite heated opposition, the Indian Appropriation Act for a new school in Riverside, California, passed in the U.S. Senate on 31 May 1900.[12] The secretary of the interior subsequently approved an appropriation of $75,000 for the purchase of land and erection of new buildings. This represented only a fraction of the $250,000 originally requested by the Indian Office. In June 1900, the commissioner of Indian affairs instructed Supervisor of Indian Schools Frank Conser to investigate a forty-acre site located on Magnolia Avenue, five and one-half miles from the center of Riverside and three-quarters of a mile from Arlington Station on the Santa Fe Railroad, in northwestern Riverside County (fig. 1.1). Conser approved the school site, and on 31 July 1900, the Department of the Interior granted permission to negotiate with Frank and Alice Richardson for the purchase of the land. On 18 August 1900, the Richardsons executed a deed conveying the land to the U.S. government for the sum of $8,400.00.[13] Later acquisitions included a ten-acre sewerage tract and a hundred-acre school farm.

As the twenty-fifth nonreservation boarding school built in the United States, Sherman Institute benefited from lessons learned at previously established schools regarding student health. The school's first superintendent, Harwood Hall, was a professional Indian school administrator, having previously been the superintendent of three other nonreservation boarding schools.[14] Hall's experience made him fully cognizant that health played a vital role in the education and "civilization" of Indian students. Perhaps more to the point, however, Hall envi-

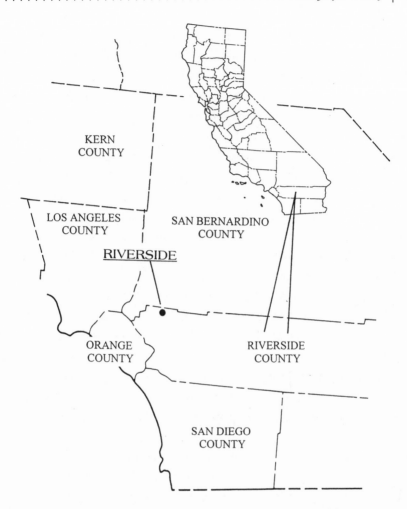

Figure 1.1. Location of Sherman Institute in Riverside, California.

sioned Sherman Institute as the quintessential Indian boarding school of the West and would do almost anything to insure that the school fulfilled his dream; illness and death were not part of his vision for the new school. As such, he endeavored to be an active participant in the establishment of Sherman Institute, particularly in the school's design.

Hall's interest in the school's design had complex origins. First, as an experienced Indian school administrator, he understood that a school's

physical plant represented its first line of defense against student morbidity and mortality. A school with substandard facilities, inadequate sanitation, or both, stood little chance in combating the diseases that
occurred in often-epidemic proportions among Native American peoples.
Second, by all accounts, Harwood Hall was a warm, caring individual
who endeavored to be a surrogate father to his youthful charges. As
such, he envisioned an attractive, safe, and comfortable school. Since his
family lived at the school, this had obvious personal benefit, but he also
recognized the appeal of a beautiful physical plant to students and their
parents. Third, a healthy school environment helped Hall "sell" the
school to prospective students' teachers and parents. In his correspondence with various interested individuals he noted, "Each dormitory is
complete in itself, lavatories, baths, closets, etc., in each and planned for
convenience and *health*."[15] This stress on health was especially important
in order to combat the perception many Indian families held of nonreservation boarding schools being death factories. Finally, since Hall
ultimately planned to turn Sherman Institute into a community and
tourist mecca, it made good business sense to create an attractive and
safe school. The white community surely would not patronize a school
full of sick and dying children; neither would an unattractive campus
hold much appeal to tourists.

The day after the Department of the Interior granted permission to
purchase the Riverside site, Hall sent the commissioner of Indian affairs
a copy of the architect's plans for the new school, with suggested
changes. A lengthy letter accompanied the plans. Selected excerpts from
his letter indicate his state of mind regarding the mental and physical
health of his charges. "It is very unwise, I find, to have a mixed set of
employees to room in childrens' quarters, outside of matrons' and disciplinarians,'" Hall wrote, "as the children cannot feel free and are always
subject to the whims and idiosyncracies [*sic*] of tired, sick, and nervous
employees." In his experience, Hall observed, "The herding of larger children in dormitories simply breeds disease and immorality, and lessons
[*sic*] a larger boy or girl's self-respect. They can have no individuality or
privacy in dormitories, as every thing is of a necessity held in common

and no privacy for anyone." So abominable did Hall find dormitories that he found them suitable only for nursery school pupils, "especially where tuberculosis has to be fought continually."[16]

Hall's letter suggested changes to virtually every portion of the architect's plan, from landscaping to the positioning of buildings on the site. His previous experiences at nonreservation boarding schools had taught him a great deal about creating a healthy and attractive environment for his students, and he determined that such elements should be present at the new school. Realistically, many of Hall's ideas were not born of compassion so much as of a desire to maximize assimilation and expedite the "civilization" of his young Indian students. His paternalistic demeanor reflected an attitude common in Indian school administration during most of its history. However, if viewed in the context of the time, Hall's plans for the new school were revolutionary because they took into consideration the individuality and vulnerability of the Indian students.

The first phase of construction at Sherman Institute included completion of four large dormitory buildings, two for girls and two for boys. Bearing names such as Ramona House and Minnehaha Home, the Indian Office architect designed each Mission-style dormitory to comfortably house one hundred students (fig. 1.2). As noted by Jones, these new school buildings possessed such modern features as steam heating, electrical lighting, and interior water closets and lavatories, all of which the older schools lacked. Yet what made these dormitories unique, possibly among all nonreservation boarding schools at the time, was the configuration of residential spaces.[17]

At Hall's insistence, the architect changed the plans for Sherman Institute from the large dormitory-style rooms commonly found at nonreservation boarding schools to small dormitories and individual rooms. Small dormitory rooms housed younger students, while dormitories divided into rooms occupied by only two or three individuals housed the older students. Hall encouraged students to decorate their rooms with personal belongings, thus making them as homelike as possible (fig. 1.3). This configuration served two purposes. First, it provided students with personal space, thus facilitating the transition from home to school life and

Figure 1.2. Girls' dormitory, Minnehaha Home.

Figure 1.3. Two-bed dormitory room for older girls.

offering a respite from the generally regimented organization of the school itself. This had the effect of restoring the students' mental and emotional well-being. A further benefit of this configuration was that it served as a quarantine mechanism. Doctors, nurses, and administrators could contain illness much easier with residential space broken into small units.

In many ways, Hall's involvement in the school design was a study in contradiction. He paid attention to the smallest detail, such as window and door screens, writing, "The window and door screens are very essential for purposes of protecting the inside of the buildings from the ravages of flies and other insects." He maintained, "Without the screens, the walls, woodwork, electric features, etc. etc. would be disfigured and injured in a short time." In typical fashion, Hall also worried about the impact of windows and screens in the transmission of disease. "Flies also carry disease," he wrote in 1902, "and are dangerous in an institution as well as being annoying."[18]

Yet despite Hall's understanding of the critical importance of a hospital in providing medical care for students, the school's initial construction schedule did not include such a facility. A room in Ramona House served as a hospital from the time the school opened in 1902 until the Indian Office finally built a small hospital in 1905. Though contractors built a commodious kitchen during the first stage of construction, an ice and cold storage plant, essential to curtailing food spoilage in Riverside's hot climate, would not be constructed for five more years. Hall evidently prioritized obtaining funding for an auditorium with a capacity of not fewer than six thousand people, "in order to accommodate the people of Southern California, tourists and residents, who will flock to the school when located at the beautiful and convenient spot on the famous Magnolia Avenue," ahead of facilities integral to maintaining student health.[19]

Sherman Institute formally opened on 8 September 1902 with an enrollment of 350 students, comprised primarily of students transferred from the Perris Indian School, as well as eight children from the Pima Reservation in Arizona. Unfortunately, problems obtaining furnishings and supplies in a timely manner necessitated sending 43 of the younger children back to the Perris school location. Hall postponed the formal dedication of Sherman Institute until 10 February 1903, so that the school could be better prepared financially and aesthetically for the onslaught of visitors that he expected to attend the dedication ceremonies. Large crowds attended the daylong ceremonies, and several prominent men in the community voiced their pride in the fact that the government was visibly doing something to better the education of the Indians. However, despite the grand showing, serious financial difficulties plagued Sherman Institute, at one point leading to the firing of all but the most necessary employees and having the students themselves take over the day-to-day operation of the school.

At the time Sherman Institute opened, eleven buildings comprised the physical plant: four three-story dormitories, a two-story classroom building, a steam laundry, a warehouse, a large barn, an office, an employees' quarters, and a one-story building for the dining hall and kitchen (fig. 1.4). With the exception of the employees' quarters, contractors constructed all buildings of brick covered by rough cast plaster, with tile roofs. They built the employees' quarters and buildings at the school farm with wood frame construction, with wood siding and wood-shingle roofs, despite the fact that at the time Indian Office regulations strongly discouraged frame construction due to the potential fire hazard.

The Riverside Land and Water Company provided water for domestic and irrigation purposes at the school, although at a very high cost. This water, said to be from a deep artesian aquifer, had actually been one of Hall's lobbying points in moving the school from Perris to Riverside. The abundant availability of pure, healthful water in Riverside obviously served as an effective counterpoint to the limited quantity and poor quality of available water in Perris. In fact, approval of a new boarding school in Southern California rested solely on the issue of healthful water.[20] Unfortunately, Sherman Institute's farm, where all agricultural operations were conducted and many children lived, did not benefit from the famous artesian water. Instead, a well and an irrigation canal supplied the farm's water needs.

Nonreservation boarding schools often experienced problems with their methods of sewage treatment, resulting in an adverse impact on

Figure 1.4. View of Sherman Institute shortly after completion (photo courtesy of the Riverside Municipal Museum).

students' health. Untreated sewage contaminated groundwater and acted as a breeding ground for disease.[21] Sherman Institute's method of sewage treatment, despite Hall's planning and precautions, proved troublesome from the first day of operation. Unlike many nonreservation boarding schools, Sherman Institute did not contain sewage within facilities at the school site. Instead, sewer pipe carried raw sewage to a ten-acre tract of land one-half mile down a slope from the school. This manner of treatment had been designed to safeguard the school from the problems often associated with raw sewage left in close proximity to living spaces. However, the problems Hall sought to avoid at the school plagued people residing in the neighborhood of the ten-acre tract, and they complained bitterly to the City Board of Health. As a result, within a month of Sherman Institute's opening, Hall had been called before the City Board of Health twice regarding the issue, and the city health officer condemned the ten-acre sewerage tract. The Board of Health strongly suggested Hall seek permission from the Indian Office to dig cesspools on the forty-acre school site. As an alternative to this action, which Hall deemed infeasible due to a lack of available space, he proposed extending the sewer line to the sand beds along the Santa Ana River, approximately two and one-half miles distant.[22] The $6,000 cost of the proposed extension proved too expensive, and sewage continued to be deposited on the ten-acre tract for several years, despite continuing complaints from its neighbors and the City Board of Health. By 1908, the City of Riverside resolved the problem by transporting Sherman Institute sewage through an eight-inch sewer main owned by the city to a septic tank approximately one and one-quarter miles from the school.

Hall emphasized certain health-related design elements at Sherman Institute, such as individual rooms, clean water, and the method of sewage treatment, for a number of reasons. Much of his concern came from personal experience at other nonreservation boarding schools and a genuine regard for the students' health. Yet many of Hall's actions also emanated from important ideological changes regarding health that occurred in the Indian Office around the turn of the century. At this time, government officials began to focus more on the health of students at boarding schools than on their rapid assimilation. These changes ultimately resulted in official health policies with which Hall chose to comply in the design and administration of Sherman Institute.

Beginning in the late nineteenth century, Progressive Era reformers put increasing pressure on Commissioner Jones of Indian Affairs to improve boarding schools, particularly regarding the extraordinarily high incidence of tuberculosis. As a result of this unrelenting pressure, on 1 July 1903, near the end of his term in office, Jones directed Indian service physicians to conduct a health survey, with special reference to the health of Indian students.[23] He thus ordered the first comprehensive study of morbidity among the Indian population of the United States. The survey would prove to have a significant impact on the improvement of health among Native Americans in general and among nonreservation boarding school students in particular.

The final conclusions of the physicians' survey had not yet been drawn when, in September 1903, Jones issued a series of directives to alleviate

some of the glaringly obvious problems existing at nonreservation boarding schools. The importance placed on health, and the acknowledgement
of the role school facilities played as the first line of defense against student morbidity and mortality, are amply illustrated by Jones's admonish-
ment to school superintendents, "Health is the greatest consideration."
Indeed, he argued, "Indian children should be educated, but should not,
however, be destroyed in the process." Jones ordered school superintendents to decrease the student population, "if you cannot accommodate your
present enrollment without lowering the vitality of the pupils." As if going
into battle, Jones ordered superintendents to wage a war upon "dust, filth,
foul odors, and all disease breeding spots." He also recommended that adequate ventilation and antiseptic methods be adopted, especially in dormitories, and that cuspidors and individual towels should be provided for the
students' use. For the first time, Jones stated that, "the rules relating to
the health of pupils must be strictly observed."[24]

Jones's admonitions to boarding school superintendents continued
emphatically: "There must, *most positively*, be *no overcrowding* in the dormitories to the detriment of the children sleeping in them." He told
superintendents categorically that they "must specifically and clearly
know that this Office does not wish you to enroll or retain any more children than you can safely and hygienically accommodate and therefore
in carrying out these orders you will be commended and not censured."[25]

This represented a dramatically different stance than Jones took earlier in his administration, when his aggressive enrollment policies paid
no mind to the fact that children, often diseased, were frequently stacked
like logs in already inadequate dormitory buildings. Through the survey
findings came the incontrovertible truth that a physical plant inadequate
for the number of enrolled students, and not kept in a thoroughly
hygienic condition at all times, rendered maintaining student health at
nonreservation boarding schools an impossibility. These findings forced
Jones to reconsider his previous policies and act accordingly.

Commissioner Jones's health policies, while of noble intent, were
nonetheless relatively ineffectual. He disseminated policy information
through circular letters to school superintendents, even though the effec-

tiveness of circulars was notoriously suspect. Many Indian Office field service employees never read the established service rules, let alone the numerous circulars sent out on a regular basis. Jones relied solely on school superintendents to comply with his directives, despite the fact that Indian school service inspectors rarely enforced them. The inspectors did not enforce the policies because they realized that adequate funding to implement change was usually not readily available. In some cases, years passed before schools received funding for improvements, despite the fact that the students endured primitive and unhealthy living conditions. The time intervals between inspectors' visits further hindered effective enforcement. As a result, elevated morbidity and mortality rates, particularly from tuberculosis, continued unabated even after Jones's policy directives of 1903.

The new health and sanitation directives issued by Jones had little bearing on Sherman Institute, since Hall had already implemented most of the practices prior to them becoming official Indian Office policies. Harwood Hall took great care to insure that the sanitary condition of the school's physical plant remained exemplary, generally going beyond official regulations. Daily inspections of every building, as well as the school grounds, became fully established procedures shortly after Sherman Institute commenced operations, and continued throughout Hall's tenure. Matrons, teachers, and disciplinarians directed the work of students in cleaning the facilities, and inspected their own departments. Hall also subsequently conducted inspections of selected departments to insure compliance with his sanitation regulations. Hall's vigilance in maintaining the sanitary condition of the school continued even in the midst of a typhoid fever epidemic in 1904. He chastised the school disciplinarian, "The general appearance of the various quarters are not satisfactory. It would seem that the sickness now prevailing is used as a reason for general neglect, which should not be the case." As a result of what he considered lax sanitation, Hall ordered "extra effort," so that the school buildings would be "kept as immaculate as ever."[26]

This was a far different scenario than existed at many nonreservation boarding schools, such as the Genoa Indian School in Nebraska.

There, Indian Inspector Arthur Tinker reported, "I was surprised to find the boys building and chapel in such dirty condition." He remarked that, "The disciplinarian and the boys matron commenced at once to clean up the boys building, and I doubt if it has had such a cleaning up for several months."[27]

Hall utilized a number of measures on a regular basis to improve the sanitary condition of Sherman Institute. Employees disinfected rooms in which ill children had been housed by "kalsomining" or by the use of chloride of lime.[28] When every type of normal fumigation for bedbugs in one dormitory proved fruitless, Hall ordered the entire building vacated and thoroughly fumigated with sulphuric acid and cyanide of potassium. Hall required floor dressing on a regular basis, "to keep down dust, from a sanitary standpoint." He recognized that "the dust arises and it is the means of spreading disease." Hall believed that, "using this floor dressing" would help "maintain health to a better degree."[29]

As a result of Hall's emphasis on maintaining the sanitary condition and attractive appearance of Sherman Institute, Indian school inspectors' reports glowingly praised the school's physical plant. In only one instance during Hall's tenure as superintendent were deficiencies noted. In 1905 an inspector wrote that the sanitary condition of the kitchen left much to be desired. Acting Commissioner C. F. Larrabee reprimanded Hall. "Unsanitary kitchen surroundings, badly cooked food, and disorder are not to be tolerated in an Indian school," Larrabee scolded, "and there is no reason why such conditions should occur." He ordered Hall to remedy the situation immediately.[30] Hall had a difficult time explaining why the kitchen, of all places, had been permitted to operate in an unsanitary manner.

Although Sherman Institute opened with only 350 students, enrollment grew at a steady pace, necessitating an aggressive expansion of the school's physical plant. By 1904, the student population in residence had grown to almost 450 and could no longer be housed comfortably in the original four dormitories and on the farm. The necessity of bringing the remaining children from Perris Indian School to Riverside, because of immediate threats to their health posed by unhealthy water, exacerbated the situation. The need for additional student housing demanded more dormitories. However, although students provided virtually all construction labor, funding for materials was generally slow in coming. As often happened, the demands of nonreservation boarding schools exceeded available funding. Instead of crowding the additional children into the existing dormitories, as was commonly done at other nonreservation boarding schools, with two or even three children sharing a bed, Hall purchased eight large canvas tents from Wilcox-Rose Mercantile at a cost of $485. He used the tents to house the children until additional dormitories could be constructed. Similar tents had already been purchased to house employees. While not ideal housing, the region's temperate climate permitted this solution, and it appeared to be a better alternative than crowding children into the finite dormitory space available.

By the end of 1905, the physical plant had grown to twenty-six buildings, and by 1906, to thirty-four buildings. Despite continuing expansion of the physical plant, the school never had sufficient room to accommodate the growing student population. Construction of additional dormitories took priority, providing ample room for student housing. The school sorely lacked other facilities, however. Four years after opening, the kitchen and dining room were woefully inadequate to serve the needs of the school, and appropriations for a much-needed cold storage and ice plant had still not been received. Hall saw these shortcomings as a serious threat to student health, writing that, "I do not wish to annoy the Office, but the need of an addition to our dining rooms, a new kitchen, and cold storage and ice plant are very great indeed."[31] At the time, the Sherman Institute dining room had forty-four tables in use, with fourteen students at tables that should have seated only eight. In Hall's opinion, the requested 50' × 50' addition would solve the seating problem, as well as expanding the kitchen and providing for a very necessary ice and cold storage facility. In requesting funding for the addition, Hall lamented, "We have a great deal of trouble in keeping our meat and other perishables. When the ice and cold storage is installed, it will assist in preserving perishables. It is almost impossible now to keep our meat from spoiling." Pressing the point, Hall added, "There is one case now of typhoid fever, and while it doubtless did not come through any filth in the school, yet we are in constant dread all the time of an epidemic of that kind breaking out on account of the overcrowded condition of the Mess in every respect."[32] Construction of the cold storage and ice plant occurred shortly after Hall's letter, with the dining room expansion completed the following year. Apparently, the kitchen retained its original size, at least until 1928.[33]

For most of his administration, William Jones's successor, Francis E. Leupp (1905–9), did nothing to promote Indian health, particularly in nonreservation boarding schools, since he adamantly opposed their existence. However, in 1908 Leupp began an aggressive campaign to improve Indian health. Eradication of tuberculosis among Native Americans created the impetus for his campaign, but wide-ranging benefits to the general health of Native peoples resulted. Tuberculosis research conducted in 1908 by Drs. Aleŝ Hrdlička and Paul Johnson, financed by the Smithsonian Institution to facilitate development of a museum exhibit on Indian morbidity, formed the foundation of Leupp's campaign.[34] Utilizing data compiled during this research, Leupp instituted a number of Indian Office health policies as part of his campaign, although few pertained to nonreservation boarding schools. In fact, Leupp seized upon evidence gathered by Hrdlička and Johnson to rail against the continued existence of nonreservation boarding schools.[35] Without a doubt, Leupp's most significant contributions to Indian health at nonreservation boarding schools were the appointments of Special Agent Elsie Newton as supervisor of schools and of Dr. Joseph A. Murphy as medical supervisor of schools. With these appointments came the first comprehensive inspections of nonreservation boarding schools and rigorous enforcement of health policies.

The year 1909 represented a landmark for nonreservation boarding schools in regard to the issue of student health. This marked the beginning of a greater awareness of the impact the physical plant had on student health and a stronger determination to remedy past deficits in school construction and sanitation. Optimism about programs for improving Indian health reflected Progressive Era ideology that had faith in the power of scientific method, education, and efficient organization to improve society.

Upon assuming office in 1909, Commissioner Robert G. Valentine succinctly voiced the new focus of the Indian Office that was to guide its actions on health issues for many years: "The reduction of the death rate is not its [the Indian Service's] primary interest." Instead, Valentine held that the Indian Office worked "rather to increase the vitality of the Indian race and to establish for it a new standard of physical well-being. *The work is being scientifically developed along lines which have already been successfully tried out by modern preventive medicine.*"[36] With this agenda, the Indian Office sought to take a proactive stance toward Indian health, not simply to react to the crisis of mortality.

In 1909, Frank Conser became the second superintendent of Sherman Institute, following Harwood Hall's appointment as supervisor of Indian schools, a position Conser had previously held. With his move to Sherman Institute, Conser brought knowledge acquired during years of observation and administration at nonreservation boarding schools across the country. This knowledge included recognition of the tremendous importance of maintaining the health of his students, as well as improving it. Experience defined Conser's approach to this arduous task.

As had been the case with Harwood Hall, the foundation of Sherman Institute health practices under Conser was twofold: consistent, strict compliance with Indian Office policies and site-specific improvements on policy, based on personal experience. In addition, Conser realized that in a large institutional setting such as Sherman Institute, constant vigilance and monitoring became necessary in order to alleviate health problems before they began. This approach proved particularly relevant when dealing with physical plant issues pertaining to student health.

In keeping with his belief that proper sanitation formed an integral part of good health, Conser rigorously enforced physical plant sanitation, implementing practices even more regimented than those established by Hall during the early years of Sherman Institute. He required that daily inspections of the entire plant be made on Monday, Tuesday, Wednesday, and Thursday of each week by the superintendent of industries, the nurse, the disciplinarian, and the matron, respectively. Employees posted reports of the daily plant inspections in every building and department immediately after the completion of the inspection of that building or department, as well as in Conser's office. No portion of the campus escaped the requisite inspections. "The entire plant should always be kept in first class condition," Conser ordered, "Special attention is invited to the matter of keeping every corner clean." He expected employees to inspect every part of every building on campus and at the farm in their inspections, including the children's lockers and clothing rooms, making note of "all untidy or unsanitary conditions." In addition, Conser instructed that special attention should be given to baths, washrooms, and toilets, including grease traps and plumbing. Employees received daily reminders that, "Sanitary conditions must be looked into very carefully at all times."[37] In addition to the daily sanitation inspections, Conser instructed students and staff to be constantly aware of the appearance of the school as well, patrolling the grounds to pick up stray debris and making note of landscaping or buildings in need of repair.

As previously noted, Indian Office health policies beginning in 1908 focused on the eradication of tuberculosis, with the first battlefield being the nonreservation boarding schools. One of the critical issues of the time centered on whether children with tuberculosis should be sent home to reservations immediately or retained and treated at the schools. In fact, Indian Office policy regarding this issue remained ambiguous until 1912. A recommendation for the establishment of tuberculosis camps at the nonreservation schools seemingly offered a solution to the debate. Students could be kept at school, but would be able to live in an open-air environment conducive to recovery. Realistically this was not a feasible option at most schools. Such camps necessitated the expenditure of far more resources than schools generally had available, and students housed at the camps would not be contributing members of the school population, placing a further burden on the administration.

The innovation of sleeping porches attached to school hospitals provided a relatively inexpensive alternative. Children could be retained at the schools while reaping the benefits of an open-air environment conducive to recovery. In 1909 the first porches were built at Carlisle Indian School, and within two years twenty-one schools had porches either in

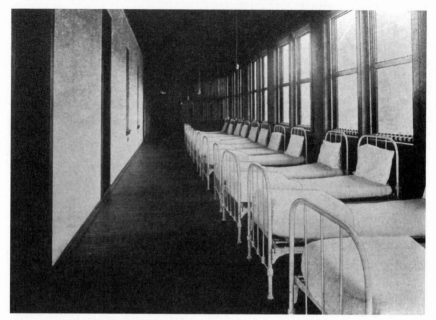

Figure 1.5. Screened sleeping porch.

use or under construction.[38] Medical Supervisor Murphy recommended, where practicable, that every school construct screened porches as sleeping quarters for students whose physical condition was not up to standard.[39]

Conser took Murphy's recommendation one step further. Sherman Institute became one of the first nonreservation boarding schools to construct sleeping porches. However, instead of adding them only to the hospital to facilitate the care of tubercular students, Conser added screened sleeping porches to every dormitory (fig. 1.5). By 1911, sleeping porches to accommodate three hundred students had been completed, with more planned as funding became available. Conser firmly believed that the porches would be of great benefit in maintaining the good health of the student body, because porches enabled students to almost live "outdoors for most of the year."[40] At the time, health practitioners considered circulation of fresh air, especially while sleeping, to be an integral defense against the transmission of disease because it kept the disease from "settling" and infecting the individual. Further, the common belief that Indians had an "inherited need for fresh air" prevailed.[41]

In 1913 the Indian Office recommended that all schools follow the lead taken by Conser: "Ample sleeping porches should be constructed on all dormitories and hospitals." Whereas in the past, the Indian Office had funded sleeping porches only at hospitals for use by sick children, the 1913 *Rules for Indian the School Service* recommended that "Children who are not thriving should be required to sleep on these porches when directed by the physician." It was further recommended that, "So far as space permits the same privileges should be extended to healthy children."[42]

Sherman Institute clearly had the advantage of a temperate climate in the utilization of sleeping porches. Further, despite Conser's genuine enthusiasm for their health benefits, sleeping porches realistically offered the added benefit of providing an inexpensive way of increasing dormitory space to house a growing student population. With Indian Office regulations requiring that dormitories supply five hundred cubic feet of air space for each pupil accommodated, sleeping porches permitted compliance that might not have otherwise been possible. These open-air dormitories permitted healthful living space for the students, but they did not provide the personalized spaces originally intended by Hall to offer respite and a homelike environment. However, evidence indicates that students may have had access to both regular dormitories and sleeping porches at Sherman Institute.[43]

As part of the new proactive stance taken by the Indian Office toward student health, government officials made an attempt to make non-reservation boarding schools somewhat less regimented and theoretically, more healthful.[44] Based on Hrdlička's criticism of boarding schools, Commissioner Leupp proposed the addition of more recreational time into the students' daily routine, but he left office before this became a reality. Commissioner Robert Valentine ultimately accomplished the interjection of more recreational activities into students' daily routines in December 1909, when he prohibited students with lung trouble from choosing indoor occupational activities and encouraged more outdoor activity for everyone. After learning of the "playground" concept from

Figure 1.6. Playing fields and the basketball court at Sherman Institute (photo courtesy of the Riverside Municipal Museum).

Lillian Wald of the Henry Street Settlement in New York, Valentine adopted the idea and urged all nonreservation boarding school superintendents to set aside playgrounds for the children's amusement and health.[45] Not all superintendents welcomed Valentine's proposal, as some felt that a child's surplus energy should be expended in some productive labor, not play. Nevertheless, by 1913 the Indian Office mandated inclusion of playgrounds in every school's physical plant. "Adequate and separate playgrounds must be provided," Valentine wrote, "one for boys and one for girls, and supplied with apparatus, such as swings, teeters, slides, turning poles, and the like." He felt that the "small boys and large boys should have separate playgrounds."[46]

Active participation by all students in a variety of outdoor sports, athletic contests, and free play formed an integral part of the daily routine at Sherman Institute. Both Hall and Conser encouraged students to spend as much time outdoors as possible, since both subscribed to the idea that fresh air guaranteed good health. Playing fields (fig. 1.6) had been part of Sherman Institute's physical plant since 1902, but in compliance with Valentine's proposal of 1909, Conser created separate open-air playgrounds for the boys and girls, which children used on a daily basis. In furtherance of the playground idea, Conser requested funding for a gymnasium in 1916, noting, "It would stand very close to the sleeping porches and hospital in the preservation of health and prevention of disease."[47] He continued to lobby for the gymnasium, using this rationale, until the Indian Office authorized funding for its construction in 1919. The fact that the Indian Office allocated funds for this project based solely on Conser's claim of its contribution to student health indicates the government's orientation at this time. Other schools besides Sherman Institute received funding for gymnasium construction, but, interestingly, many schools with a greater need due to adverse climatic conditions did not receive such funding. As was often the case, appropriations for physical plant improvements at nonreservation boarding schools followed no logical course, and some schools received seemingly preferential treatment.

Sherman Institute did not have a health care facility until 1905, when a twenty-five-bed hospital was completed. Hall gave little priority to providing an adequate health care facility for the students, instead settling first for a room in Ramona Home, and then for a painfully small, poorly designed and constructed hospital. Conser considered this situation unacceptable. He realized that without an adequate hospital to care for the students, he could do little to insure the students' good health. As a result of Conser's persistent lobbying, the Indian Office authorized $15,000 for the construction of a state-of-the-art hospital at the school in 1912. Once completed, Conser considered the hospital facilities equal to any in the Indian Service and superior to those found in the average small city.[48]

Two specific components of Sherman Institute's physical plant—toilets and baths—played an important part in the maintenance of student health, and both proved problematic. Each dormitory building had three toilets on the first floor, three on the second, and six in the basement. Considering the fact that over one hundred students lived in each dormitory, twelve toilets were clearly inadequate, particularly since half that number was in the basement, where no residential spaces were located. Odors from the basement toilets, especially in the boys' dormitories, presented an ongoing problem as they filtered up into the first-floor dormitory rooms.[49]

During the early years of Sherman Institute, neither the number of toilets nor their odors constituted a serious hardship on students simply because the facilities were new and the student population not overly large. By the time of Conser's administration, however, the situation had changed considerably. The ever-increasing student population sorely taxed the already inadequate facilities located near the dormitory rooms. Below-grade plumbing hindered adequate drainage of the basement toilets, resulting in frequent stoppages and overflowing sewage. Further, basement toilet rooms allowed only limited natural light and ventilation, exacerbating the unpleasant atmosphere, growth of mold and mildew, and concomitant structural and sanitary degeneration.[50]

The problem of basement toilets was not unique to Sherman Institute. In 1911 the Indian Office acknowledged the pervasive sanitation problems associated with basement toilets throughout the boarding schools and directed all plumbing to be installed above grade in separate structures connected with each dormitory through covered passages.[51] The same directive noted, "Removal from basements of all rooms used by students for any purpose whatsoever will make a distinct sanitary advantage." On a surprisingly astute note, Valentine instructed school superintendents to abolish "half-underground playrooms," because their "gloomy cheerless atmosphere of which is utterly antagonistic to any spirit of healthful play," would accomplish more "by freeing the children from most depressing influences."[52] Of course, expedient funding for the specified improvements was rarely forthcoming. In fact, every dormitory at Sherman Institute continued to have basement playrooms, and basement toilets were not completely removed from all Sherman Institute buildings until 1922, fully eleven years after the Indian Office directive.

Curiously, Indian Office medical inspectors did not have a problem with either the inadequacy or the poor location of toilets at Sherman Institute. Instead, government officials levied the harshest criticism for the lack of privacy the toilets offered, a perceived threat not to the students' physical health but their mental health. In 1916, an Indian Office health inspector, Dr. Newberne, first called attention to the lack of privacy created by the use of partitions between toilets, but no individual doors enclosing the stalls; curtains were used in lieu of doors.[53] Newberne repeatedly claimed that the toilets constituted the weak spot of the entire school because of the privacy issue. While admitting the clear desirability of fully enclosed toilets, Conser rather pointedly noted that the inadequacy and poor condition of the toilets created the underlying problems, particularly in the basement. "My special reasons for not having doors on these rooms were for the purpose of providing as much light and air as possible in these toilets," Conser wrote tersely, "as the more exposure we can have for these toilets the cleaner they can be kept."[54]

Conser further remarked that the children were undoubtedly more exposed to each other in their dressing rooms and dormitories than in the toilets. Although he understood that privacy in toilets was "a special hobby of Dr. Newberne's," he did not see it as a necessity, and until the Indian Office solved the problems of inadequacy and location, he preferred to keep the existing system, since it guaranteed the most sanitary environment.[55] Obviously, the Indian Office did not view the privacy issue as strongly as did their health inspector, since funding for toilet improvements did not arrive for almost six years.

Bathing facilities at nonreservation boarding schools had long been a detriment to student health. The Indian Office recognized adequate ventilation and a sanitary physical plant as integral to maintaining a healthy student population, yet, for some reason, the facilities used for keeping children clean were often overlooked. This is ironic, considering the emphasis placed on cleanliness being a requisite for "civilization." Schools provided a limited number of washbasins and bathtubs for the use of students, but unfortunately, many students generally shared the same water. At schools with a limited water supply, this was an especially common practice. Sharing bathwater potentially had a tremendous adverse impact on student health, particularly in the case of trachomatous or scrofulous children. Infectious disease could easily be transmitted from one child to many through the contaminated bathwater. Furthermore, even when employees changed the water, they rarely cleaned and scrubbed the tubs.

By the late nineteenth century, bathing facilities received overdue attention as being important to student health. A critical improvement occurred when schools replaced bathtubs with "ring baths," a system Commissioner Daniel Browning first introduced into nonreservation boarding schools.[56] The "ring bath" system involved individual shower stalls with pipes that surrounded and sent out water from head to foot upon an occupant of the stall. Students soaped their bodies thoroughly, then rinsed by stepping into the stall, where "properly tempered water is evenly distributed, carrying away with it the dirt and filth with which it is contaminated."[57] The system proved an efficient and effective method of cleaning large numbers of children, and one wholeheartedly approved of by boarding school staff.

Sherman Institute dormitory buildings each contained four ring baths and two bathtubs to serve a minimum of one hundred students. This limited number of bathing facilities rendered the logistics of arranging weekly baths for each student extremely difficult, even during the early years when the school had a relatively small population. As enrollment increased and dormitories housed more students than they had originally been designed for, the level of difficulty increased measurably. Further, although the Indian Office required that all nonreservation boarding schools provide at least one bath per week for each student, this hardly proved sufficient to maintain clean students, considering the types of labor performed during the course of a normal school day. Washbasins in dormitory rooms helped somewhat, but the bathing situation at Sherman Institute remained marginal at best.

In 1906, Hall proposed that in addition to the dormitory bathing facilities, a separate plunge and bath building be constructed. Hall believed, "A plunge and bath house would certainly be a great improvement in regard to bathing for the pupils." In addition to bathing, students would also be able to "enjoy a swim, for, at this location, there are no streams or water short of the Pacific Ocean, where they can take a swim." He admitted that a pool and bathhouse would be a luxury, but argued that "it would be more, it would be healthful and would assist materially in the cleanliness of the pupils."[58]

At a cost of $15,000, Hall's request certainly did represent a luxury addition to the school. The following year, he again made the request, this time placing increased emphasis on the health benefits. "A plunge bath and building where the pupils may take their baths and be healthy is one of the very necessary improvements at Sherman Institute," Hall argued, "From a sanitary standpoint this is important." According to Hall, only with a plunge and bath building would the large student population be able to "have unrestricted bathing privileges."[59]

Apparently, the commissioner of Indian affairs concurred with Hall's assessment, eventually authorizing construction of a separate bath and plunge building. This facility proved to be of great benefit to Sherman Institute students. In comparing the bathing facilities at Sherman Institute to those at other nonreservation boarding schools, Lewis Meriam noted that at Sherman Institute, "these quarters are open practically all the time and they are used freely," resulting in children being cleaner, and "this is reflected in the clean bed linen seen."[60]

Bathing facilities at most boarding schools were often kept locked and opened for use only on specified occasions. Typically, children received only one or two baths each week at boarding schools, but Sherman Institute allowed children to bathe anytime—day or night— making the institute exemplary among nonreservation boarding schools. Undoubtedly, the opportunity offered by this portion of the school's physical plant played an important part in maintaining the health of the students at Sherman Institute.

CHAPTER 2

Prevention

PREVENTIVE HEALTH PROGRAMS INSTITUTED AT NONRESERVATION BOARD-ing schools marked the second line of defense against student morbidity and mortality. These programs provided a necessary complement to regulations governing the physical plant design. Each facilitated and strengthened the other. Programs based on interpretations of prevailing medical thought concerning disease transmission offered multifaceted, often innovative, approaches to preventing disease at the boarding schools. In their "vigorous battle" against disease, the Indian Office attempted to utilize every measure considered even marginally effective in impacting disease incidence. These preventive health programs focused on education, observation, nutrition, exercise, and disinfection.[1] As the early twentieth century progressed, Indian health became an increasingly relevant issue. School superintendents used health as an argument for a variety of funding requests, with claims that seemingly every facility and program had some integral function in preventing disease and maintaining student health. Superintendents Hall and Conser lobbied relentlessly for such funding. More importantly, however, they combined strict compliance with Indian Office health campaign policies with preventive practices specific to Sherman Institute in their attempts to prevent student morbidity and mortality.

EDUCATION

Education was the core of preventive health programs at nonreservation boarding schools. The earliest attempts at health education focused primarily on teaching personal hygiene, emphasizing the importance of cleanliness in preventing disease. In the 1901 *Course of Study for the Indian Schools,* Superintendent of Indian Schools Estelle Reel admonished teachers, "Show the Indian child that it is unhealthy to eat on the floor, where disease germs are numerous and are waiting to be carried with the food into the body."[2] Inferring that Indian children did not naturally understand the concept of personal cleanliness, Reel instructed teachers to include lessons on the skin, pores, and benefits of frequent bathing, even if it meant spending an entire day on the lessons. By repeatedly focusing on personal cleanliness, she speculated, "it will soon be so agreeable to the children to be clean that there will even be a rivalry about it."[3]

Teachers were also expected to provide rudimentary information on physiology and disease prevention. For example, Reel's instructions stated that teachers had to explain that, "secretion of the nasal passages is germicidal," and "that malaria enters the system when the mouth is used for breathing." Breathing, as a result, should be "through the nose," in order to prevent "poisonous bacteria from entering the blood."[4] Reel felt that teaching Indian children to breathe correctly would necessarily improve their health.

The Indian Office placed importance on health education for a number of reasons. In keeping with the common perception that a clean Indian was a civilized Indian, full assimilation demanded that Indian students be instructed in "proper" personal hygiene. Progressive Era belief in the power of education to effect change, coupled with the prevailing medical dogma that linked disease to filth and germs, made health education in the boarding schools an obvious choice. By teaching Indian students about personal hygiene and disease prevention, the excessive morbidity and mortality at nonreservation schools would decrease, it was thought. Further, according to assimilationist ideology, if students were taught about personal cleanliness and disease prevention at boarding school, they, in turn, could teach their families when they went home to the reservations. As succinctly stated by Dr. Joseph Murphy, "The Indian children will be the best promoters of new ideas in the homes and will be able through the training received at school to advance materially all efforts along other lines."[5]

While this was generally considered to be an effective method of preventing disease transmission, familial divisiveness and discord often resulted instead as children attempted to instruct their parents in the white man's ways. Illustrative of this unfortunately common situation is Sherman Institute student Polingaysi Qoyawayma, a Hopi girl, who upon returning home after four years at school scolded her parents for maintaining their traditional ways,

> Why haven't you bought white man's beds to sleep on? And a table? You should not be eating on the floor as the Old Ones did. When I was a little girl I did not mind sleeping on the floor and eating from a single bowl into which everyone dipped. But I am used to another way of living now, and I do not intend to do these things.[6]

Polingaysi's parents tried to make the changes she demanded, but the divide between school and home, new and traditional lifeways, was simply too great to bridge effectively.[7] The Indian Office had not envisioned this situation in their health campaign.

From the time Sherman Institute opened in 1902 until 1907, teachers provided no health education beyond that specified in the 1901 *Course of Study*. Harwood Hall, an Indian Service bureaucrat, did not consider doing less, but neither did he do more during this period. As part of the regular curriculum, students received instruction in bathing, tooth brushing, and hair care. Basic physiology lessons included discussions of how to care for various body parts and ways to prevent disease. Teachers led deep breathing exercises several times each day so students could partake of the healthful Riverside air. Students received detailed instruction on such minutiae as the proper way to make beds to insure adequate airing, the best clothing to wear in order to optimize healthful sleeping conditions, and the amount of sleep necessary to maintain good health and growth. Most importantly, teachers instructed students that individual towels, soap, toothbrushes, combs, and brushes could never be shared, because such sharing could lead to transmitting "disease germs" to each other. Hall repeatedly stressed to teachers, matrons, and disciplinarians that the "no sharing" policy be strictly enforced for the safety of the students and the school. For Indian children whose traditional lifeways included sharing personal items as a means of showing trust and friendship, one can only imagine the difficulty they experienced in internalizing this particular lesson in a place where friendship was sorely needed.[8]

Beginning in 1907, students at Sherman Institute began publishing a school newsletter, *The Sherman Bulletin.* The newsletter included articles on health, personal cleanliness, and other relevant issues in each issue, usually on the front page. Sherman Institute nursing students wrote a number of essays for publication in the newsletter as part of their curriculum requirements. Other articles included speeches from guest lecturers, excerpts from various publications, or health-related articles written by knowledgeable members of the newsletter staff. Both Hall and Conser strongly supported the inclusion of health articles in every *Bulletin,* and this practice continued through 1922. With the exception of curriculum-based material, *Bulletin* articles formed the core of preventive health education received by students at Sherman Institute.

It is probable that *The Sherman Bulletin* articles made a forceful impact on the students, serving to reinforce lessons learned in the classroom. The power of the articles came from the fact that they were written from the perspective of fellow students, and as such, took on a personal tone. Children and young adults are always more willing to listen to advice and information given by their peers instead of by adults, because it somehow seems more trustworthy and less likely to have an ulterior motive. Articles covered such wide-ranging topics as "The Human Body," "What Are Your Eyes Worth," "Infection," "Hygiene and Sanitation," "Is the Cockroach a Menace," and several articles entitled simply "Health." An article written by a staff member in 1910 exhibits the type of relatively well-written, informative, and convincing prose typical of *The Sherman Bulletin:*

> Without health there is no real enjoyment of life, and while in school we should learn to take proper care of ourselves in order to keep well and strengthen our bodies. The essentials to the preservation of health are pure air, wholesome diet, regular exercise, scrupulous cleanliness, proper clothing, and regular diet.[9]

With the increased focus on student health at nonreservation boarding schools that began in 1909 came stricter Indian Office requirements for preventive health education. Virtually every program had its roots in the war on tuberculosis but most applied to health issues in general. The Indian Office required that practical sanitation and hygiene, as well as the cause, prevention, and treatment of tuberculosis and trachoma be taught to every child at every school.

In 1911, Valentine attacked the problem of disease prevention through education in a far different manner than had previously been tried. He instructed Indian Service physician Dr. Ferdinand Shoemaker and a full-time photographer to prepare a series of stereopticon slides and motion picture films for presentation to students through the Indian Service. The slides primarily dealt with tuberculosis and trachoma, while the films depicted healthful and unhealthful hygiene, "to illustrate in juxtaposition the ordinary habitations of careless Indians and the pleasant, healthful homes of Indians who have taken advantage of the opportunities the government has given."[10] Since most schools did not possess lantern slide projectors, Shoemaker spent much of his time traveling to Indian schools and agencies of California, Arizona, New Mexico, and Montana, showing the film and slides, while giving a simple lecture. Shoemaker's lectures included such diverse topics as wet-mopping, outdoor exercise, ventilation, disposal of garbage, care of milk, sleeping porches, sterilization of eating utensils, water supply, tuberculosis, trachoma, and separate combs and brushes. During his tour through the Southwest in 1911, he gave fifty-two lectures to over ten thousand

Indians and Indian Service employees. Dr. Shoemaker presented lectures at Sherman Institute during the evenings of 13 and 14 March 1911.[11] As an extension of this program, Medical Supervisor Murphy carried sets of slides with him, and after completing his inspection of a school, presented illustrated lectures in the evenings. Murphy also gave school superintendents copies of his slides, along with typewritten lectures, to present to the students during the year.[12] Superintendent Conser frequently made use of these materials during his Sunday evening chapel lectures to Sherman Institute students.

The appointment of Cato Sells as commissioner of Indian affairs in 1914 brought preventive health education programs to a higher level, particularly in regard to tuberculosis and trachoma.[13] He promoted the health campaign in schools by requiring teachers to attend annual institutes that included health and hygiene topics. In 1914, for example, teachers attended illustrated lectures on disease and prevention, saw demonstrations on fumigation and disinfection methods, and witnessed a demonstration on the treatment of trachoma.[14]

Sells also frequently sent bulletins published by the United States Public Health Service to school superintendents, teachers, and physicians.[15] Upon receipt of these bulletins, Conser circulated them to all staff members and included them in *The Sherman Bulletin* for student perusal. Most of the public health notices published in the newsletter were rather dry and not particularly relevant to boarding school students. Periodically, however, notices written in a very different manner appeared, one apparently meant to appeal to Indian youths:

> The scratch of a lion's claw is almost as deadly as his bite, for he never cleans his nails and always carries them under rotting meat that is rank with deadly germs. Flies and water bugs do the same things on a smaller scale; "Don't forget," says the U.S. Public Health Service, "that they never wipe their feet."[16]

Sells also increased the number of health-oriented periodicals sent to boarding school administrators and physicians. There is no evidence that Sherman Institute received such periodicals, particularly since the school's physician had a private practice and undoubtedly maintained his own journal subscriptions. Conser regularly ordered pamphlets such as "Indian Babies—How to Keep Them Well" for distribution to all employees and students. Responsibility for disbursing the pamphlets fell to the resident nurse, who also made sure students read and used them appropriately. The pamphlets generally supplemented special programs that included lectures, demonstrations, and relevant articles published in *The Sherman Bulletin*.[17] This multilevel educational approach resulted in greater comprehension of the health issue, as well as heightened retention.

OBSERVATION

Medical observation equaled education in the Indian Office's preventive health program. In fact, they created more new policies and regulations under the guise of observation than any other health program, largely because preventive medical observation had essentially been ignored during the first two decades of nonreservation boarding schools. In the quest to "civilize" as many Indian students as quickly as possible, Commissioner Jones had ordered school superintendents to fill their schools to capacity. In many cases, this meant enrolling unhealthy children without physical examinations and permitting diseased children to remain at the schools in close contact with healthy children. This all too common scenario resulted in increasingly elevated student morbidity and mortality rates at nonreservation boarding schools.

Between 1879 and 1902, the Indian Office did not encourage the enrollment of unhealthy children or the retention of diseased children, yet neither did it enforce existing health policies. Regulations regarding contagious disease were actually quite specific and rigid, but school superintendents often chose to ignore them in order to maintain high enrollment figures, and suffered no repercussions from the Indian Office.[18]

Not until 1903, with the preliminary results of the physicians' survey in hand, did Jones issue the first directive actually forbidding nonreservation boarding school superintendents from receiving students who lacked a medical certificate attesting to their physical soundness.[19]

Interestingly, the directive did not say that an unhealthy child could not be enrolled, only that the student had to have a medical certificate stating his or her condition. By 1904, Jones issued directives to remedy this oversight. Each student had to be examined by a physician prior to enrollment, and if the physician observed any signs of tuberculosis, the child could not be enrolled at school.[20] The directive said nothing about excluding children observed to have other illnesses.

The following year, Indian Office regulations became more comprehensive in scope, mandating that superintendents, "Enroll only *sound and healthy* pupils" in their schools. However, once students enrolled at the boarding schools, Jones's rules for dealing with their illnesses became considerably more lenient. Any pupil observed to have symptoms of diseases "which may be corrected or cured by returning home" had to be sent home immediately by the superintendent. Jones, however, did not specify exactly which diseases could be better cured or corrected on reservations than in boarding schools. Students suffering from communicable diseases were also to be sent home immediately, "provided they cannot be properly segregated," although Jones did not provide guidelines as to what constituted proper segregation. To alleviate the potentially serious epidemiological—and public relations—problem resulting from superintendents waiting too long to send critically ill children home, Jones emphatically directed, "*Do not wait* until such pupils are ready to succumb to the disease before returning them to their homes, to become foci of infection for the defenseless Indians and whites that may be living near."[21] Finally, Jones strictly forbade nonreservation boarding school superintendents to receive students without proof of their physical soundness. Superintendents who broke this rule had to personally pay for the student's transportation home.

In the two-year period from 1903 to 1905, medical observation of Indian students became a critical factor in preventing disease at nonreservation boarding schools. No longer would it be possible to enroll and retain unhealthy children in order to boost enrollment—at least theoretically. Realistically, while most schools complied with the requirement of obtaining a medical certificate for each new student, many schools continued the practice of allowing ill children to remain at the campus. This proved particularly true of children with signs of tuberculosis, even though tuberculosis prevention had been the original purpose of the regulations, and the Indian Office did not permit the retention of children suffering from tuberculosis. Superintendents often felt they could provide better care for the student at school than would be possible at the child's reservation home, since many reservations had neither hospitals nor physicians. Unfortunately, many boarding schools also did not have adequate medical care facilities or personnel, and by the time superintendents finally sent a child home after realizing he or she would not recover, it was too late and the child died shortly after returning home. Although some superintendents undoubtedly sent critically ill children home to die out of compassion for the child and his or her family, in reality, most superintendents did this out of a desire to minimize the number of student deaths recorded at the boarding school. Unfortunately, aside from the devastating experience of having one's child die shortly after arriving home, this practice served to spread disease from the child to family members on the reservation.

The new Indian Office regulations had little impact on Sherman Institute. Medical observation had been an integral preventive health program at the school since it opened, implementing procedures that had been established in 1891 at its predecessor, Perris Indian School, located twenty miles south of Riverside.[22] Between 1891 and 1902, students entering Perris Indian School had to have a certificate of examination from the physician either at a previous school or at the child's reservation agency. Hall continued this tradition when the school moved to Riverside, as Sherman Institute, in 1902. When students arrived at Sherman Institute, the school's contract physician, Dr. Parker, subjected them to a rigorous physical examination. If Parker observed any signs of disease, he immediately sent the child home. The difference between Sherman Institute and many other nonreservation boarding schools was that Superintendent Hall strictly enforced dual certification of good health. Hall could afford to be selective and admit only perfectly healthy children because far more students sought enrollment than the school could hold. By enrolling only children observed to be healthy, Hall sought to prevent the introduction of disease into the student population, thus controlling the level of morbidity and mortality.

Beginning in 1909, the Indian Office instituted additional preventive health policies involving medical observation. The difference between these policies and those of the 1903–5 period was that the new policies were not strictly enforced. Instead, they appeared in the form of official suggestions made by Medical Supervisor Murphy to individual boarding school superintendents. Murphy based most of the suggested policies on prevailing medical concepts of tuberculosis prevention, and some were experimental in nature.

On 25 May 1909, Dr. Murphy paid an inspection visit to Sherman Institute and made a number of recommendations in his subsequent report, several of which related to preventive medical observation. In general, Murphy's report was very positive. He wrote that Hall's "hearty support and cooperation" in his work had given him a great deal of pleasure, as had "seeing the spirit which has been manifested in the school by the employees and pupils toward the endeavor to improve the health conditions here."[23] Murphy recommended that, "The experiment of monthly weighing of pupils by teachers for the purpose of keeping check on delicate children is recommended to be tried," and that the index card system of recording the physical conditions of pupils entering school should be continued.[24]

An Indian Office tuberculosis advisory committee originally had recommended both measures in a report dated 29 December 1908, but the measures had not been formalized as policy.[25] In accordance with the committee's recommendations, Sherman Institute's contract physician, Dr. A. S. Parker, implemented the index card system in January 1909. Monthly weighings had not been implemented because there were no scales at the hospital. Apparently, weighing had not been a regular part of students' enrollment examinations prior to this time. Following Murphy's recommendation, Conser arranged for the purchase of scales for the hospital, and the task of weighing each student during the first week of each month fell to the principal teacher.

Murphy also recommended that employees closely examine each child during bathing for the purpose of eradicating scabies. This practice was incredibly intrusive and demeaning, particularly for the older students. While it is true that scabies presented an ongoing, pervasive problem at the school, the staff was usually well aware of the infected students without bath-time examinations. Since intense itching is a characteristic symptom of this burrowing mite infestation, students readily volunteered for treatment at the hospital. Yet, in the spirit of prevention, Conser complied with Murphy's recommendation.

The year 1912 represented a landmark for preventive health programs that focused on medical observation. At this time, Commissioner Valentine created new forms for reporting on health issues involving children at nonreservation boarding schools. Valentine designed one of the forms for use by physicians during their examination of students at the beginning of every year and during periodic reexaminations throughout the year. This report required information that could be sent to the Indian Office for easy tabulation, permitting consistent statistical reporting and analysis of health data from all nonreservation boarding schools. He designed a second new form for teachers to record monthly weights of students. Both teachers and the school physician carefully watched any student evidencing a significant weight loss, since this was considered to be one of the first signs of tuberculosis. Recording monthly weights over time sometimes enabled early identification of a problem and permitted timely treatment with a combination of rest and an enriched diet. Recording of monthly weights also served to identify students who were doing poorly for reasons other than tuberculosis.

At Sherman Institute, the head nurse had responsibility for maintaining a case record for each student in the hospital office. The nurse filed all health records in the case folder, including the physician's examination forms and monthly weighing forms. In this manner, she exercised tight organizational control over the records. She could access and compare all health data, for any student, from records maintained in a single location.

In 1913, the *Rules for the Indian School Service* established protocol for preventive health measures that remained in place through 1922. Many of the rules dealt with medical observation. The majority of these measures previously had existed in a less stringent form, but had not been formal Indian Office policies. The measures also lacked rigorous enforcement until 1913. Inclusion in the *Rules* added strength to these preventive measures.

Whereas monthly weighing had previously been a recommended "experiment," the *Rules* now required weighing immediately upon admission to the school and once each month, with the weights recorded on official forms filed in the school office. Further, the formal policy now required school physicians to examine weight records at regular intervals and give special attention to students who lost weight and to those who did not properly gain weight.[26] The Indian Office instructed employees to supervise pupils to insure that they properly cleaned their teeth each morning and evening, using tooth powder at least once a day. The Rules for Indian Service Schools also directed any employee who noticed evidence of disease in a student to take immediate steps to see that the case was promptly reported to the school physician.[27]

The *Manual of Sherman Institute* of 1912–13 included many of the same preventive measures found in the *Rules,* but in a number of cases, they represented a far more stringent orientation. The *Manual* reflected Conser's strong focus on maintaining student health at the school, even to the extent that he mandated preventive measures that stripped students of their dignity and presented an inferred belief that Indians were inherently unclean. "Immediately on the arrival of all pupils whether returning from their homes after vacation or new pupils they shall be given a bath," read the first sentence of the *Manual.*[28] This set the tone for the entire volume. Whereas the *Rules* stipulated that any employee who noticed evidence of disease should take steps to see that it was reported to the physician, the *Manual* was far more specific:

All employees should constantly observe the physical condition of all pupils in their classrooms or on their details, and any apparent physical ailment of any kind should be reported immediately to the disciplinarian or matron in order that they may be sent promptly to the hospital for treatment. Any case

that seems to require immediate attention should be sent to the hospital
directly from detail or classroom and disciplinarian or matron so notified. [29]

By 1912, the bath inspection recommended by Dr. Murphy in 1909 to
eradicate scabies had become a procedure firmly incorporated into the
students' daily routine. Conser required that a "responsible person"
inspect every girl and boy on bath day, and further stipulated that all
matrons remain in the buildings during the entire time of bathing, "even
though it may be after five o'clock."[30] The girls' inspector also observed
the menstruation pattern of each girl and made note of it in the girl's
medical case file. Although at first glance it may seem that the purpose
of the latter was to check for pregnancy, most medical authorities considered cessation of menstruation an early sign of tuberculosis. For this
reason the girls' inspector recorded menstruation data; they did not consider pregnancy a possibility among Sherman Institute students. Under
the guise of disease prevention through observation, Conser essentially
removed all semblance of privacy available to the students. The bathing
experience thus degraded students instead of providing enjoyment and
pleasure.

NUTRITION

During the early years of nonreservation boarding schools, food was seen
merely as a necessary commodity. Little thought was given to food's nutri-
tive value, taste, or freshness. Incorporation of traditional native foods
into the students' diet never received consideration, since it would have
been antithetical to the assimilationist focus of the schools. Instead, cost
was the critical factor. Commodities provided by the Indian Office were
largely determined by which food could be purchased in greatest quantity for the least amount of money, such as flour, rice, beans, and bacon.
The Indian Office expected farms attached to nonreservation boarding
schools to supplement the commodities with fresh fruits, meat, dairy
products, and vegetables. Unfortunately, since farm production varied
greatly, many schools depended primarily on government commodities to

feed the students. Rapidly expanding populations and minimal yearly appropriations often resulted in diets inadequate in both quality and quantity.

By the end of the nineteenth century, the Indian Office exhibited a growing recognition that nutrition had a significant impact on student health. This was based primarily on prevailing medical theories that increasingly emphasized the value of fresh, wholesome food in maintaining strong bodies, which in turn fought disease. This recognition by the Indian Office is clearly evidenced in the 1898 *Rules for the Indian School Service,* which advised nonreservation boarding school superintendents that, "Good, healthful, and well-cooked food should be supplied in abundance." The *Rules* directed that meals be comprised of various foods, "served regularly and neatly." To supplement commodities supplied by the Indian Office, the *Rules for the Indian School Service* stipulated that nonreservation boarding school farms "should provide an ample supply of vegetables, fruits, milk, butter, cottage cheese, curds, eggs, and poultry." In furtherance of the idea that diet influenced health, the *Rules* directed school superintendents to furnish coffee and tea sparingly, that "milk is preferable to either, and the children should be taught to use it."[31] While the authorized subsistence rations still emphasized quantity and cost over quality, the Indian Office at least made a provision for the purchase of vegetables when they could not be grown on the school farm.[32]

Subsequent to issuance of the *Rules,* Jones ordered that the established subsistence rations be changed, substantially decreasing the amount of meat-based protein. He based this rationale on the premise that by providing a more varied diet, Indian students would be broken from their predominantly meat-based diets, which in his opinion excluded many nutritional items necessary to maintain good health.[33] Although many criticized the new subsistence rations as being inadequate for the needs of growing Indian children, Jones received strong support from Department of Agriculture Office of Experiment Stations experts. Their report concluded that while the older diet contained more protein, the two diets supplied the same amount of "energy," as well as all of the nutrients needed by the body in amounts that exceeded those found in the diet of "the average working American."[34] With a typical Progressive Era reliance on the opinions of experts, Jones's orders were seemingly vindicated. However, both Jones and the experts failed to insure that important foods such as eggs, dairy products, and vegetables formed an integral and consistent part of the new school diet. Theoretically, every nonreservation boarding school had a farm that could supply these foods; realistically, few did so adequately.

By the time Sherman Institute opened in 1902, recognition of the value of nutrition in preventing disease had been strengthened by recommendations made by medical professionals that victims of tuberculosis be treated with an enriched diet, primarily comprised of dairy products and eggs. If such a diet could be used to treat individuals already stricken by the disease, it seemed logical that an enriched diet could also be used to prevent tuberculosis. As was usually the case, Indian Office policies created to deal with tuberculosis in the boarding schools proved to be equally beneficial when applied to student health in general. By this time, the Indian Office had also stipulated that school curriculum include lessons discussing the connections between diet and health: "Teach that tea and coffee may work injury to the development of the bones and muscles, strong coffee injuring the nervous system."[35]

One of Sherman Institute's strengths in the campaign to maintain student health lay in being able to provide an abundance and variety of nutritious foods for the students. Regardless of any other factor influencing their health, students at Sherman Institute ate well. While restricted to subsistence rations mandated by the Indian Office, Sherman was fortunate in that its farm provided supplemental foods such as dairy products and fresh fruit and vegetables on a consistent basis. These foods not only supplied the vitamins, minerals, and amino acids sorely lacking in the starch-rich commodity foods, but also offered a tangible link to dietary components familiar to the children from their days at home.

The farm encompassed one hundred acres, located approximately four miles from the 40-acre school site. Compared with other nonreservation boarding school farms, such as Chilocco Indian School with 8,640 acres, or Chemawa Indian School with 345 acres, Sherman's farm was clearly minimal, particularly since its student population was considerably larger than that of these schools.[36] Yet for the first ten years of operation, the farm was sufficient in size to produce an abundance of food for the students. In 1906, for example, students produced over one thousand gallons of tomatoes that they canned for winter use by September, as well as a large amount of strawberries, loganberries, and blackberries. A ranch wagon brought milk, eggs, and vegetables from the farm to the school twice a day throughout the year.[37] This was in stark contrast to the Rapid City Indian School, where, despite intensively farming over 300 acres of land, potatoes were the only crop raised for the direct consumption of students.[38] Indian Office inspectors regularly reported that Sherman had a far greater amount of fresh fruit and vegetables than was commonly found at nonreservation boarding schools.[39] Students wrote home describing the "wagonloads of oranges, the fields of watermelon, the sweet potatoes and squash, the cheese and butter."[40]

The increased attention given to Indian health that began in 1909 resulted in additional Indian Office policies pertaining to nutrition as a preventive health measure. After his annual inspection of Sherman Institute, Medical Supervisor Joseph Murphy communicated this enhanced focus directly to Conser. He wrote, "For the purposes of building up children who are not thriving, a special diet table should be provided." Further, Murphy told Conser that any pupils recommended by the school physician, by matrons, or by teachers, "because of apparently delicate health or loss of weight should be given milk and eggs in addition to their regular diet at this table."[41] Murphy suggested that in order to supply more eggs for this diet table, poultry and egg raising be made a specialty at the farm, and if possible, Conser should find a way to produce more milk.

The emphasis on diet and nutrition as preventive health measures was directly connected to the Indian Office's "war" on tuberculosis, particularly in regard to the dairy products that comprised an enriched diet. Medical professionals and lay persons alike considered a diet rich in eggs, cheese, buttermilk, and cream integral to recovery from tuberculosis.

Interestingly, the insistence on more dairy products possibly did more harm than good to Native American students. Over 75 percent of Native Americans are currently lactose intolerant, and there is no reason to believe this percentage differed significantly one hundred years ago. This common food allergy manifests itself with lethargy, nausea, diarrhea, flatus, and abdominal cramps. The diarrhea associated with lactose intolerance may be severe enough to purge other nutrients before they can be absorbed.[42] Clearly, forcing lactose intolerant children to consume large quantities of dairy products would have resulted in a great deal of illness—inexplicable at the time—a weakened constitution, and resultant immunological vulnerability to numerous disease organisms.

Eggs, milk, and other dairy products had been an integral part of the Sherman Institute diet since Hall established the farm in 1902, so the impetus behind Murphy's expectations of increased production are unclear. In a typical year, the Sherman Institute dairy herd produced enough milk to provide approximately five pints of milk per child each day of the year.[43] Few schools provided as much as a pint of milk a day for each student, and at many schools, milk and butter were two things unknown to the children.[44]

Though Conser complied with Murphy's edict to increase egg and milk production, it became increasingly difficult to provide abundant fruit and vegetables for students at Sherman Institute. As the student population grew, the original one hundred acres of farmland could no longer produce food in the quantities Conser determined necessary to maintain student health. Since appropriations for the purchase of additional farmland were long in coming, Conser rented additional farmland as close to the Sherman Institute farm as possible. By 1916, students farmed six additional parcels of land. This permitted the continued supply of abundant fresh produce to the school, and in fact, during vacation periods, when attendance was considerably reduced, there was a surplus of food. Conser sold the surplus to local stores for several hundred dollars each year, using this money to fund the rental properties and add improvements to the farm to increase food production.

EXERCISE

In its quest to provide abundant and nutritious food for the health of its students, Sherman Institute clearly benefited from good soil, adequate water, a temperate climate, and the vision of Superintendents Hall and Conser. The latter two elements, climate and vision, also benefited another important preventive health program at the school—exercise. In many ways, the exercise element of student health was more complex in both its origins and expected results than any other preventive program mandated by either Indian Office policy or practices specific to Sherman Institute. Military drills, regimented exercise, free play, and competitive sports comprised the exercise program. The professed goal of these elements as they pertained to health was twofold: to encourage outdoor activity with its concomitant healthful fresh air and to build strong bodies and minds.

Military drills had played an integral role in nonreservation boarding schools since the establishment of Carlisle Indian School in 1879. During the following two decades, school officials did not enforce drills for the purposes of maintaining a healthy student population, but simply because they believed that rigid discipline and structure aided in the rapid assimilation of Indian youth. By the end of the nineteenth century, however, the Indian Office increasingly rationalized military drills as being necessary to the health of nonreservation boarding school students. This was partially in response to pressure placed on the Indian Office by Progressive reformers who questioned the continued need for such tactics, and partially because of the increasing focus on health by the Indian Office. Further, the tenets of the powerful Public Health and Sanitary Movement of the late nineteenth and early twentieth centuries emphasized fresh air and exercise as integral to preventing disease. What better way to justify the continued use of military drills, which all boarding school superintendents perceived as necessary to assimilation, than to claim they were effective preventive health measures? In addressing a conference of Indian Office physicians in 1899, Dr. Johnson G. McGahey of the Standing Rock Agency summarized the prevailing Indian service medical opinion on the value of such drills. McGahey wrote that in the past, "when game was abundant and the aboriginal inhabitants of this country roamed at will in search of his food, he found also rude health of the game he pursued; but the Indian today is cut off from his former nomadic existence; his vitality is impaired." The medical doctor argued that, "The judicious use of military drill, coupled with improved dietetic conditions, would do more to eradicate tubercular diseases among the Indians than all the drugs in the material medica." Clearly, he felt that "systematic drill will have great value in preventing the many digestive disturbances of the Indian."[45]

McGahey continued, stressing another beneficial aspect of military drills, saying that, "discipline will also teach him self-control, so that in the future he may be able to do not what he likes, but rather, willing to do what he ought." Contrary to traditional views, McGahey felt that girls should also receive some military drill as well: "The day has come for the athletic white girl, and her Indian sister has the same need for physical development in accordance with hygienic laws." McGahey concluded his discourse on the value of military drills with the thought that "The question of the physical development of the Indian child touches upon the future of the race."[46]

Another vocal proponent of military drills as preventive health measures noted that the simple callisthenic exercises, particularly arm swinging, improved health and exercised nearly all the muscles of the body, causing pupils to become straight and supple and strong. This resulted in increased self-confidence and a heightened ability to learn both literary and industrial lessons.[47] In other words, there was not much that military drills could not accomplish, and all for the benefit of the Indian students.

Despite proclamations of the health benefits that military drills imparted, the Indian Office did not take a particular stance regarding their use as a preventive health measure. Nonreservation boarding schools universally used military drills, and with the exception of Progressive reformers there was no inclination on the part of school administrators to remove them as established procedures. Consequently, the Indian Office saw no need to regulate.

Figure 2.1. Military drills at Sherman Institute, circa 1902 (photo courtesy of the Riverside Municipal Museum).

Military drills had been part of the normal routine since Sherman Institute opened in 1902, but perhaps administrators placed less emphasis on rigid militaristic details than at other schools. Unlike some schools, such as Rapid City Indian School and Phoenix Indian School, Sherman Institute girls did not wear uniforms during the drills. Furthermore, rigid military formation and attention were not always enforced during the drills (fig. 2.1). Neither Hall nor Conser stressed the health benefits of military drills. Instead, they viewed drills primarily as a method of imparting order, organization, and discipline to several hundred students, most of whom were adolescents and young adults—a formidable task at best.

Hall and Conser placed a great deal of emphasis on the health benefits of exercise, free play, and competitive sports, however. Before the turn of the century, physical activity in the form of exercise and free play was virtually nonexistent at nonreservation boarding schools. Days were filled with the work of assimilation, and there seemed no tangible benefit to expending energy on activities not directly relevant to productivity and learning. By 1901, the Indian Office had recognized the value of exercise in maintaining health and had added appropriate recommendations to the *Course of Study for Indian Schools:* "Exercise makes the heart beat faster, so that it forces the blood more rapidly through every part of the body. The blood on its way carries new food to each part of the body and carries away what has worn out." The importance of muscles in maintaining healthy bodies did not go unnoticed, although there seemed to be an imperfect understanding of muscle physiology: "The muscle which is often and vigorously exercised is hard and firm because all its parts have been often changed, and all are young and strong. This is why the healthfulness and vigor of the body depends upon the amount of exercise we take."[48]

The Indian Office further acknowledged that some type of physical training might actually be necessary, if for no other reason than to counterbalance the Indian student's inherent weaknesses and better prepare him or her for the real world. "In order to get the best out of life, it is necessary to look into the physical condition of pupils," the *Course of Study* stated, adding that physical training, "will counteract the influences of unfortunate hereditary and strengthen the physique." Improving the physical condition of Indian youth would not only make them healthier in general, but through this physical training, "they may be able to bear the strain that competition in business will impose."[49]

The Indian Office did not require the compulsory integration of physical training into the curriculum, but rather merely suggested it. Interestingly, by this time virtually every nonreservation boarding school fielded a variety of competitive sports teams. Participation in these baseball, football, basketball, and cross-country marathon teams apparently did not constitute physical training in the eyes of the Indian Office. Perhaps this was because the Indian Office viewed the teams more as an advertisement for the schools, promoting individuality and instilling the American competitive spirit in Indian youth, than as providing physical conditioning. Alternatively, it may be that since competitive sports teams had been an integral part of nonreservation boarding schools since 1879,

Indian Office officials perceived school teams as established realities at the schools, not a viable solution to physical training.

Not until 1909 did the Indian Office develop policies regulating exercise and free play at boarding schools. As discussed earlier, after the landmark study conducted by Hrdlička and Johnson in 1908, Commissioner of Indian Affairs Francis E. Leupp determined that nonreservation boarding schools should become less regimented and, theoretically, more healthful. Though he was unable to act decisively on this matter while in office, his successor and friend, Robert Valentine, succeeded in interjecting more recreational activity into the students' daily routines. In December 1909, in an action based on the war against tuberculosis, Valentine prohibited all students with lung troubles from choosing indoor occupational activities and encouraged more outdoor activity for everyone. For the first time, the Indian Office acknowledged that a healthy student population was not one whose days were comprised solely of study and work. Valentine felt that recreation and play "of pupils and a proper balancing of work and play in the several schools has been made an important part of the health programme and the Indians' inherited need of fresh air has been met by encouraging football, baseball, basketball, and other forms of outdoor amusement."[50] To facilitate his proposal, Valentine adopted the concept of playgrounds and urged all boarding school superintendents to set aside outdoor space for the students' amusement and health.

By 1913, the Indian Office's stance toward exercise as a preventive health measure at nonreservation boarding schools had strengthened considerably. What began as a proposal became policy, subject to strict enforcement. The *Rules for the Indian School Service* stipulated that every school "should have systematic physical training," and this policy "must be made of utmost importance, reaching all pupils." The required physical training included breathing exercises once or twice every school session, a great amount of outdoor exercise and outdoor occupation, and the use of well-equipped playgrounds. By providing this training, the *Rules* noted paternalistically, "the constitutional tendencies and weaknesses of Indian pupils are to be vigorously combated."[51] The Indian

Office mandated inclusion of playgrounds in every school's physical plant, and appropriations for playground equipment, such as "swings, teeters, slides, turning poles, and the like," were readily forthcoming.[52]

During Hall's tenure at Sherman Institute from 1902 to 1909, he expressed no particular inclination toward using exercise as a preventive health measure. This was not surprising. Since the Indian Office had not yet formulated official policies regarding this issue, bureaucrat Hall did not institute any practices. He encouraged students to spend as much time outdoors as possible, because he was a firm believer in the healthful climate of Riverside and the benefits fresh air imparted to the children, but he did not encourage exercise or any other physical activity. Large playing fields had been part of Sherman Institute's physical plant since opening in 1902, but these were for the express use of the competitive sports teams, not for general free play or exercise. Throughout his career, Hall had been a great supporter of his school's football, basketball, and baseball teams, but not because they provided healthful physical training. Instead, Hall looked at these teams as powerful marketing tools. Sherman Institute's teams traveled throughout California, playing against all the major college and university teams, often winning. Hall used this exposure to elicit "friends" of Sherman Institute, garnering support for the school and for him.

It was not until Conser assumed the superintendency of Sherman Institute in late 1909 that exercise became an important part of the school's preventive health program. One obvious reason for this was Valentine's proposed integration of exercise and play into boarding school curriculum. However, Conser's personal belief in the importance of exercise in maintaining a healthy student population led him to embrace Valentine's proposal when many other superintendents did not. In compliance with Valentine's proposal, Conser immediately had separate open-air playgrounds constructed for boys and girls that the children could easily access and use on a daily basis. Throughout Conser's administration, active participation by all students in a variety of outdoor sports, athletic contests, and free play formed an integral part of the school's daily routine. Competitive football, baseball, and marathon teams for boys, and basketball teams for girls, continued to abound, and according to Conser, "Sherman students have seldom failed to win the prize in any athletic contest they have entered."[53] Conser encouraged students to spend as much time as possible outdoors in recreational pursuits with other students. In addressing the official Indian Office policies of 1913, Conser wrote that he expected "a reasonable amount of work and study," from students, but that he did not "lose sight of the fact that a healthy and prosperous institution must provide for proper recreation and social amusement and as much freedom and social intercourse is permitted the students as is consistent with proper discipline."[54]

While Conser encouraged a balance of work, play, and informal student recreation, by 1919 he felt that with the number of enrolled students, an exercise program supervised by a professional would be of far more benefit than one led by regular staff. In requesting authorization to hire an exercise director, Conser strengthened his argument by noting that properly supervised physical exercises would be a great factor in physical development, "as well as prevention of disease."[55]

Unfortunately, due to the minimal salary authorized by the Indian Office, Conser had great difficulty obtaining the services of a qualified individual until 1922, and then he could find only a girls' physical director; the disciplinarian continued to provide guidance for the boys. Yet Conser acceded that even under the direction of only one professional, the athletic games directed "have done much to maintain the general health of the students and have added to the good spirit of the institution."[56]

DISINFECTION

The fifth type of preventive health program developed by the Indian Office and implemented at Sherman Institute focused on disinfecting materials used by students at nonreservation boarding schools. This type of preventive program centered on specific sanitation within the school, such as clean bedding, books, and musical instruments, as well as personal hygiene. The intent of the preventive health program was to cleanse materials (and students) of anything that could transmit infectious disease. Over time, concepts of what caused disease and the best methods of disinfection changed, but at all times the school used some method of disinfection in an effort to prevent disease. Sherman Institute administrators used three distinct types of disinfecting agents: fresh air, sterilization, and chemicals. A fourth method of disinfection involved the "no sharing" policy previously discussed.

The medical profession had long considered fresh air important to preventing disease, hearkening back to a belief in the miasmatic theory of disease transmission. When the germ theory of disease emerged as the prevailing medical doctrine in the late nineteenth century, fresh air continued to be viewed in this light, because it prohibited germs from "settling" and infecting an individual with disease.

Following a misplaced belief that, "Air becomes contaminated by decomposition of animal and vegetable matter, causing many diseases," the 1901 *Course of Study for the Indian Schools of the United States* emphasized fresh air as the most important of disinfecting agents, simply by its existence.[57] Therefore, it specified measures for insuring that school plants maintained adequate ventilation and fresh air in both their construction and operation. In addition, Indian Office regulations mandated that employees clean all materials within the school on a regular basis with fresh air. Indeed, the Indian Office ordered that "Once a week, all mattresses should be thrown across the foot of the bed, so that air may circulate around them." Officials directed that "Buckets or boxes used in dormitories at night should have lids and be put into rooms the last thing at night, taken out the first thing in the morning, and aired outside all day."[58] The purpose of these regulations was to freshen the materials and cleanse them by exposure to fresh air that "is the great natural disinfectant, antiseptic, and purifier."[59]

By 1904, with the results of the 1903 physician's survey coming to light, regulations concerning exposure of school materials to fresh air became even more stringent, particularly concerning bedding. A circular issued in 1904 set forth very specific instructions on the methods of making beds for "the preservation of good sanitary conditions."[60] The circular required that mattresses be aired every morning, bed covers thrown back over the foot of the bed, and blankets sunned every week in the open air. School officials never allowed children to sleep in clothes worn during the day, because to do so would dirty the bedding and trap unhealthy materials under the covers. Instead, children had to hang clothes up overnight, where the clothing could be exposed to fresh air and thus cleansed for wear the next day. School employees stressed the importance of closely following these instructions, "as nothing is more conducive to health of mind and body than sound refreshing sleep in clean beds and well ventilated rooms."[61]

As discussed earlier, Sherman Institute superintendents Hall and Conser diligently complied with Indian Office regulations regarding physical plant ventilation. They also complied with the use of fresh air in disinfecting bedding, with an established routine that began shortly after the school opened in 1902 and lasted at least through 1922. Students threw their bedding over the back of their beds upon rising each morning, where it could be aired until after breakfast, when the beds were made up. On Saturday mornings, children took all blankets outside and placed them on the lawn or lines, where they aired until just before dinner, when the beds were remade.[62] Compliance with other regulations concerning fresh air disinfecting was negligible. Since each dormitory floor had toilets, there existed no pressing need for chamber pots or buckets to be aired. Students slept in nightwear, but since they hung their clothes in lockers, the exposure of clothing to fresh air overnight was minimal.

By 1913, the Indian Office placed less emphasis on fresh air as a disinfecting agent and more on other, less natural, methods. Though daily airing of mattresses and bedding continued, policy also required sterilization of bedding on a regular basis. As specified in the 1913 *Rules for the Indian School Service,* Indian Office policy mandated that all bedding be thoroughly disinfected twice a year, although it did not specify the precise method of disinfection. Further, no bedding used by an ill student could be used by anyone else until it had been sterilized with steam or boiling water or disinfected by formaldehyde or another efficient agent.[63]

At Sherman Institute, a steam laundry had been one of the first buildings constructed. Steaming and boiling on an as-needed basis cleaned sheets, towels, and students' clothing. Considering the size of the student population, it is highly unlikely that such cleaning occurred frequently, at least of the bedding. Since students generally possessed only one set of everyday clothes and one set of good clothes, it is also unlikely that their clothes received frequent cleaning at the laundry. Individual "Pullman" towels constituted the primary focus of disinfection by sterilization at the laundry.

As early as 1895, Superintendant of Indian Schools William Hailmann had condemned the prevailing roller towel system used at nonreservation boarding schools as a major contributor to the spread of disease, particularly trachoma. In keeping with Hailmann's recommendation, the 1901 *Course of Study* specified that every student be provided an individual towel. However, few boarding schools complied. Eleven years later, Circular 602 directed the use of individual towels that students were required to hang in separate assigned spots to avoid possible contact with other towels. No more than one student was ever to use a towel before it had been freshly laundered. Where schools had adequate laundries to handle the additional load, Valentine urged that the "Pullman" towel system be utilized.[64] This towel system, as used on Pullman train cars, provided each person with small hand towels to be used but once, then discarded to be laundered. Again, few schools complied with Circular 602, despite recognition that the recommended towel system could considerably decrease disease incidence. Superintendents protested that their already inadequate resources did not permit compliance. Existing appropriations were insufficient to cover the cost of additional towels for either the individual or Pullman systems, and they did not have enough staff to launder the towels, particularly if their school did not have a power laundry. Additional appropriations were not forthcoming, and the roller towel system remained in use at most boarding schools.

The following year, 1913, President Woodrow Wilson prohibited the use of roller towels in public buildings, which included nonreservation boarding schools. Newly appointed Commissioner of Indian Affairs Cato Sells subsequently sent every school rolls of crash to be cut into individual towels measuring nine inches by fifteen inches.[65] He ordered large schools that possessed power laundries to implement the Pullman towel system and provide each student with a minimum of four towels daily.[66]

Since Sherman Institute had a large steam laundry, the individual towel system had been implemented shortly after the school opened. How frequently students sent their individual towels to the laundry is not known, but it is improbable that they did so on a daily basis. Employees issued students bath towels as well as hand towels, the latter to be used in conjunction with lavatory washbasins between baths. Each towel was stored on either an individual hook or rack. Presumably, boys involved in farming and labor-intensive industrial training required more frequent laundering of towels than did the girls in domestic science class.

Since Conser had already put the individual towel system in place at Sherman Institute, he had little problem transitioning to the Pullman towel system in 1914. However, his response to Sells's policy circular illustrates the magnitude of such a change and explains why most boarding schools did not switch to this system. Conser told the commissioner that, relative to the Pullman system of individual towels, "we will need 3,000 towels in addition to the number that can be made from the crash now on hand." He requested that the Indian Office purchase and ship "900 yards of crash estimated at 11¢ per yard, amounting to $99.00, payable from the appropriation "Indian School, Riverside, California 1914."[67]

Fresh air and sterilization were the most common disinfecting agents utilized at nonreservation boarding schools. Yet, in many ways, the most effective disinfecting agents were chemical in nature. Chemical disinfection of school physical plants, by methods such as kalsomining or chloride of lime, had long been a common practice sanctioned by both the Indian Office and boarding school superintendents.[68] Disinfection of school supplies had been ordered periodically since the late nineteenth century, but neither the specific type of disinfection nor directions on how to accomplish it had been forthcoming. Not until 1908 did the

Indian Office specifically order chemical disinfection for materials and implements used by individual students and provide the necessary directions to proceed.

During the Hrdlička and Johnson tuberculosis study of 1908, the researchers found tubercle bacilli on the mouthpieces of wind instruments examined at Phoenix Indian School.[69] Since almost every non-reservation boarding school had a band comprised primarily of wind instruments, the implications of Hrdlička's discovery were obvious. Wind instruments posed a clear danger to student health by transmitting tuberculosis. Upon learning of Hrdlička's discovery, the Indian Office immediately sent a warning to school superintendents of the potential danger to band members. Schools had to report the names of each band member, their degree of Indian blood, name of their tribe, their age, and their number of years at school to the Indian Office.[70] Detailed instructions followed in Education Circular No. 246, explaining step–by step how to chemically disinfect the instruments. All mouthpieces had to be removed from the instruments and then soaked for one half hour in a 50 percent solution of alcohol. After cleaning all remaining parts of the instrument with alcohol, the employee had to further fumigate the entirety of the instrument with formaldehyde. The Indian Office gave school officials three alternate methods of formaldehyde disinfection. The instruments could be placed in a tightly sealed room accompanied by a hanging sheet soaked in formaldehyde for twelve hours; permanganate of potash could be mixed with formaldehyde in a tightly sealed room and the fumes from the chemical reaction be allowed to disinfect the instruments for at least twelve hours; or a fumigating generator could be used.[71] On 18 November 1908, the Indian Office issued instructions for disinfecting books in a similar manner.[72] The Hrdlička and Johnson study made no mention of books as potential carriers of tuberculosis, but as a precautionary measure, Circular No. 254 directed school superintendents to fumigate all books used by children, not just those with tuberculosis.

As seen in figure 2.2, Sherman Institute's band was comprised almost exclusively of wind instruments. Yet there is no evidence that Hall complied with the directive to disinfect either the mouthpieces or all books

Figure 2.2. The Sherman Institute band, 1902 (photo courtesy of the Riverside Municipal Museum).

in the school. Considering Hall's bureaucratic nature and his concern with students' health, one would expect to find prompt compliance. Further, in 1905 Hall had purchased a Trener-Lee Formaldehyde Disinfector, so disinfection would have been relatively simple. While it is probable that Hall did in fact comply, supportive documents have not been found despite an otherwise complete documentary record during this period.

By 1913, chemicals became a common method of disinfection for personal items used by students. Any school materials used by more than one student were subject to daily disinfection with formaldehyde, a costly and potentially harmful practice.[73] The increased emphasis on disinfection coincided with a greater focus by Valentine on preventive health measures, particularly as they related to tuberculosis. The *Rules for the Indian School Service* ordered, "Every precaution must be taken to prevent the spread of infectious disease." When two or more students used lead pencils, penholders, books, or other articles in succession, the *Rules* mandated that the school supplies "must be kept completely disinfected through the use of formaldehyde. If articles are distributed and collected each day, in the evening they are to be placed in small boxes with sponges moistened with formaldehyde."[74]

Students at Sherman Institute rarely had to share school supplies, so daily disinfection proved unnecessary. Conser budgeted accordingly to provide each student with the basic supplies. Generous donations by community "friends" generally could be counted on to supplement the budget if the school experienced a shortage of supplies. Conser complied with the disinfection of books as required by the Indian Office because books were expensive and could not readily be replaced.[75]

In most cases, Sherman Institute had sufficient textbooks to provide each student with his or her own copy. Therefore, students did not have to share books or have them sanitized. Upon advancement to the next grade, students passed their books on to other students, once the books had been disinfected with formaldehyde and recovered. However, any books used by students suffering from an infectious or contagious disease could not be issued to another student. School officials burned books used by infected students.

Disinfection by fresh air, sterilization, or chemicals provided a final method for preventing disease. If all other preventive health measures failed and disease occurred among the student population, disinfection kept the disease from being spread to other students. The officials at Sherman Institute used disinfection as a primary method of preventing disease, but they never ignored the importance of primary medical care.

CHAPTER 3

Medical Care

MEDICAL CARE HAD A MONUMENTAL IMPACT ON STUDENT MORBIDITY AND mortality at nonreservation boarding schools, with the dual function of providing both prevention and intervention. Facilities and personnel responsible for providing medical care represented the third line of defense against disease and death. Integrated with physical plant considerations and preventive health programs, they facilitated the maintenance of a healthy student population. Yet when these lines of defense failed and children became the victims of disease, illness, or accidents, the same medical facilities and personnel worked to heal the children and make them whole again.

Considering the increasing focus on health issues by the end of the nineteenth century, one would assume that providing adequate hospitals, medical supplies, doctors, and nurses at every nonreservation boarding school received priority attention. This was rarely the case. Instead, a crippling web of bureaucracy often entangled medical care for boarding school students, threatening, rather than facilitating, student health. Chronically inadequate appropriations for hospitals, modern surgical instruments, and medicines significantly affected the quality of medical care at every nonreservation boarding school. Low pay and political machinations limited the pool of Indian Service physicians from which the boarding schools could draw. Many schools had only part-time medical care from contract physicians, depending on resident nurses for both prevention and intervention.

Though the Indian Office expressed great concern over student health at nonreservation boarding schools and implemented a number of important changes, inadequacies in medical care continued through most of the early twentieth century, and as a consequence, student morbidity and mortality levels remained elevated. Only at schools where the superintendent placed a premium on student health and found ways to insure that students received consistently good medical care did morbidity and mortality levels decrease.

Sherman Institute did not have a facility specifically designed for health care until 1905. The school's original site plan did not include a hospital, and Superintendent Hall seemed unconcerned about the absence of a medical facility. In his lengthy discourse on school design sent to Commissioner Jones in 1900, Hall made detailed recommendations regarding virtually every element of Sherman Institute. Yet not once did he mention the need for a hospital, despite the fact that he was fully cognizant of the importance of such a facility. Instead, he focused on the need for an auditorium to seat no less than six thousand people.[1]

The reasons for Hall's inattention to the detail of providing a hospital are complex. First, he had an abiding belief in Riverside's healthy environment. Having experienced the oppressive heat of Phoenix and the inadequate water of Perris, Hall viewed Riverside, with its temperate climate, abundant water, and lush vegetation as "the healthiest place on earth." He quite foolishly believed there would be little need for a hospital at Sherman Institute, since few children would be ill. Second, Hall saw Sherman Institute as the quintessential Indian school of the West, a showplace to display the successful assimilation of Indian children. A hospital certainly had no part in that vision. Further, by the turn of the century, student health had received increasing attention, with efforts made to remedy past wrongs. The Indian Office wanted to change the perception of nonreservation boarding schools as disease and death factories. To construct a hospital at a new, flagship boarding school would have been admitting that health problems continued to exist. Plus, hospitals were very expensive to build and furnish. With only limited appropriations, the money was thought to better serve students by constructing state-of-the art dormitories that would help prevent illness, than by building a hospital to care for the few children who became ill. Unfortunately, despite the many preventive measures instituted, children at nonreservation boarding schools continued to become ill, and those at Sherman Institute were no exception. A hospital should have been one of the first buildings constructed, not only to provide adequate medical care for the students, but also to prove to Progressive reformers that the Indian Office was indeed making important changes at nonreservation boarding schools. By not providing a hospital, the Indian Office and Superintendent Hall showed a clear disregard for the health of Sherman Institute students.

Between 1902 and 1905, medical personnel cared for ill students in one of the older girls' dormitories, Ramona Home.[2] This three-story building had forty individual rooms on the second and third floors, dormitory space on the first floor, sitting rooms on each floor, and a playroom in the basement. Exactly where ill children were cared for is not known, but it appears that much of the building was used for this purpose at one time or another. When the hospital was finally built in 1905, Hall noted that the entire building needed to be kalsomined to make it healthy for its occupants.[3] This certainly brings up an interesting question—where were students living while rooms of their dormitory were being used to care for ill children? An answer for this rather provocative question is not immediately forthcoming. Conceivably, students whose rooms were used in Ramona House may simply have traded places with ill students, sleeping in their quarters while the ill students were being treated in the pseudoinfirmary.

The lack of a designated health care facility did not seem to be a problem until the autumn of 1904, when a devastating typhoid fever epidemic struck Sherman Institute.[4] Over a period of three months, forty-two children fell victim to the disease, with seven eventually perishing. With so many seriously ill children and no hospital, school officials did not have enough room in Ramona Home, so they distributed the children equally among the four dormitory buildings. With ill children spread over such a large area of the school, officials had difficulty providing adequate medical attention with the limited staff. Treatment of typhoid fever demands rigorous sanitary procedures that would have been extremely difficult to maintain for children housed in four separate dormitories.[5] The lack of a proper medical care facility may actually have exacerbated the length and severity of the epidemic.

By the summer of 1905, Hall had a small hospital constructed at Sherman Institute. The two-story brick building had a twenty-five-bed capacity and contained five wards, three private rooms, a kitchen, a drug room, and a dispensary.[6] A resident nurse lived at the hospital in order to provide around-the-clock care when necessary. Girls in the domestic science classes prepared all meals for ill students in the hospital kitchen. During the first two years of the hospital's operation, different girls took turns, a week at a time, preparing meals for students being cared for in the hospital. By 1907, the system had changed so that a single girl was detailed to take full charge of the hospital kitchen and dining room for each term. The domestic science teacher and resident nurse designed this change to provide more comprehensive training for the girl and to contribute to a more cohesive organizational plan for the hospital. Presumably, the girl in charge received help during periods when the hospital was at capacity, since preparing meals for twenty-five patients with varying dietary needs would have been a difficult task and surely not a situation conducive to the well-being of either patients or the domestic science student. This system continued until 1911, when a hospital cook staff position was finally established.[7]

Though Hall placed little importance on having a hospital at Sherman Institute and was quite satisfied with the one built in 1905, Frank Conser definitely did not share Hall's sentiments. As one of Conser's first acts upon assuming his position as superintendent in 1909, he requested a $5,000 appropriation for the purpose of improving the efficiency of the hospital. Conser considered the hospital very poorly arranged and sought funding to make necessary changes in its layout. "The health of the pupils must always receive primary consideration," he told Commissioner of

Indian Affairs Francis Leupp. In his opinion, proper medical care for five hundred to six hundred children demanded a first-class hospital, and he noted, "I confess that I have not seen a hospital recently that seems so poorly arranged for a school of this kind as ours."[8]

Conser's argument for a "first-class hospital," coupled with a recommendation from Supervisor of Indian Schools Charles that a new hospital be constructed at Sherman Institute, resulted in a decision by the Indian Office to seek appropriations for a new hospital instead of remodeling the old one. Considering the fact that Sherman Institute's hospital had been constructed only five years earlier, it is interesting that the Indian Office gave approval for a new hospital so readily.

In this case, timing was everything. As previously discussed, 1909 was a landmark year for aggressive action on student health at non-reservation boarding schools. The administrations of Francis Leupp and Robert Valentine put a priority on improving Indian health, and although Leupp despised nonreservation boarding schools and in fact had argued against the government providing hospitals for Indians, support was given to those schools showing the most promise as viable educational facilities, particularly for health–related issues.[9] Sherman Institute clearly qualified. Consequently, 1909 was an advantageous time for Conser to claim the need for a new hospital.

An Act of Congress (Public No. 114), approved 4 April 1910, appropriated $15,000 for construction of a new hospital at Sherman Institute.[10] Conser utilized specifications and blueprints for hospitals at Carlisle Indian School and Haskell Institute in designing the new hospital, modifying them to allow for the environmental differences of Riverside. Eliminating a ventilating system for the new hospital proved to be one of the more significant modifications Conser made to the plans. According to Conser, the elaborate ventilating systems used in the dormitories were absolutely worthless and a needless expense in Riverside's climate, so he eliminated the system from the hospital design. Conser argued that windows kept open throughout the year would amply provide ventilation. He also required that the hospital's brick walls be strengthened with iron rods in case of "probable earthquake."[11] Most of the changes Conser made, such as lowering the first story by six inches and substituting metal roof shingles in areas that could not be seen, were to reduce construction costs.

Workers completed the new hospital in 1912 (fig. 3.1). The one-hundred-bed facility employed exhaust steam heating, electric call bells in each ward, hot and cold running water, medicine chests, a nurse's office, reception rooms, a dental room, and an operating room with sterilizer, operating tables, and other necessary equipment. Screened porches were also provided to expedite the recovery of ill patients and minimize contagion. Once they were completed, Conser claimed that the hospital facilities were equal to any in the Indian Service and superior to those found in the average small city.[12]

Despite having what was considered a state-of-the-art operating room, surgery could not be performed on students until four months after the hospital opened. By that time, the original hospital had been converted into a girls' industrial building, so surgical cases, such as trachoma or tonsillectomies, had to be postponed. The problem originated with lost instructions for operating the sterilizer (fig. 3.2). Though it had been installed in the operating room in September, no one could figure out exactly how the sterilizer worked because instructions had not been included in the shipment. Correspondence with the supplier, Sun Drug Company, and the manufacturer, the American Sterilizer Company, brought instructions for operation, and the sterilizer could then be used for sterilizing surgical instruments. However, due to the placement of the sterilizer in the operating room (fig. 3.3), steam escaping from the machine rendered the administration of ether in the room impossible. Not until the end of December, when the manufacturer provided educational materials on the physical properties of water and steam, was the problem alleviated so that surgical procedures could commence. The hospital staff had simply been boiling water in the sterilizer too vigorously.

In addition to students and employees, Sherman Institute's hospital served Indians from nearby reservations, regardless of age, if they were in need of medical or surgical attention and could not afford to pay for the services elsewhere.[13] The school hospital provided medical care for

Figure 3.1. Sherman Institute hospital, 1912 (photo courtesy of the Riverside Municipal Museum).

Figure 3.2. Hospital operating room with sterilizer (photo courtesy of the Riverside Municipal Museum).

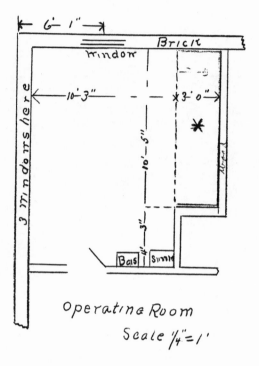

Figure 3.3. Original schematic of the operating room.

these individuals without cost. Every month between one and three patients from Southern California reservations were cared for at the hospital for a variety of ailments.[14] With the exception of Soboba Hospital near Banning, Sherman Institute provided the only medical care available for most Indians in the region.

Unlike many nonreservation boarding schools, Sherman Institute did not have a staff physician. Instead, a contract physician directed medical care at the school. This was an unusual situation for a school as large as Sherman Institute, since most schools without a staff physician had significantly smaller student populations.[15] Large nonreservation boarding schools typically had Indian Service physicians who had passed the Civil Service exam. The exam generated a list of eligible appointees, and those physicians with the most political influence generally received the appointments. In special cases, a physician could petition to be given a noncompetitive examination, and if the secretary of the interior approved, that person could be appointed immediately after taking and passing the test.[16] Contract physicians, on the other hand, evaded the Civil Service rules and were thus not required to pass a competency examination. They kept their private practices and were paid quarterly by the Indian Office for services rendered on a part-time basis.[17]

All methods of obtaining physician services for boarding schools held the opportunity for abuse, and this often resulted in poor-quality care for Indian students. While Indian Service physicians had proved at least competent enough to pass the Civil Service examination, those who received appointments were not necessarily those with the greatest medical skills, but usually those with the greatest political pull. New physicians often saw the Indian Service as an opportunity to gain experience in patient care, practicing their medical skills on the captive Indian students. Other physicians joined the Indian Service as a way to escape problems in their earlier lives, either professional or personal.[18] Of course there were also many competent Indian Service physicians who dedicated themselves to providing optimum care to Indians on reservations and in boarding schools. A few of these physicians, such as Dr. W. J. Minthorn of the Chilocco Indian School, served the dual function of school superintendent and physician.[19]

Contract physicians, on the other hand, provided only part-time care for boarding school students, with resident nurses given daily responsibility for student health care. While this situation clearly did not provide the best possible health care at boarding schools, the contract physicians were usually more experienced and often possessed higher-quality credentials than did regular Indian Service physicians. Since they maintained private practices while under contract to the boarding schools, they were able to provide equipment and specialized expertise not common among Indian Service physicians. Unfortunately, contract work was ancillary to their private practices, and as a result, some physicians gave their work at the nonreservation boarding schools less than optimal priority.

By 1902, Jones had expressed a desire to replace all Indian Service school physicians with professionally trained nurses, supplemented by contract physicians. He felt that trained nurses would provide better health care than that rendered by staff physicians, although he never articulated the basis for this opinion.[20] Compliance with Jones's preferences was not the sole reason Hall decided to contract for physician services instead of hiring a staff physician. More important was the fact that Hall doubted that for the limited amount of money prescribed by the Indian Office for staff physician wages he would be able to obtain as qualified an individual as he could by contracting with an outside physician. Recommendations for a local physician, made by prominent Riverside citizens who had been integral in bringing Sherman Institute to Riverside, strengthened Hall's resolve to avoid hiring a full-time Indian Service physician.

Shortly before Sherman Institute opened in 1902, Hall requested authority to contract with Dr. A. S. Parker for medical attendance at the school. He argued that "with 350 pupils it is quite imperative for the health of the school that good medical attention be given." Good medical attention could certainly be given by Dr. Parker, who stood at the head of his profession in the City of Riverside. "He is an energetic, able man in every particular," Hall noted, "and will give the school the best attention. He is a "regular," or "old school," and is an excellent surgeon as well."[21]

The medical community considered Parker one of the most highly qualified physicians and surgeons in Riverside County. He had begun his medical education at the University of Southern California, and then had transferred to Tulane University, where he received his medical degree in 1893. Dr. Parker had his first practice in 1896 at Fallbrook in San Diego County, and then moved to Riverside in 1897. He was elected secretary-treasurer of the Riverside County Medical Association in 1899, president in 1901, and delegate to the state meeting of the Medical Association in 1906.[22] Parker maintained a thriving medical practice in downtown Riverside and did not need additional work. However, he agreed to be Sherman Institute's contract physician at the request of his friend, Frank Miller, and also because, like many prominent Riverside citizens, he felt a certain amount of paternalism toward Indian students at the school.

Dr. Parker's contract provided for an annual payment of $600 in exchange for specified medical services. His contract required him to visit Sherman Institute whenever school officials needed his professional services. At a minimum, his contract required him to visit the school at least three times per week for the purpose of improving the sanitary and hygienic conditions there.[23] Since he was not considered an employee of the school, the Indian Office could revoke his contract upon fifteen days' notice. At the end of each quarter, Parker submitted vouchers, filled out in triplicate, upon which he itemized the number of visits made to the school and the services performed during each visit.[24]

Despite his contractual obligations, there is no indication that Dr. Parker actually spent much time at the school.[25] In fact, with his private practice located across town from the school and office hours of 9:00 to 11:00 A.M., 1:00 to 3:00 P.M., and 7:00 to 8:00 P.M., there would have been little time during the week for Parker to have visited Sherman Institute, let alone provided more than cursory patient care.[26] Since Sherman Institute did not have hospital facilities until 1905, and even then lacked a formal operating room until 1912, Parker performed few surgeries at the school. His work focused on routine medical examinations at the beginning of each school year, minimally implementing and enforcing physical plant sanitation, and consulting with the resident nurse on individual patient care.

Not until the typhoid fever epidemic of 1904 did Parker spend appreciable time caring for students at Sherman Institute. During the duration of the epidemic he visited the school daily to check on children who had fallen victim to the disease, but his function primarily involved consulting with the two resident nurses and giving orders to "irregular" nurses hired to provide additional medical care during the epidemic. Though the epidemic continued for two weeks, Parker did nothing to investigate its source. Not until being chastised by Commissioner of Indian Affairs Leupp did he even speculate as to the cause of the epidemic, and then offered two conflicting reports.[27]

Parker resigned his contract position at Sherman Institute in 1909, citing his health as the reason. Shortly before resigning, he had been appointed one of two Riverside County physicians, alternating with Dr. William W. Roblee on a monthly basis, to provide services for the indigent of the county.[28] Maintaining a private practice, serving as contract physician for Sherman Institute's 555 students, and rotating duties as the county physician apparently took its toll on Parker's health, for he resigned from the county position concurrent with his resignation from Sherman Institute.[29] Parker recommended that his associate, Dr. Roblee, be hired to fill the vacancy at Sherman Institute. Conser concurred, and Roblee assumed the position of contract physician at Sherman, a position he was to hold for the next twenty-eight years.[30]

William W. Roblee, like Dr. Parker, was an eminent physician and surgeon in Riverside at the time of his association with Sherman Institute. He attended Emporia College in Kansas and went on to become the physical director of the Oakland YMCA in 1891. He attended the Cooper Medical College in San Francisco, where he obtained his medical degree in 1895. After moving to Riverside and starting a medical practice in 1895, he also served as physical director of the Riverside YMCA for a few years. Roblee continued his education by spending a year in Europe in 1902, where he took extensive courses on bacteriology and microscopy in Vienna and Heidelberg. Upon returning to Riverside, Dr. Roblee was elected president of the Riverside County Medical Association in 1905.[31]

Despite the fact the Roblee was a contract physician and thus not technically an Indian Service physician, he remained subject to Indian Office regulations regarding patient care.[32] The Indian Office had long provided guidelines pertaining to the duties of physicians, but exact job duties of physicians at nonreservation boarding schools not been formalized or enforced. This changed with the issuance of *Rules for the Indian School Service* in 1913, a guide that was to remain in effect at least through 1922.

According to section 177 of the *Rules*, school physicians, "Shall make regular, frequent, and thorough examination of the pupils, with special attention to infectious diseases of all sorts." In addition to physical examinations, nonreservation boarding school physicians had to attend to the "individual needs of pupils in nutrition and physical welfare," and institute appropriate treatment. The duties of school physicians extended to making "constant examinations of all parts of the school to see that the insanitary conditions of all kinds are rigorously prevented." Finally, the *Rules* required that physicians give intelligent instruction to students "concerning sanitation, tuberculosis, trachoma, and the cause and prevention of disease."[33]

In addition to caring for students, the school physician made a thorough examination of all employees and members of their families who either lived on the school grounds or associated with the students in any way. The purpose of the examinations, conducted during the first month of the school year and at any other time necessary, was to find evidence of any communicable disease that might be transmitted to students, as well as to diagnose cases of pulmonary tuberculosis.[34]

Interestingly, the 1913 *Rules* emphasized prevention of smallpox, with little mention of tuberculosis or trachoma, despite the fact that smallpox had not posed a large health hazard in the schools since the late nineteenth century. The Indian Office required physicians to vaccinate each pupil before he or she was enrolled in school, unless the pupil presented satisfactory evidence of a recent successful vaccination. All employees and their children were also to be vaccinated before reporting for duty unless they could prove they had already had smallpox or had been successfully vaccinated in the recent past. If a smallpox scare in the vicinity of the school arose, all pupils and employees, regardless of whether they had already been vaccinated, were to be revaccinated by the school physician. The *Rules* admonished every school to keep a complete record of the dates and names of persons vaccinated on file in the school office at all times.[35]

In addition to vaccination records, the Indian Office directed school physicians to keep permanent records of every case treated, and using the data from these records, make semiannual reports on the sanitary conditions of the school and all cases treated. Physicians sent the reports to the commissioner of Indian affairs through the school superintendent on July 1 and January 1 of every year. As previously discussed, the required physician reporting forms had been specifically designed by

Valentine to facilitate consistent collection of health statistics from schools across the country.

School physicians, whether staff or contract, were directly responsible to the school superintendent. The *Rules* stipulated that physicians were in charge of the school hospital and directed all hospital employees, but the superintendent assigned their duties. Physicians were required to instruct "a class of the more advanced and intelligent girls in nursing and in the care of the sick." The formalized rules for physician duties went so far as to specify which diseases—smallpox, measles, mumps, scarlet fever, epidemic cerebro-spinal meningitis, infantile paralysis, whooping cough, acute conjunctivitis, and scabies—physicians had to quarantine. Again, the fact that tuberculosis was not mentioned as a disease to be quarantined is curious.

Roblee's service as Sherman Institute's contract physician proved intensive, despite the fact that his contract required only a part-time presence. While his contract called only for visits to the school three times per week, he often made daily visits, and he was on call for special cases or emergencies. Should Dr. Roblee be unavailable, one of his associates, either Dr. C. VanZwalenburg or Dr. T. A. Card, would attend to the students. This clearly represented a significant improvement in the level of medical care over that provided during the seven years of Dr. Parker's tenure as Sherman Institute's contract physician.

Upon construction of the new hospital in 1912, Roblee specialized in surgery. Operations held there regularly included cases of appendectomy, mastoiditis, empyema, osteomyelitis, tonsilectomy, and trachoma. One of his associates always assisted in the operations, but nursing students also participated, as surgery comprised an integral part of their training.

Of perhaps equal importance to Roblee's care of medical and surgical patients were the secondary benefits the school acquired through his large private practice. Roblee provided medical equipment and diagnostic procedures that regular Indian Service physicians rarely, if ever, had access to in their care of Indian students at nonreservation boarding schools. Roblee's office in Riverside had "a plant thoroughly equipped for bacteriological and chemical work together with modern X-ray equipment." He provided "all the bacteriological work necessary in the handling of contagious diseases and everything necessary both in photography and X-ray treatments," at no charge to the Indian Office, with the only additional charge ever made "being the actual cost of the X-ray supplies."[36] Since one of the most common complaints from Indian Service physicians concerned the lack of up-to-date medical and surgical equipment, the fact that Roblee's private practice supplied these diagnostic tools virtually free of cost was an important factor in the health care of Sherman Institute's students.

Unfortunately, Roblee could not completely stock the Sherman Institute hospital with surgical instruments from his private practice, and consequently often shared Indian Service physicians' consternation regarding the lack of up-to-date or appropriate tools. In one instance, the hospital possessed no instruments for performing tonsillectomies, yet there were a number of students with enlarged tonsils needing the operation. Tired of waiting for an instrument order to be filled through the appropriate channels, Roblee finally told Conser to request an emergency authorization for the purchase of instruments on the open market.[37]

In addition to problems obtaining surgical equipment, Roblee shared a problem common to every Indian Service physician at nonreservation boarding schools—lack of medicine. Sherman Institute suffered from a chronic shortage of both medicine and medical supplies, particularly as the student population expanded. This was partially the result of Conser's mandate that any child exhibiting the slightest symptoms of illness be sent to the hospital for treatment. Each year the hospital went through dozens of clinical thermometers, checking the temperature of every child sent for observation.[38] Furthermore, physicians ordered medical supplies from the Indian Office only once a year, and accurately anticipating the coming year's health needs often proved difficult. As a result, Conser, like Hall before him, requested emergency purchases of medicine on the open market several times each year, each instance being "imperative for the preservation of life and health of Indian pupils at the school."[39]

Both Indian Service physicians and Roblee also complained that the standard Indian Office supply list was outdated and lacked the flexibility

to provide for special cases. If physicians strayed from the list and purchased different medicines on the open market, they were called to task
over the matter. In one case, Roblee made several such purchases and
Sells demanded an explanation from Conser. In defense of Roblee's
actions, Conser explained to Sells, "There are several different reasons
why these purchases were made, the principal one being that we were out
of the particular drugs purchased, that those desired were not on the
annual estimate, and were needed immediately for special cases."
Although whenever possible, Conser noted, "we have endeavored to
make our patients fit the drugs on hand," in some cases it proved impossible, and "it is necessary to have drugs suit the patients or the peculiarity
of the disease or to cause the individual to suffer hardship and danger."[40]

As a career Indian Office bureaucrat, Conser automatically responded
to official Indian Office policies with strict compliance. However, in dealing with the health of students at Sherman Institute, experience and
instinct shaped his compliance. Conser left decisions about patient care
to Roblee simply because Roblee was the medical professional. In the
rare instance that Roblee's actions did not conform to official policy,
Conser offered support and justification on his behalf to the Indian Office.
A telling example of this occurred when Sells questioned Roblee's unauthorized use of eucamal in treating coughs. Conser told Sells that Roblee
considered the use of eucamal especially good for the children, but since
he wanted to comply with official orders, he hesitated to continue using
the medicine. In defending Roblee's use of eucamal, Conser rather caus-
tically added, "I therefore wish to suggest that in my opinion, it is in the
best interests of our children to be governed by the discretion of our
health officers."[41] Conser went on to request that the continued use of
eucamal be permitted even though it might not have been found on the
United States dispensatory.

Roblee preferred to use eucamal for treating coughs at Sherman
Institute because it did not contain any opiates, unlike the cough
medication prescribed by the Indian Office. In noting his faith in this medicine Roblee noted, "I have been using this largely in my private practice
as well as in my own family in place of the ordinary expectorants." He

found it to be very effective in the treatment of most coughs. Roblee explained his reasons for using eucamal instead of the cough medicines authorized by the Indian Office: "The main objections to the use of the ordinary cough mixtures for children is that they all contain opium or its derivatives," adding, "This to me is very objectionable with any patient and especially for children." In his defense, Roblee closed, "I felt that I was rendering the Indian children under my care good service when I recommended that it be purchased for their use."[42]

Unfortunately, the Indian Office did not encourage physicians to prescribe unauthorized medicines, and as such, did not give Roblee permission to prescribe eucamal, despite the fact that it was a safer cough medicine. Although Roblee abhorred the thought of giving Indian children cough medicine that contained opiates, physicians throughout the United States commonly prescribed this type of medicine to both children and adults, therefore making it acceptable to the Indian Office.

In part, restricting physicians to the use of only specifically authorized medications represented a control and safety factor, particularly considering the fact that even the Indian Office knew Indian Service physicians were not always among the most highly qualified physicians. Medicines included on the standard supply list were generally conservative, time-tested remedies. Their use precluded individual physicians from experimenting or following their own theoretical inclinations and possibly endangering the lives of the Indian students being treated.[43] However, from a purely practical and financial standpoint, the annual bidding process fixed the cost of all medicine on the supply list. Allowing physicians to purchase unauthorized medical supplies would have potentially wreaked havoc with the Indian Office's budget.[44]

With the exception of trachoma, medical care at Sherman Institute did not include treatment of eye problems. Both Parker and Roblee conducted cursory vision examinations for any student complaining of sore eyes, difficulty seeing, headaches, or problems studying. Teachers referred students for examinations when they observed them to have any of these problems, even if the child did not personally complain. The physicians treated students with trachoma at the school, but referred those with regular vision problems to a local oculist. Interestingly, the Indian Office did not automatically authorize payment for these referrals, but required justification for any for treatment on an individual basis. In each case, Sherman Institute superintendents reported that after inspecting the pupil's eyes, the physician claimed the child required glasses, "without same their eyes were being very damaged. Upon his recommendation, I had them examined and glasses furnished."[45]

By 1916, the Indian Office had recognized the importance of safeguarding Indian students' eyesight, primarily because trachoma had reached almost endemic proportions at every nonreservation boarding school. As the foundation for this new emphasis in eye care, Commissioner Cato Sells authorized arrangements with the A. S. Aloe Optical Company to provide eyeglasses for Indian students through the St. Louis warehouse, at prices ranging from $.60 to $3.15 each. Sells then admonished school superintendents to consider the position of desks, windows, and curtains so that students' eyes would not be injured by improper light as they performed their schoolwork: "Light should never enter from the front and shine in the pupil's eye." Exhibiting a distinct lack of understanding of the cause of trachoma, Sells added, "This is especially important in the Indian service in view of the high percentage of trachoma." Sells's directive further ordered that "The window space should not be less in area than one-fifth of the floor space," a somewhat arbitrary requirement that nonetheless benefited students.[46] To insure compliance with his directive, Sells instructed school superintendents to submit cost estimates for any necessary structural improvements to the Indian Office.

At Sherman Institute, the number and size of existing classroom windows made structural improvements unnecessary. Classroom arrangements had taken both light and ventilation into consideration from the beginning, with desks generally positioned so that window light came from the side or slightly behind the students. Consequently, compliance with this portion of the directive proved easy. On the other hand, Sells's directive to purchase eyeglasses from a central purveyor did not sit well with Conser, and compliance was not immediately forthcoming.

Referring to Circular No. 1170 relative to the furnishing of eyeglasses to Indian pupils, Conser notified Sells that he had spoken with a specialist in Riverside regarding the cost of professional eye examinations and glasses. The doctor charged $5.00 for an examination, plus the costs of the glasses. Conser admitted, "the prices quoted by Dr. Walker for examination and glasses are somewhat higher than his examination and obtaining these glasses from the St. Louis Warehouse." However, in his opinion the extra cost was worthwhile: "I believe that the satisfaction of obtaining theses glasses immediately from the local doctor would more than compensate for the additional price."[47]

Conser's wariness regarding ordering eyeglasses from a central purveyor through the St. Louis Warehouse was understandable. Orders for commodity goods from regional warehouses often took months to fill, and it was unlikely that a pair of eyeglasses ordered for a pupil across the country would receive priority treatment. By the time school physicians referred a student for an eye examination, a problem had already become evident, and Conser did not want the child's vision problems exacerbated by a lengthy wait for glasses to arrive from St. Louis.

On a somewhat more pragmatic note, both Hall and Conser nurtured strong ties between the school and the citizens of Riverside, depending on the largesse and paternalism of the community to support the school. Patronizing a local doctor to serve the vision needs of Sherman Institute's large student population made infinitely more business sense to Conser than did strict compliance with Sells's directives. Sells's response to Conser is not known, but it is assumed that he did not fully consent to a local provider of eyeglasses. Requests for authorization of "emergency eyeglasses" from the local doctor continued on a regular basis, suggesting that Conser had not received permission to bypass the mandated procedure for obtaining glasses.

For most of the period from 1902 to 1922, Sherman Institute did not provide dental care for students at the school. In fact, there is no evidence that students received any regular dental examinations or preventive care until 1911. School officials sent children with tooth injuries or whose teeth were in extremely bad condition to a private dentist in

....

Riverside. While the school paid for injuries, students assumed responsibility for paying for any other dental work. Generally, the dentist examined a student's teeth and sent a diagram, such as the one shown in figure 3.4, accompanied by a written estimate for the cost of the necessary dental work to the superintendent. Superintendent Hall or Conser then sent a letter to the student's parents, requesting the specified amount of money prior to authorizing any dental work. Only in emergencies or when the student could not possibly afford to pay, did the school pay for dental work.

The inattention to regular dental examinations and preventive care at Sherman Institute reflected the orientation of the Indian Office during this period. The importance of proper care and cleaning of teeth had long been recognized, but not emphasized. Though focusing at length on other aspects of physiology and personal hygiene, regarding teeth the 1901 *Course of Study* noted only that students should be taught not to pick their teeth with metal lest it break the enamel, nor should they drink very hot or cold beverages lest they crack the enamel and cause tooth decay.

In 1911, the dental care program in nonreservation boarding schools changed dramatically. In recognition of the important role dental hygiene played in general health, Commissioner Valentine ordered all Indian school superintendents to provide each student with a toothbrush and to supervise the brushing of teeth twice daily. The Indian Office also considered employing dentists to treat the teeth of students in nonreservation boarding schools, and solicited opinions from various superintendents on how this might best be accomplished. They directed each superintendent to contact local dentists to arrange for regular dental services for students, securing estimates for the costs of filling cavities and extracting and cleaning teeth. Conser took this one step further by contacting the California Association of Dentists representative in Riverside for input on establishing a dental care system. The recommendation that instead of contracting with private dentists, the school hire a full-time staff dentist, Conser deemed impracticable.[48]

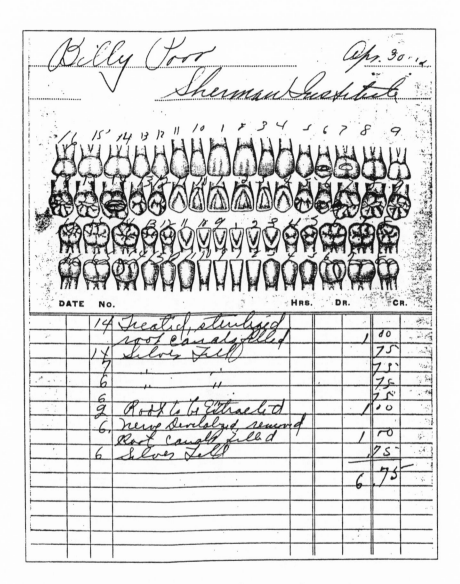

Figure 3.4. Sample dental examination diagram and cost estimate.

The Indian Office created seven staff positions for dentists in 1913, each at a salary of $1,500 per annum, roughly double the salary of Indian Service physicians. The dentists traveled to various schools to care for students' teeth during the school year and adults' teeth during vacation periods.[49] The Indian Service dentists apparently never reached Sherman Institute. The school continued to depend on private dentists in Riverside to provide dental care, with the students responsible for payment when at all possible.

With the increased Indian Office focus on providing dental care for all Indian students, the cost of sending students to private dentists soon proved a hardship on Sherman Institute's budget. Conser complained that all his students had to go to Riverside for their dental work, usually accompanied by an employee. In these cases, cost became a critical factor, "Streetcar fare to Riverside and return costs 20¢. Where an escort is needed one trip to Riverside costs 40¢ in addition to the dental work."[50]

As a solution to this problem, Conser recommended purchasing a dental chair, a dental engine, and a small cabinet for a cost of approximately $200, installing this equipment in a corner of the hospital, then enticing a local dentist to come to the school and work on the students instead of sending the students to the dentist.[51] The Indian Office approved his request, and Conser established a small dental office in the southeast corner of the hospital. Conser then contracted with a local dentist to provide routine cleaning, extractions, and fillings for students on a weekly basis.[52] Not until a number of Hopi and Navajo children requiring considerable dental work arrived at the school in 1920 did Conser seek additional help for the local practitioner by requesting that an Indian Service dentist be detailed to care for these pupils.[53]

Providing toothbrushes and dentists did not instill an automatic appreciation for dental hygiene in either students or school employees. The concept of dental hygiene was new for many Americans, and some Indian Service employees thought regular tooth brushing was just a fad.[54] To promote appreciation of good dental hygiene, the Indian Office distributed dental textbooks to physicians, included dental care in Dr. Shoemaker's lectures and stereoptican slide show, and supplied school

Figure 3.5. Dental hygiene advertisements in the *Sherman Bulletin*.

newspapers with articles and quotations designed to stimulate interest in dental hygiene. The *Sherman Bulletin* regularly published these articles and advertisements (fig. 3.5).

Despite these efforts, dental care remained poor throughout the Indian Service schools, primarily because of apathy on the part of school officials. Matrons often complained that supervising tooth brushing twice a day took them away from more important tasks. Superintendents often purchased poor-quality toothbrushes, or an inadequate quantity to insure a separate toothbrush for each child, or neglected to enforce twice daily brushing. Further, the methods used for brushing teeth ranged from merely ineffective to unsanitary and even dangerous as far as the transmission of disease. Until Commissioner Sells required that racks be built at each school to keep toothbrushes separated, students reportedly traded toothbrushes, put them in their pockets, played with them, or even threw them away.[55]

Fortunately, this situation did not exist at Sherman Institute. Whether Frank Conser actually recognized the important role dental hygiene played in good health or whether he simply complied with Indian Office directives is not known. Both factors probably entered into his establishment of regular dental care at Sherman Institute. The fact that a dentist visited the school weekly beginning in 1913 and continued throughout his tenure at the school undoubtedly had an impact on Conser, as well. He witnessed the dental problems of students and endeavored to prevent as many as possible from occurring. As such, Conser consistently ordered enough toothbrushes to insure each student had his or her own, enforced the supervision of tooth brushing by employees, had students label toothbrushes with their names, provided racks for storing toothbrushes separately, and provided individual cans of tooth powder to each student with instructions on the proper method of application. Realistically, it is unlikely that each of these measures was successfully implemented all the time. The fact that Conser attempted to instill good dental practices among the students is significant, however, considering the difficulty encountered in this regard at many schools by the Indian Office.

Nurses constituted both the strongest and weakest component of medical care at Sherman Institute. They provided the majority of patient care on a daily basis, yet it was difficult to find and retain competent nurses who could also manage the heavy workload. Consequently, turnover was high, and long-term stability lacking.

As previously discussed, Sherman Institute never had a staff physician, instead relying on part-time contract physicians. However, the Indian Office hired a resident nurse for the school who had full responsibility for the daily medical care of both students and employees. The nurse lived at the medical care facility, which at first was located at Ramona House before the Indian Office funded hospitals in 1905 and 1912. In this way, nurses provided round-the-clock care to patients. The nurse received a salary of $600 per year, the same amount as most teachers, the seamstress, the baker, and the cook.[56] Although Sherman Institute superintendents provided her a room, the resident nurse paid for her board at the "employee mess," or dining room, as did all Sherman

Institute staff. Between 1902 and 1907, the resident nurse had no assistance except during the 1904 typhoid fever epidemic. For the one-month duration of the epidemic and recovery period, Superintendent Hall hired an assistant resident nurse and five "irregular" nurses to help care for the thirty-five children stricken by the disease.[57] The remainder of the time, the resident nurse was virtually on her own as far as patient care, since the contract physician, Dr. Parker, spent little time at the school.

Between 1902 and 1907, Sherman Institute had at least one new nurse every year. In some cases, the nurse simply could not handle the amount of work expected or the responsibility the position entailed. This proved to be an ongoing problem throughout the research period. All too frequently, a nurse's incompetence led to her discharge, a problem Hall found extremely frustrating. Every time he reported yet another vacancy and asked for a new nurse to be sent, he reiterated, "A *trained* nurse is very necessary for this position, one that has experience."[58] The fact that Hall made this plea so frequently is interesting, since Indian Service nurses had to pass the Civil Service examination in order to be placed on the eligibility list. Apparently, as had been the case with Indian Service physicians, the ability to pass this test did not accurately reflect competency. One of the major problems with nurses at Sherman Institute was that few had any hospital experience, yet the Indian Office policy regarding medical care personnel effectively put them in charge of running the school hospital.

In 1907, a significant change in the quality of nursing care occurred. The Indian Office sent Miss Mary Israel to fill the resident nurse position at Sherman Institute. In reality, Miss Israel was not a nurse at all, but a physician. She had received her medical training in Baltimore and Washington, D.C., and had been hired as the Medical Inspector in the Marine Health and Public Hospital Service when a lack of funds to pay salaries caused the cancellation of her appointment. As a result, she took the position of nurse at Sherman Institute. Israel had considerable experience in the treatment of trachoma, as well as patient care and surgery. In essence, when Mary Israel came to Sherman Institute, the school enjoyed the care of a full-time physician for the first time.

Figure 3.6. Nursing students at Sherman Institute pictured with a woman believed to be Mary Israel.

One of the first and most important things Israel accomplished was the establishment of a comprehensive nurse's training program at Sherman Institute. Although before her arrival some students had helped the resident nurse and thus received limited training, Israel created a program based on medical school curriculum. Since Israel had trained as a physician, not a nurse, she shaped the nursing program according to the only training she knew. She did not intend to train the nursing students to be physicians, but to insure that their hospital training was complete enough to provide optimum patient care at Sherman Institute and to prepare them for jobs when they completed their training (fig. 3.6).

At first, Israel divided the nursing program into three grades, the first of which had two classes, A and B. The first years' work included care of the hospital itself, such as cleaning and making beds, as well as preparation of food and "the little attentions essential to the comfort of patients."[59] By the second half of the first year, nursing students were learning about the preparation of simple drugs, taking temperature, pulsation, and respiration, administering dressings, and the use of disinfectants. Second-year students made stock medicines from the crude drugs, and learned prescription Latin, the use of medicinal terms, how to keep patient charts, how to administer medicines hypodermically, and how to dress wounds. These students also cared for special cases, such as pneumonia and typhoid fever. By the third year, the curriculum consisted of diet cooking, knowledge of the principles of modern surgery, surgical care, anesthesia, hemorrhage, shock, and other emergency treatment, and special operations.[60]

Shortly after the nurse's training program began, Israel relieved the students from general cleaning and ward work, assigning "ward maids" to do these chores. She felt that these menial jobs wasted the skills of her nursing students. In this way she allowed nursing students to focus on their studies and on the practice of medicine, rather than on housekeeping.[61] Israel's actions represented a major philosophical change in the way Indian students were perceived. Most whites thought Indians were too stupid to learn a profession, instead relegating them to "industrial training" or "domestic science" jobs. These jobs required little education beyond basic reading, writing, and arithmetic, at best. Mary Israel, however, believed that the Indian nursing students at Sherman Institute had the intelligence and capabilities to become true nursing professionals, not simply to provide manual labor in the hospital.

The new course of study reflected Israel's belief in the students' intelligence. Required courses included anatomy, physiology, hygiene, and general nursing. Since the school hospital had facilities for only minor operations, Israel and Dr. Parker arranged for advanced students to have the opportunity to observe and help in operations conducted at Riverside General Hospital. At the end of every month students took practical examinations, gave public demonstrations of their work, and wrote articles on health matters that the *Sherman Bulletin* published. In this manner, nursing students effectively served as public health educators to the rest of the student population.

Within a short period of time, the coursework assigned to nursing students became very sophisticated, and their level of training under

Miss Israel proved problematic, in that they lacked a sufficient patient base on which to put their academic knowledge to work.[62] Hall addressed this problem in a request to Commissioner Leupp that the Sherman Institute hospital be permitted to care for Southern California Indians requiring medical care. The school had a fairly well equipped hospital and a class of nursing students, "taking training under our most competent trained nurse and physician." But, "as there is not sufficient sickness among our pupils to give these girls proper experience and training," he wrote, "it has been suggested that the Indians from the reservations of Southern California who require surgical treatment and lying-in, be, so far as practicable, entered in the school hospital."[63]

Considering the fact that Sherman Institute would not receive extra compensation for this care, and that Hall's budget had little room to pay for additional meals and medication, his request is significant. Hall's offer indicates that he had faith in the abilities of the Sherman Institute nursing students to elevate the level of their learning and become nursing professionals. This is particularly evident in his mention of patients requiring surgical treatment. Assisting in surgery required a great deal of knowledge and expertise, both of which Hall obviously felt the nursing students capable of in offering their services. As an aside, Hall's letter also suggests that the student population at Sherman Institute in 1908 was generally healthy, leaving the nursing students little work to do.

Leupp approved Hall's request, and from that time, nursing students at the Sherman Institute hospitals provided medical care for any Indian living in Southern California. Hall's only caveat to this situation was that it would necessitate rules "eliminating whole families with children, and horses, and teams, and dogs, from remaining at the school."[64] In the past, Southern California reservation Indians seeking medical attention had arrived at Sherman Institute with "entire families, their relations, and others," accompanying the sick ones and desiring "to board at the school or camp there indefinitely." In view of his considerable budgetary constraints, Hall requested that this be eliminated.[65]

Mary Israel's tenure at Sherman Institute lasted until 1909. Shortly after her arrival at Sherman Institute, she applied for a position as an

Indian Service physician, but the Indian Office did not hire her as a doctor until two years later, when an assistant physician position opened at the new Phoenix Indian School trachoma hospital. After her departure, the resident nursing situation resumed its unstable nature, with a seemingly endless parade of nurses rotating thorough the doors of the school hospital.

Fortunately, Israel had established a firm foundation for the nursing program. Under the direction of Dr. Roblee and a variety of resident nurses, it continued to thrive, eventually expanding to include four years of training. In 1913, a former Sherman Institute student, Miss Ellen Norris, enrolled in the University of California, Berkeley, premedical course with the ultimate goal of becoming a physician. While at Sherman Institute, Ellen had completed the four-year nursing program in two years, and she credited the program with her desire to become a physician. "It was there that I first decided to become a doctor," said Miss Norris, "I liked the nursing, but I felt that would never satisfy me, and I wanted to be a doctor."[66] Not all nursing students fared as well as Norris, but several obtained professional nursing jobs after graduation. In 1917, Conser endeavored to have the nursing program recognized by the Bureau of Registration of Nurses of the California State Board of Health so that students could obtain credit toward their nursing licenses through their studies at Sherman Institute. Unfortunately, an agreement could not be reached. In order to be registered nurses in the State of California, Sherman Institute nursing students had to apply to, and graduate from, a "regular" nurse's training program, in addition to their four years of training at Sherman Institute.[67]

By 1916, it became apparent that a single nurse could not handle the amount of work required with so large a population, by this time averaging over seven hundred students. Conser asked the Indian Office for authority to create a second resident nurse position, payable from the "Relieving Distress and Prevention of Disease Among the Indians Fund." In further support of a second position, he noted that it would be more economical to employ a second nurse regularly than to pay for irregular nurses during emergency situations. Despite a strong commitment to improving student health at nonreservation boarding schools, Commissioner Sells disagreed with Conser, suggesting instead that nursing students be used to relieve the resident nurse. A second position was thus denied.

Between 1902 and 1922, Sherman Institute students received medical care from a single resident nurse, a part-time contract physician, and after 1907, an average of ten nursing students. In times of emergency, irregular nurses provided supplemental medical care. Considering that enrollment reached over one thousand students during this period, depending on such a small force to provide medical care seems almost unbelievable. This situation was not unique to nonreservation boarding schools. Rapid City Boarding School, Chilocco Indian School, Flandreau Indian School, and Haskell Institute had similar medical staffing. However, what did make Sherman Institute unique was that it had a larger student population than did any of these schools.[68] In a perverse sense, however, the size of Sherman Institute's student population proved fortunate at least once. At the time of the school's greatest medical crisis—the 1918 Spanish Influenza pandemic—Conser found irregular nurses in extremely short supply and virtually unavailable to provide help at the school. Consequently, he put every well student and employee to work caring for the sick, until, that is, they became sick themselves. In this case, a large student population from which to draw for medical care made a difference in mortality resulting from the epidemic.

Both Hall and Conser recognized that medical care personnel and facilities played an important role in the daily operation of nonreservation boarding schools. In addition, they came to understand the significance of doctors and nurses most acutely when epidemics, accidents, and illnesses struck Sherman Institute.

———

CHAPTER 4

Morbidity and Mortality

As one of the last nonreservation boarding schools built by the Indian Office, Sherman Institute benefited from lessons learned through past mistakes, particularly those dealing with health issues. Excessive student morbidity and mortality had long been a problem at the early boarding schools, resulting in a lasting perception of these schools as death factories for Indian children. Primarily as a result of pressure from Progressive reformers, improving student health at the boarding schools became an important issue. Therefore, during the first two decades of the twentieth century preventive health measures implemented by the Indian Office included everything from physical plant design to health education, from sanitation inspections to monthly weighing of students. The intent of these measures was to prevent continuing elevated morbidity and mortality rates at nonreservation boarding schools.

The many preventive measures implemented at Sherman Institute between 1902 and 1922 have been discussed in the first three chapters of this study. The question to ask is, did they work? Were the preventive health programs implemented by the Indian Office and by the school superintendents effective in preventing disease, in maintaining a healthy student population, and in curtailing the upwardly spiraling morbidity and mortality rates historically present at nonreservation boarding schools? Did the preventive measures make a significant difference in the health of Indian students attending Sherman Institute?

The answers to these questions are both yes and no. Students at Sherman Institute continued to be plagued by epidemics, accidents, and a variety of illnesses throughout the research period. Preventive measures, though seemingly comprehensive, did not shield these children from all adverse health impacts. Tragically, many children died while still at school or shortly after being sent home. The epidemiological dynamics of a relatively closed institution housing so many children and young adults simply precluded continual good health. This, combined with the imperfect state of medical science and technology during the early twentieth century, resulted in children suffering from disease, and some succumbing to it. Yet the number of children with serious illnesses and the number of children who died were far lower than would have been expected without the implementation of preventive health measures. Though for every parent whose child was sick or died the number was too large, the preventive health measures implemented at Sherman Institute successfully kept that number from being greater.

It is difficult to place Sherman Institute's student morbidity and mortality rates into a meaningful context, because comparative health data from other nonreservation boarding schools is virtually nonexistent. While primary source material dealing with health is undoubtedly available for all of the other boarding schools, it has not been detailed in any of the current historiographic works. Furthermore, where descriptions of morbidity and mortality do exist, they are largely cursory and qualitative in nature, lacking any substantive quantitative data.

This chapter offers a comprehensive picture of student health at Sherman Institute between 1902 and 1922, using both qualitative descriptions and quantitative data derived from all available sources.[1] The data offered does not profess to be complete, but it is all the data that exists for Sherman Institute. Data from any single source is generally incomplete, because each reported different aspects of morbidity and mortality during the twenty-year research period. However, the sources are complementary, with one providing data not included in another. For example, a *Descriptive Statement of Pupils at Sherman Institute* notes when officials sent students home sick, when they were dropped from the school rolls, and when they died, but does not list the illness or cause of death. This information, in turn, can be found in official correspondence from the school superintendent, in case files, death certificates, or Sherman Institute *Bulletin* articles. Unfortunately, information is not available describing the illness or death of every student, because relevant documents are often missing. Consequently, while the *Descriptive Statements* provide a complete list of all students who were sent home sick, dropped from the rolls, or died between 1902 and 1922, the causes of many of these cases remain unknown.

The *Descriptive Statements* list only students who died at school or whose illnesses were serious enough to warrant sending them home instead of continuing treatment at school. Information regarding less serious illnesses or accidents is generally found only in correspondence, articles in the Sherman Institute *Bulletin,* and reports to the commissioner of Indian affairs. Further, data pertaining to epidemics at the school may only be extrapolated from the *Descriptive Statements,* with substantiating data derived from the aforementioned sources.

The intent of this chapter is not only to quantify student morbidity and mortality at Sherman Institute between 1902 and 1922, but also to provide baseline data for future comparative research. Currently, historiographic work on health at other nonreservation boarding schools simply does not exist. Since data similar to that found for Sherman Institute undoubtedly exists for other schools, future scholars will be able to place their data into a comparative context with Sherman Institute, thus painting a far more comprehensive picture of student health at nonreservation boarding schools than is now possible. The following offers all existing student health data for Sherman Institute, with comparisons made to white populations, Southern California native populations, and other nonreservation boarding schools when possible.

Between 1902 and 1922, Sherman Institute students experienced six diseases in epidemic proportions, thirteen different types of illness, and numerous accidents.[2] In many cases, available documents do not record the type of illness or the number of victims, simply that some illness existed. Table 4.1 lists the known epidemics, accidents, and illnesses that

TABLE 4.1

EPIDEMICS, ACCIDENTS, AND ILLNESSES

School Year	Smallpox	Measles	Chicken Pox	Typhoid Fever	Spanish Influenza	Diphtheria	Pneumonia	TB	Trachoma	Other	Accidents	Unknown
1902–03	–	–	–	–	–	–	1	2	U	1	–	9
1903–04	45	86	–	–	–	–	2	9	U	1	–	7
1904–05	–	–	–	35	–	–	2	1	U	–	–	1
1905–06	–	–	–	–	–	–	–	4	U	1	–	9
1906–07	–	–	–	–	–	R	1	1	U	–	1	2
1907–08	–	–	–	–	–	–	–	7	U	–	2	3
1908–09	–	–	E	–	–	–	1	10	125	1	–	6
1909–10	–	36	–	–	–	–	2	11	270	2	–	5
1910–11	–	–	–	–	–	150	–	13	152	4	–	8
1911–12	–	–	–	1	–	–	1	18	36	1	–	10
1912–13	–	–	–	–	–	–	–	11	88	1	–	7
1913–14	–	1	–	1	–	–	–	12	41	3	–	10
1914–15	–	122	–	–	–	–	–	16	85	–	2	4
1915–16	–	–	–	–	–	–	–	21	51	5	1	6
1916–17	–	87	–	–	–	–	–	22	65	1	–	7
1917–18	–	–	–	–	569	–	–	18	53	2	–	2
1918–19	–	–	–	–	–	–	–	30	56	–	1	3
1919–20	–	–	E	–	–	–	–	11	86	–	2	1
1920–21	–	E	E	–	–	–	1	13	96	–	2	9
1921–22	–	–	–	–	R	R	–	20	327	–	–	3

E = Epidemic recorded, but number of students affected unknown

R = Incidence recorded, but number of students affected unknown

U = Unknown data

Pneumonia = as primary illness only

Other = includes Bronchitis, Systemic Blastomycosis, Meningitis, Acute Nephritis, Fever, Appendicitis, Inflammatory Rheumatism

Unknown = Reflects incomplete data; illness noted but not identified in available sources

45, 86, etc. = Reflects number of known cases

occurred during the research period, as well as the number of victims each claimed. The table also lists cases of unidentified illness.

Although medical care practitioners treated the vast majority of students with health problems at the school hospital, in some cases they sent ill students home. This generally happened when parents requested that the student be sent home, or if the school physician felt that a change in environment would be beneficial and aid in the child's recovery. In most cases, these students eventually returned to school, but sometimes school officials dropped the ill student from the rolls either immediately or after a period of time. Information regarding the sickness for which a student was sent home and dropped is not always forthcoming. However, based on the records that are available, a pattern emerges that indicates students sent home sick and immediately dropped probably suffered from tuberculosis. In every known tuberculosis case, this pattern predominated. With diseases other than tuberculosis, the school physician sent students home sick, but they were not dropped until some later time. The possibility of recovery allowed these students time to heal before being dropped from Sherman Institute; officials did not give children afflicted with tuberculosis such an opportunity, since they never expected recovery. Finally, in some cases students were sent home sick, were dropped, and then died. While most of these cases were tuberculosis victims, some were not, and not all died from the disease for which the officials sent them home. Some students sent home in this manner died several years after originally being dismissed and dropped from school. Usually, these children went home either because of a parental request or because nothing further could be done for them at the school hospital. Table 4.2 lists the number of students on a yearly basis that school superintendents sent home sick, the number who were sent home sick and dropped, and the number who were sent home sick, were dropped, and then died.

Sherman Institute documents do not record the ailments of every child sent to the hospital for observation, only the number of patients admitted. Hospital admittance records are somewhat misleading because they tabulate every student who entered the hospital for *any* reason. This

TABLE 4.2

STUDENTS SENT HOME SICK, DROPPED, AND DIED

School Year	Sent Home Sick	Sent Home Sick Dropped	Sent Home Sick, Dropped, Died
1902–03	3	6	4
1903–04	3	10	2
1904–05	0	3	0
1905–06	5	8	2
1906–07	0	5	0
1907–08	1	5	3
1908–09	1	14	4
1909–10	2	4	0
1910–11	1	8	4
1911–12	3	7	11
1912–13	1	4	5
1913–14	0	12	8
1914–15	0	6	5
1915–16	1	10	2
1916–17	3	4	7
1917–18	0	1	4
1918–19	0	6	5
1919–20	0	3	1
1920–21	0	8	5
1921–22	3	15	2
TOTAL	27	139	74

included students receiving daily treatment for trachoma, every student referred by school employees because he or she did not look quite right, students requiring minor first aid, and of course, seriously ill students. Further, hospital admittance records were based on cases, not individual students, so it is impossible to denote whether many students were ill or a few students were ill, many times. Hospital records also include, but do not differentiate, nonstudents treated at the hospital. While not large, the number of Indians from Southern California reservations treated at the hospital, particularly after 1912, generally averaged one to three patients each month.

After Frank Conser became superintendent in 1909, the number of recorded hospital cases increased dramatically, not necessarily because more students were sick, but because he instructed school employees to constantly observe every student for signs of illness and to immediately send any student to the hospital for observation that evidenced the slightest irregularity. This also represents the period when more children received treatment for trachoma at daily hospital clinics and when student demographics begin to change, admitting more at-risk children.

Unfortunately, hospital treatment and admittance records are available for only the years 1902–5 and 1910–22. The early records are in the form of monthly reports and include data on the number of patients admitted to the hospital, the number discharged, and the number remaining in the hospital at the end of the month. Students sent home sick or those who died at school were also listed. Records from the latter years were annual statistical reports that offered a plethora of data, including the number of students treated at the hospital, the number admitted, discharged, and remaining at the end of the year, the number sent home sick, and the number who died while hospitalized. In addition, complete data on the number of students examined for tuberculosis and trachoma, as well as examination results by gender and disease are provided. Table 4.3 offers a summary of data common to both: students admitted to the hospital, students discharged, students remaining in hospital at the end of the year, students sent home sick, and those who died while hospitalized.

Tragically, several children died as the result of epidemics, accidents, and illnesses at Sherman Institute. Most of the students died in the hospital while under the care of the physician and nurses, but a few died of accidents away from the school. As seen in Table 4.4, tuberculosis caused twice as many deaths as any other diseases or accidents. The policy at Sherman Institute had always been to send tubercular children home as soon as possible after diagnosis, but in some cases the disease was in acute form and there simply was not enough time to send the child home. In other cases, environmental conditions at the child's reservation precluded transport in a timely manner.

TABLE 4.3

SHERMAN INSTITUTE HOSPITAL RECORDS

School Year	Enrollment*	Admitted	Discharged	Remaining	Died
1902–03	389	98	98	0	0
1903–04	638	335	327	8	4
1904–05	722	205	184	12	9
1905–06	596	NR	NR	NR	2
1906–07	687	NR	NR	NR	0
1907–08	699	NR	NR	NR	2
1908–09	672	NR	NR	NR	1
1909–10	555	NR	NR	NR	1
1910–11	712	208	197	8	3
1911–12	631	228	216	15	5
1912–13	639	464	471	7	1
1913–14	690	407	400	12	2
1914–15	744	252	251	11	2
1915–16	790	640	639	8	4
1916–17	787	779	775	10	2
1917–18	862	654	661	3	0
1918–19	879	650	632	9	12
1919–20	974	687	682	14	0
1920–21	1030	836	824	20	6
1921–22	1059	1293	1287	4	6

*Enrollment figures do not reflect the actual number of students attending school, since many children participated in the outing program and though enrolled, did not attend school on a regular basis.

NR = no records found

As is clearly evident from Table 4.1, tuberculosis and trachoma dominated the disease environment of Sherman Institute, at least after 1909. Tuberculosis represented the single greatest health problem in all non-reservation boarding schools, and Sherman Institute was no exception. Though virtually every preventive health program implemented by the Indian Office throughout the first two decades of the twentieth century had as its purpose the eradication of tuberculosis, it continued to be a dangerous presence. Due to the importance of tuberculosis in considering student morbidity and mortality at Sherman Institute, a separate

TABLE 4.4

CAUSES OF STUDENT DEATHS AT SHERMAN INSTITUTE

School Year	Tuberculosis	*Influenza	Pneumonia	*Typhoid Fever	Other Illness	Accident	Unknown
1902–03	–	–	–	–	–	–	–
1903–04	2	–	1	–	–	–	1
1904–05	–	–	3	6	–	–	–
1905–06	1	–	–	–	–	–	1
1906–07	–	–	–	–	–	–	–
1907–08	1	–	–	–	–	1	–
1908–09	–	–	–	–	1	–	–
1909–10	–	–	–	–	1	–	–
1910–11	1	–	1	–	1	–	–
1911–12	3	–	–	1	1	–	–
1912–13	–	–	–	–	–	–	–
1913–14	1	–	–	–	1	–	–
1914–15	1	–	–	–	–	1	–
1915–16	1	–	–	–	2	1	–
1916–17	1	–	–	–	1	–	–
1917–18	–	–	–	–	–	–	–
1918–19	2	8	1	–	–	1	–
1919–20	–	–	–	–	–	2	–
1920–21	3	–	1	–	1	1	–
1921–22	2	1				2	–
TOTAL	19	9	7	7	9	9	2

* Listed cause of death, even if secondary (i.e., Typhoid Fever was primary disease, but pneumonia listed as
cause of death or primary disease was measles, but TB developed and was cause of death)

chapter is devoted to this disease and it will not be included in the following discussion of epidemics, accidents, and illness. Trachoma represented the second-greatest health problem in all nonreservation boarding
schools, and as such, it is also discussed in a separate chapter.

Based on statements made in every *Annual Report* from 1902 to 1922,
it is clear that both Hall and Conser considered student health at Sherman

Institute exemplary, marred only by occasional epidemics. Analysis of data contained in Table 4.1 seems to substantiate their claims. With the exception of tuberculosis, trachoma, and various epidemics, Sherman Institute experienced surprisingly little sickness and few accidents during the twenty-year period from 1902 to 1922, particularly considering the size of the student population. Tables 4.2 and 4.4 indicate only a small percentage of the student population in any given year was sick enough to be sent home, was dropped from school, or died after going home sick or at the school. Yet, on 21 October 1904, Harwood Hall remarked,

> I am compelled to return sick pupils to their homes very frequently, such pupils have passed the physical examination for entrance, but go into a decline thereafter.[3]

Less than one month later, he noted, "In fact we seem to have no little sickness all the time."[4] If the health environment at Sherman Institute was actually as good as it appears to have been, what could have driven Hall's laments? Was student health far worse than that claimed by the school superintendents or as documented in official records?

At the time of Hall's statements, student health was cumulatively at its worst. During October of the previous year, Sherman Institute had experienced an epidemic of smallpox involving forty-five students, and in the spring of 1904, several children had been sent home for "weak lungs," one girl died of tuberculosis, a boy died of pneumonia complications from meningitis, and an eighty-six-student measles epidemic occurred, ultimately claiming the lives of two more children. Plus, as noted by Hall, "Upon the active opening of school each September there is always considerable sickness on the part of pupils, owing, doubtless to change of location, climate, etc."[5] In the autumn of 1904, a typhoid fever epidemic swept Sherman Institute, affecting forty-two students and killing seven, followed by a scabies infestation. Clearly Hall did not exaggerate when he said that there was no little sickness all the time.

Although hospital records are incomplete, the period of exhaustive illness and death noted by Hall does not seem to be wholly representative of the early years at Sherman Institute. Smallpox, measles, and typhoid fever epidemics occurring in the one-year period between autumn 1903 and autumn 1904 clearly devastated the school population and accounted for the majority of hospital admittances. Yet with the exception of these epidemics, there appears to have been very little disease or illness, including tuberculosis, during the early years.

In the first year of operation, resident nurses admitted ninety-eight students to the hospital, which roughly equates to one admittance or visit every four days.[6] Not considering students suffering from the smallpox and measles epidemics in 1903–4, hospital admittance in the 1903–4 and 1904–5 school years was 204 and 205, respectively. This equates to one admittance or visit every two days. Considering the fact that school employees sent every child that did not feel well to the hospital, regardless of symptom severity, and the fact that student populations in the three years for which records are available ranged from 389 in the 1902–3 school year, to 638 in 1903–4, to 722 in 1904–5, this is a very low morbidity ratio.

By way of comparison, in just one month at Flora Vista Elementary School, a twenty-first-century upper-middle-class elementary school with a student population of 544, there were 287 absences due to illness.[7] This does not include all the children who attended Flora Vista with colds, coughs, and other ailments common to children between the ages of five and twelve, only those deemed sick enough to stay home from school. At Sherman Institute, all children exhibiting any signs of illness went to the hospital for observation. The difference, of course, is that parents of twenty-first-century schoolchildren generally do not have to worry about diseases reaching epidemic proportions if not treated in time. Sherman Institute superintendents did not have that luxury.

It is surprising that Sherman Institute did not experience more health problems during the early years of its existence. For the first three years, the school had no health care facility other than rooms in one of the dormitory buildings. This situation certainly exacerbated the contagion level during epidemics, since the rooms offered little opportunity for quarantine. In addition, lack of a suitable health care facility resulted in a higher incidence of secondary infection, particularly pneumonia, since students could not be optimally cared for in dormitory beds. The poorly designed twenty-five-bed hospital, built in 1905, proved inadequate for most patient care, especially surgery. Dr. A. S. Parker, the school's contract physician, paid little attention to the preventive health care needs of the students, visiting the school only half as many times as his contract minimally called for, with most of those visits in response to epidemics. Nurses responsible for the daily care of students were often ill-trained for running a hospital facility and caring for so many students single-handedly. The school frequently possessed no medicines and children were forced to wait while Hall sought permission for open-market purchases. Yet with all these hindrances, good health prevailed for Sherman Institute students.

Undoubtedly, an important reason for the generally healthy population is that most of the early students came directly from Perris Indian School, where they had been under the strict attention of Mission-Tule Agency physician Dr. C. C. Wainwright. Rigorous entrance physical examinations permitted enrollment of only the healthiest children at the school, and it was this population that comprised the majority at Sherman Institute. As enrollment increased over time, the addition of children from other agencies and schools compromised the essentially healthy population of Southern California Indians with which Sherman Institute began.

Arguably, the most significant reason for generally good health during these early years was that Hall diligently complied with Indian Office policies and implemented his own school-specific policies regarding health. From a school design that broke dormitories into small, quarantine-manageable areas, to strict enforcement of sanitary practices, to providing a diet substantial in fresh fruit and vegetables, Hall established an environment conducive to the maintenance of good health. By firmly establishing this environment from the very beginning, there were no old habits and practices to be broken at the school, only new ones to follow. Hall complied with Indian Office health policies because he was a bureaucrat, but he established school-specific health practices for a number of reasons, not the least of which was that he and his family lived at the school. Ill health among the students, especially in epidemic form, posed a very real threat to the continued well-being of Hall's wife and children. Regardless of why Hall prioritized health at Sherman Institute, the fact remains that his actions proved beneficial to the students. By establishing and enforcing health-relevant policies, Hall set the tone for the school's future health environment.

The health environment established by Hall in 1902 continued unabated throughout Conser's administration, though it evolved and strengthened in many ways. By the time Conser assumed the superintendency of Sherman Institute in 1909, student population dynamics had changed. Most of the original students who came from Perris Indian School had graduated or left school, enrollment was continuing to increase at a steady rate, fewer young children were attending the school, and more students were coming from reservations outside Southern California, particularly in Arizona and New Mexico. Further, the outing program grew in proportion to its continued success, resulting in exposure of more students to the community at large.

All of these factors, except that pertaining to the number of younger students, had the potential to negatively impact student health at Sherman Institute. The founding students' good health was arguably one of the most important reasons for continued good health at the school during the early years. Increased enrollment resulted in more opportunities for transmission of disease, particularly during the periods between physical plant expansions. The inclusion of a growing number of students from Arizona and New Mexico, both areas with exceptionally high tuberculosis and trachoma rates, posed an important health threat to students at Sherman Institute. Finally, expansion of the outing program, where students worked in the homes and businesses of white families, removed students from the seclusion of the boarding school and exposed them to health risks in the general community.

Surprisingly, despite the potential negative impacts on student health posed by these population changes, the changes had little impact on morbidity and mortality at Sherman Institute, except for tuberculosis and trachoma. As shown in table 4.1, epidemics occurred with approximately the same frequency as during the early years, albeit with larger numbers of affected students. Illnesses classified as "Other" increased considerably, but there is no evidence that changing population dynamics influenced these individual disease occurrences. Accidents also increased, but since they were primarily the result of sports or off-campus activities, population change did not factor. Pneumonia cases decreased substantially, particularly after 1912, not because of population change, but because construction of the new state-of-the-art hospital permitted far better medical care than previously available.

Construction of the new hospital also figured greatly in the number of students sent home sick. Previous facilities did not have sufficient room to house patients for any length of time. Consequently, students requiring extended care or convalescence were sent home to free available beds for other patients. The new one-hundred-bed hospital alleviated this problem to the point that, as illustrated in table 4.2, Conser sent only eleven sick children home in the ten years between 1912 and 1922. Interestingly, the number of children sent home sick and dropped did not decrease measurably after the hospital was built, but in fact, increased slightly. Tuberculosis morbidity undoubtedly contributed greatly to the increase, since most of these children had been diagnosed with "weak lungs," "tubercular tendencies," or the "early stage of tuberculosis." Sending tubercular children home had long been standard practice at Sherman Institute, but reported cases of tuberculosis increased after 1909, and as a result, Conser sent more children home sick and dropped them from the school rolls. This was particularly true after 1912, when the official Indian Office policy required immediate dismissal of any child diagnosed with tuberculosis. Consequently, the availability of a large hospital proved irrelevant when considering tuberculosis. This also applied to children sent home sick and dropped, who later died. The majority of these cases were those diagnosed with tuberculosis and hence, could not be kept at the hospital for treatment.

Hospital records are incomplete for the years 1905–10, but those years for which data is available paint an intriguing picture of student health at Sherman Institute. Figures recorded for hospital admittance and discharge pertain not to the actual number of students, but to the number of cases. This is similar to modern attendance-recording practices at schools throughout the country, where the number of absences due to illness is recorded on a monthly basis, but not whether many or few individual students were ill. Therefore, it is impossible to discern whether many students with few illnesses were admitted to the Sherman Institute hospital, or whether a few students with many illnesses were admitted. Further, resident nurses recorded as being admitted any student sent to the hospital for any reason, whether for observation or treatment, surgery or life-threatening illness.

Although information regarding epidemics, accidents, and illnesses is not currently available for nonreservation boarding schools other than Sherman Institute, information is available regarding the general health environment at other schools. Table 4.5 offers a comparison of school enrollment, hospital capacity, morbidity and mortality figures for all nonreservation boarding school hospitals during the 1911–12 school year. In analyzing these figures, it is apparent that Sherman Institute fared very well in comparison to schools of similar size. Hospital admissions at Sherman Institute equate to 36 percent of the enrolled students, while those at Carlisle Indian School equate to 78 percent, those at Haskell Institute to 92 percent, and those at Phoenix Indian School to 64 percent of the enrolled population. Interestingly, the mortality figures at Sherman Institute are considerably higher than at every school except Phoenix Indian School. The admissions policies of these schools are unknown, so it is not possible to determine whether superintendents sent every student exhibiting signs of illness, no matter how slight, to the hospital, as Conser did at Sherman Institute. Similarly, policies of other school superintendents in regard to sending sick children home are unknown, although they may have offered insight into the recorded mortality figures.

Superintendent Frank Conser was primarily responsible for the continued good health of Sherman Institute students, despite the potentially negative population changes experienced at the school. Conser prioritized

TABLE 4.5

COMPARISON OF NONRESERVATION
BOARDING SCHOOL HOSPITALS, 1911–1912

School	Enrollment	Hospital Capacity	Remaining from June 30, 1911	Admitted	Treated	Discharged	Died	Remaining July 1, 1912
Carlisle	1031	60	14	804	818	802	1	15
Salem	325	38	10	128	128	115	1	22
Chilocco	536	30	10	617	627	612	–	15
Genoa	340	20	3	327	330	328	1	1
Albuquerque	332	35	–	212	212	212	–	–
Haskell	719	70	–	663	663	657	2	4
Carson	318	14	3	410	413	410	–	3
Fort Mojave	400	8	–	280	280	278	2	–
Phoenix	808	75	13	514	527	515	6	6
Pipestone	212	12	–	58	58	56	1	1
Flandreau	445	40	1	160	161	159	1	1
Greenville	125	12	3	15	14	15	1	3
Fort Bidwell	126	10	–	35	35	34	1	1
Rapid City	–	12	–	70	70	70	–	–
Sherman	631	100	8	228	236	221	5	15

Source: Table 21: Hospitals and Sanatoria in Indian Service, for the fiscal year ending June 30, 1912. *Annual Report of the Commissioner of Indian Affairs.*

* Data for Phoenix Indian School General Hospital only, does not include sanatorium

not only maintaining student health, but improving it as well. As such, he proved even more diligent in complying with Indian Office health policies than Hall. He implemented many school-specific policies, especially those focusing on diet, exercise, and sanitation, that in his experience as an Indian school administrator, positively impacted student health. However, Conser was also abundantly aware that Indian Office priorities had shifted significantly toward health, and that to obtain funding for literally anything having to do with the school, one had only to make a plea based on student health. During his administration, he lobbied the Indian Office relentlessly for funding to improve Sherman Institute's physical plant, usually in the name of preventive health measures. Conser served as an advocate for his students' health, even if it meant challenging the standard Indian Office protocol. Maintaining a healthy school environment was a source of personal and professional pride for Conser, but it also made good business sense. A boarding school full of sick and dying Indian children clearly posed a significant threat to continued community support for the school and the success of the outing program. Perhaps most important, however, Conser lived at the school with his family, so he had a vested interest in keeping the school population healthy. Conser had little control over accidents occurring at the school, but he did have a certain amount of control over illnesses and epidemics that impacted Sherman Institute. Consistent compliance with Indian Office preventive policies, coupled with the implementation of his own school-specific health practices, gave Conser the power to provide a reasonably healthy living environment for Sherman Institute's residents, including his own family.

CHAPTER 5

Epidemics, Accidents, and Illnesses

MORBIDITY AND MORTALITY FIGURES TELL THE STORY OF ILLNESS AND death in a way that facilitates tabulation, analysis, and comparison. What they do not do is provide information about the circumstances of illness and death, about the essential human element of these experiences. They do not provide a context within which to comprehend how they came to be. In order to fully understand student health at Sherman Institute or any other nonreservation boarding school, it is important to view morbidity and mortality rates not just as numbers but also as a way to understand the entire boarding school experience for Native American children and their families. Who were the children who sickened and died? How were they cared for? Did their parents know of their illness? Did anything change because of illness and death? These questions and others add depth and understanding to the true meaning of morbidity and mortality figures.

The following discussion of epidemics, accidents, and illnesses at Sherman Institute from 1902 to 1922 offers a human aspect to the statistics presented in the previous chapter, "Morbidity and Mortality." Students who suffered and died at the school had names and faces, friends and family; they were all someone's children. Therefore, they deserve to have their stories told, if only in a small way. The intent of these stories is not necessarily to analyze, but instead, to tell about what happened at Sherman Institute, to explain how the statistical data came to be. In all cases where names are known they are given, and in this way, recognition comes to each child who suffered away from home.

EPIDEMICS

The technical meaning of the word *epidemic* is an "excess of cases of a disease over the number expected in a given population."[1] This is an important concept because it means that an epidemic is not simply the appearance of an infectious disease or condition that attacks many people at the same time in the same geographical area. It is an epidemic only if the number of cases exceeds what may be expected and consequently strains available medical resources. Several cases of influenza may herald the beginning of the annual influenza season and not be considered an epidemic, yet two cases of a rare disease may constitute an epidemic.

Between the years 1902 and 1922, six diseases reached epidemic proportions at Sherman Institute: smallpox, measles, chicken pox, diphtheria, typhoid fever, and Spanish Influenza. With three exceptions, each epidemic disease represented a single occurrence, though isolated cases appeared periodically. Measles, chicken pox, and diphtheria epidemics occurred on a relatively regular basis throughout the research period.

Smallpox

A single smallpox epidemic involving forty-five students occurred at Sherman Institute in October 1903.[2] Little is known of the epidemic other than when it occurred and how many students were infected. The presence of a smallpox epidemic as late as 1903 is particularly surprising. Vaccination of reservation Indians had been a common procedure for several decades, and beginning in 1901, the Indian Office required vaccination of all students at nonreservation boarding schools prior to enrollment unless the student provided proof of a recent successful vaccination. The Indian Office further directed that current vaccination records be kept on file in the office of every boarding school.

In compliance with Indian Office regulations, Mission-Tule Agency physician C. C. Wainwright vaccinated all students at Perris Indian

School in 1901 and recorded the vaccinations in the *Descriptive Statements of Pupils*. Upon the move to Sherman Institute in 1902, this practice ceased. Perhaps because the founding student population was primarily comprised of children from Perris Indian School who had all been recently vaccinated, the issue of smallpox received no consideration at Sherman Institute. No evidence of vaccinations or required certifications in 1902 or 1903 has been found. As a result of this complacency, an infected child entered the school in late September, and by 12 October, the disease had spread to forty-five students.

Dr. Parker established quarantine at Sherman Institute as soon as the first case of smallpox appeared. The quarantine lasted two weeks, and children were allowed neither to leave nor to enter the school during this period. Since Sherman Institute's physical plant did not yet include a hospital, smallpox victims were housed in tents.[3] Hall hired two trained nurses to care for the forty-five smallpox victims at a rate of $6.00 per day, a sum considered exorbitant by Assistant Commissioner of Indian Affairs A. C. Tonner.[4] Parker vaccinated all students and employees immediately, regardless of whether they had recently been vaccinated or not. Subsequent to the epidemic, Parker instituted a program of systematically vaccinating every child upon entering the school, with a revaccination within five years. By leaving nothing to chance, Parker believed that "there is practically no danger from this disease."[5] This program was later modified to conform to official Indian Office policy, which allowed for certification of recent successful vaccination instead of automatic vaccination upon enrollment.[6]

After the 1903 epidemic, Sherman Institute ordered between two hundred and seven hundred smallpox vaccine points at the beginning of each school year from the Cutter Analytic Laboratory in Berkeley, California, to insure that every incoming student could be vaccinated if necessary. In 1916, the school became a regional depot for "the stowing and distribution" to schools and agencies in Southern California of smallpox vaccine, diphtheria antitoxin, and other biological supplies.[7] Prior to this, superintendents submitted requests through the Indian Office, and supplies were purchased as an exigency. The long distances and consequent time delays involved rendered this practice unsatisfactory, hence the arrangement made with Sherman Institute.

Hall and Parker's laxity in complying with the Indian Office small-pox policy is not surprising, despite the fact that Hall generally complied with all policies. Vaccination had been neglected for several years in some parts of California, the result of a complacency that came from the belief that smallpox no longer constituted a viable health threat.[8] In addition, California experienced a large number of cases of smallpox in 1903, characterized by their mild nature and the propensity of many to make a wrong diagnosis.[9] Between general complacency and a lack of information about the presence of smallpox in California, Conser and Parker had no reason to believe smallpox posed a potential threat to Sherman Institute. They obviously discovered such was not the case. After the 1903 epidemic, strict adherence to the smallpox policy prevented any further outbreaks despite the fact that smallpox epidemics continued to occur throughout the state for the following two decades.

Measles

Measles was one of the most common epidemics at every boarding school and reservation.[10] Between 1902 and 1922, not a year passed without measles epidemics occurring at numerous nonreservation boarding schools throughout the country. As noted by the superintendent of the Springfield Indian Training School, complications of the disease were usually far more serious among Indians, particularly reservation Indians, than among whites.[11] The greatest threat to boarding school students came not from the measles infection itself but from secondary infections, such as pneumonia and tuberculosis, that resulted from the immunologically vulnerable condition of the lungs following infection by the measles virus.

Sherman Institute suffered measles epidemics in June 1904 (86 cases), April 1909 (36 cases), August 1914 (122 cases), November 1916 (87 cases), and February 1921 (unknown number of cases). Fortunately, the measles mortality rate was very low. Of the 331 known cases, only one student, sixteen-year-old Johnny Sterling (Mission), died as a direct result of the measles infection, in this case during the 1916 epidemic.[12]

All other deaths were the result of secondary pneumonia and tuberculosis. After contracting measles in 1904, six-year-old Nancy Lawrence (Fort Tejon) developed pneumonia, then tuberculosis, ultimately succumbing to the latter. The measles epidemic of 1909 saw the demise of twenty-two-year-old Mina Hill (Klamath) from tuberculosis following measles. The epidemic of 1921 proved the most deadly, with four children dying from secondary infections after contracting measles. Fifteen-year-old Fernando Amago (Mission) died after contracting measles, which became pneumonia, and finally developed into tuberculosis. The same year, fourteen-year-old Elizabeth Wright (Paiute) died at Sherman Institute after developing tuberculosis following her measles infection. Eleven-year-old Sylvas Kayiyah (Navajo) died ten days after Elizabeth, in the school hospital. Sylvas developed a strep infection after contracting measles, then was stricken by tuberculosis, finally dying from a severe lung hemorrhage. Finally, on 13 January 1922, thirteen-year-old Jerry Horne (Klamath) died from tubercular meningitis following a bout with measles.

When tuberculosis developed following measles, as it did in these cases, it is probable that the students already had latent tuberculosis prior to the measles infection. Tuberculosis may lie dormant for several years, not becoming active until stress or illness weakens the individual's immunological responses. Since Sherman Institute physicians did not screen students for tuberculosis with either X-ray or tuberculin skin tests, latent tuberculosis would have been undetected until activated at the time of the students' weakened condition following measles infection.

In each epidemic, as soon as the first cases appeared, students were quarantined in the hospital, though in almost every case the number of patients exceeded the number of available hospital beds. Providing adequate patient care clearly proved a daunting task, especially in 1904, before the nursing program began. Hall did not hire irregular nurses to care for the eighty-six patients, so responsibility for attending to patients fell to the two resident nurses and Dr. Parker. The fact that only one child died during the epidemic probably says more about the virulence of the measles virus than about the excellence of the medical care given. Fortunately, by the time of the other measles epidemics, a strong nursing program had been established and student nurses aided in patient care.

Why measles posed such a serious threat to Indians is unknown. All of the so-called childhood diseases, such as measles, mumps, smallpox, and chicken pox, caused tremendous morbidity and mortality among Native Americans during the early years following the fifteenth-century European invasion of America, because they had no immunity to these diseases.[13] However, by the late nineteenth and early twentieth centuries, the majority of Indians had been exposed to these diseases and had acquired a level of immunity equal to that possessed by the white population. However, whereas other childhood diseases had ceased to pose a viable threat by this time, measles inexplicably continued to haunt Indians' health. Many boarding school superintendents, including Harwood Hall, considered measles one of the most menacing diseases to confront Indian students, correctly viewing it as a precursor to pneumonia and tuberculosis,

> Of course as you may know, I don't care to take any chances on the measles and I would ask you to kindly give it your personal supervision, for measles seem to create havoc among our Indians, going to their lungs. Out of the list of contagious diseases, I would prefer any to measles—at least that has been my experience.[14]

Concern that any measles case could lead to a more serious condition caused both Hall and Conser to be especially diligent in notifying students' families of their conditions. This was particularly true of Conser, who immediately notified families of illness and frequently sent daily updates apprising them of their child's condition. During the 1916 measles epidemic, a number of boys from the Round Valley Reservation were stricken with the disease at the same time. From 19 October through 6 November 1916, Conser sent daily updates on all the afflicted children to the superintendent of the Round Valley School so that he could keep the families up to date on the children's progress. On the first day of the epidemic, 19 October, Hall notified the superintendent that Arthur Reyes, Dewey Whipple, Clarence Wilburn, and Andrew Potter were sick with measles and that Arthur and Dewey had rather serious cases.[15] The following morning, Hall sent word, "Dewey and Arthur better this morning. Andrew Potter increase in temperature and not so well. Clarence Wilburn is not feeling as well as he did yesterday. John Wilburn and Bud Potter now have measles."[16]

Unfortunately, in some cases Conser's letters reflected an urgency borne in response to worsening health, "I regret that Dewey Whipple seems to have taken a turn for the worse."[17] According to Hall, Dewey seemed to be getting along fairly well, but not so well as the other patients. "Last evening he was somewhat delirious at times," he reported, "and I am not at all satisfied with his case."[18] Since Dewey's serious condition precluded him from returning home, Hall strongly suggested that his family come to him, despite the expense of such a trip: "I hope he will pull through all right, but if any of his people are interested I will be glad to have them come see him."[19] Understanding Conser's implications, Dewey's father came to visit as soon as he received the letter. Although the other children from Round Valley fully recovered, Dewey Whipple never regained his strength, and as Dr. Roblee feared the onset of tuberculosis, soon went home.

Chicken Pox

Sherman Institute experienced chicken pox epidemics in January 1908, March 1920, and April 1921.[20] The number of students afflicted with the disease is not known, with the only records of the epidemics' existence being articles in the *Sherman Bulletin*. The 1908 epidemic was confined to Minnehaha Home and occurred at the same time as several cases of mumps, while the other two epidemics were schoolwide. All patients received treatment at the school hospital, with no complications or fatalities noted, although it apparently took some patients of the 1921 epidemic a long period of time for full recovery. The chicken pox epidemics followed the typical pattern of appearing in winter and early spring, but obviously not that of appearing in three- to four-year cycles. The fact that epidemics occurred on consecutive years indicates that a new student probably brought in the virus and that there were enough new susceptibles in the population to create an epidemic incident.

Diphtheria

Diphtheria occurred at Sherman Institute in June 1907, November 1910, November 1921, and at some time in 1922.[21] The number of cases occurring in 1907 is unknown; Hall recorded only the fact that the school had no medicine on hand with which to treat the afflicted children.[22] In 1910, diphtheria reached epidemic proportions, with 150 students affected. Conser and Roblee quarantined the students who had a "slight form of diphtheria."[23] Additional information regarding this epidemic is not forthcoming in available documents.

In November 1921, a number of diphtheria cases appeared at Sherman Institute. To prevent additional cases, Dr. Roblee conducted a Schick Test of the entire student body and found 375 students who were susceptible to diphtheria. The Schick Test is an intradermal injection of dilute diphtheria toxin, the results of which occur three to four days later. Susceptibility is indicated by the development of a red inflamed area at the point of injection. Through Conser, Roblee requested authorization from the Indian Office to purchase the Diphtheria Toxin-Antitoxin Mixture, at a cost of $0.50 per dose, for the purpose of immunizing the students.[24] Commissioner Sells granted Conser's request and all diphtheria-susceptible students were immunized. The following year, a few cases of diphtheria appeared, and the same procedural sequence was implemented to prevent additional morbidity.

Typhoid Fever

A devastating typhoid fever epidemic struck Sherman Institute in 1904.[25] The epidemic began on 29 October, ended on 14 November, and affected forty-two students, seven of whom died from the disease.[26] This effectively equaled the cumulative mortality from all previous years at both Perris Indian School and Sherman Institute. Yet in his annual report to the commissioner of Indian affairs, Harwood Hall did not mention the deaths of these students. Instead, he stated only that in the fall of the year they had been troubled with some sickness. [27]

The epidemic received only minimal coverage in local newspapers. Those who were aware of the problem were very concerned, not by the fact that it threatened the health of Indian children at Sherman Institute, but because the possible source of contamination could infect the general Riverside population. The wells of the Riverside Water Company provided domestic water not only to Sherman Institute but also to the residents and businesses of the City of Riverside. Consequently, if the well water was contaminated, typhoid fever could potentially spread throughout the entire city. Of further concern to knowledgeable citizens was that some of the city's most influential citizens were shareholders in the Riverside Water Company. Typhoid contamination of their wells would certainly have proved catastrophic. In response to the perceived threat, the Board of Health conducted an expeditious, but ill-publicized, investigation of Riverside Water Company wells.

Although the local press did not publicize the tests the Board of Health ran on the Riverside Land Company domestic wells, they quickly printed the full text of the investigation results—even before they were formally presented to the County Board of Trustees. Both the *Riverside Enterprise* of 17 November and the *Riverside Press and Horticulturist* of 18 November 1904 carried the official report that was to be presented to the Board of Trustees at their 25 November 1904 meeting. In addition to providing a lengthy, detailed description of the source of water for the wells, they concluded that at no time was water in the wells exposed to contamination from any source. The water was pure, absolutely free from all pollution and disease. Once it was known that the general population was not in danger of being exposed to typhoid fever from the domestic water wells, nothing further was written about the epidemic at Sherman Institute; it had become an internal problem. The County Board of Trustees took no action after receiving the report, except, perhaps, to breathe a sigh of relief.

It is interesting that the County Board of Trustees did not show more concern regarding this issue, since by this time Sherman Institute and its resident Indian children had become quite a tourist attraction in Riverside. Hall maintained an "open door" policy, with several thousand people visiting the school each year. The trustees apparently did not consider the possibility, at least publicly, of tourists contracting typhoid fever while visiting the school, or of the school no longer being accessible to tourists because of the epidemic.

The source of the Sherman Institute typhoid fever epidemic was never conclusively determined. In fact, not until the commissioner of Indian affairs demanded an explanation of the epidemic did Parker investigate possible causes. According to Parker's subsequent report, there had never been a case of typhoid fever in the school prior to the epidemic. Over half the cases occurred during the first week, with equal distribution among the four dormitories; thus, he said, "This points to the conclusion that either the water or the food supply became infected at that time."[28] Since contaminated food and water generally are the primary mechanisms for typhoid fever transmission, Parker's conclusion left much to be desired. The school water supply had been cleared by the Board of Health investigation, so that left food as the causative factor in the typhoid fever epidemic. However, Parker explained, "It is decidedly uncertain as to how the food could have become infected, other than the fact that there were swarms of flies on the premises that could spread an infection once started."[29] To prevent additional cases of typhoid fever, "The grounds, kitchen, cellars, urinals, every thing that could possibly figure in contagion, were immediately and rigorously cleansed and renovated, and it was ordered that every drop of milk should be boiled."[30]

Five months later, Parker suggested that children eating watermelons, tomatoes, onions, and lettuce from a garbage wagon standing near the kitchen where there were numerous flies caused the epidemic: "These vegetables and particularly the watermelons that were cut and placed on the table sometime before meal time, were covered with flies."[31] The doctor claimed that flies from the neighborhood, in which one or two cases of typhoid had recently occurred, transmitted typhoid germs to the vegetables. In support of this theory, he claimed that football players, who ate exclusively at the training table in another building, and employees eating at the mess, did not contract the disease. Parker also noted that the cook at the school, "was not especially cleanly in her work and that the vegetable room was not always in proper condition decayed vegetables being allowed to accumulate and swarms of flies being in the vegetable room, and in the kitchen and dining room."[32]

Parker's theory, while possible, is also rather implausible. Before flies can transmit typhoid fever, they must first land on the dejecta of typhoid fever patients. Even if Parker's assertion that there were one or two typhoid patients in the neighborhood was true, a large number of flies would have to have landed on a large amount of human dejecta contaminated with typhoid in order to have been able to transmit the disease to as many students as became infected.

An alternate theory of causation is that milk from the school dairy was contaminated with typhoid fever. The farm did not have benefit of the Riverside water system, but obtained their water from a well, and the Board of Health had not tested the well water during their investigation. At the time, milk frequently proved to be source of typhoid fever, either because it had been diluted with contaminated water, or because milking implements, including udders, had been washed with water containing the typhoid bacilli. The Sherman Institute farm was located in a rural area of Riverside that had many dairy herds, with associated large amounts of manure that served as ground water contaminants, and that depended exclusively on wells to provided water. Over a period of years after the 1904 epidemic at Sherman Institute, several other typhoid fever epidemics occurred in the area around the farm, although none affected the farm. The Board of Health ultimately traced these epidemics to well water contamination by dairy herds. It is certainly plausible that this could have been at least a contributory cause of the Sherman Institute epidemic in 1904.

Five years after the epidemic, Parker recommended that screens with powerful springs be installed on all doors and windows to prevent a recurrence of typhoid fever at Sherman Institute. Fortunately, only a single case of the disease occurred during the remaining years of the research period.[33]

Based on information contained within death certificates of the Indian children who succumbed to typhoid fever, the first student became ill on 15 October 1904. Mateo Couts, a seventeen-year-old Luiseño boy from Rincon, who had come to Perris Indian School as a six-year-old, contracted typhoid fever, and he died as a result of the disease on 6 November. Couts's family buried the boy sometime thereafter in Temecula. Interestingly, in Parker's report, forwarded to the commissioner of Indian affairs, the first students (five) were said to have taken sick on 18 October, and Mateo Couts was not listed as being ill until 20 October. The reason for the discrepancies in Parker's reports is unknown, although it is apparent that he had difficulty either in maintaining consistent records or in keeping track of student identities.

Three students, including fourteen-year-old Lilly Edwards (Round Valley), seventeen-year-old Mamie Alpheus (Klamath), and seventeen-year-old John Powers (Wylachi) took ill on 22 October. Parker treated them for seven, twenty, and twenty-two days, respectively, but unfortunately, all of them died. School officials buried the children in the Sherman Institute cemetery in caskets purchased from the undertaking firm, Squire and Flagg. On 24 October 1904, two more students became ill. Their names were Dan Edwards (Round Valley) and George Summersell (Pomo). Fourteen-year-old Dan was ill for seventeen days before his death; twenty-two days passed before twelve-year-old George finally succumbed to the disease. The place of burial for each of these boys was listed as "U.S.A. Grounds," but it is unclear exactly to what this referred.

Hall diligently notified parents of their children's illnesses and deaths. The first day a child became ill, Hall sent a short letter to the family apprising them of the diagnosis. In many cases, Hall sent subsequent letters on an almost daily basis with updates on the child's condition, particularly if the child was not doing as well as expected. He assured parents that their children were receiving the finest medical care, and often invited them to visit, on the condition that they feed their child absolutely no food of any kind: "I write this because we have more trouble with relatives giving the sick food and otherwise doing things contrary to the doctor's orders."[34]

At the time of the typhoid fever epidemic, a hospital had not yet been built at Sherman Institute. Riverside County General Hospital was located on Magnolia Avenue less than one mile from the school, yet Hall did not send Indian children at Sherman Institute suffering from typhoid fever to the hospital.[35] Instead, Hall kept the children at school, where Parker and two resident nurses took care of them, aided by two employees and five "irregular nurses."[36] In a request for authorization to pay for the irregular employees, Hall stated that it was at the direction of Parker that the "most skilled nurses" were brought in to care for the children.[37]

Why Hall chose to keep the ill children at school instead of sending them to the hospital is inexplicable. As Riverside County's primary health care provider for indigent residents, the hospital accepted all patients, regardless of ethnicity or ability to pay. Consequently, Sherman Institute students would not have been discriminated against, and Hall would not have had to pay for their care from his meager budget. A possible explanation is that as residents of a federal facility, students at Sherman Institute did not qualify as Riverside County residents for admission to Riverside General Hospital.

Although neither treatment nor medication records have been found, it is known that Sherman Institute purchased drugs only on 30 September, approximately three weeks before the epidemic began, and on 31 December, six weeks after it ended. It is unlikely that the school stocked sufficient medication to treat the forty-two children suffering from typhoid fever.[38] The method of treatment utilized by Dr. Parker and the nurses can only be imagined, but it obviously was not terribly effective.

The last student to succumb, George Summersell, died of typhoid fever on 14 November 1904, and Hall had him buried in the school cemetery the same day. Additional deaths did not occur during the year.

Spanish Influenza

The Spanish Influenza Pandemic of 1918 to 1919 struck Sherman Institute with a vengeance during the second week of October 1918, and continued for the next three months.[39] By the end of the epidemic, 569 students and eight employees had been stricken, and 8 students had died. Sherman Institute's experience came in the middle of the most virulent period of the pandemic. The first known case of Spanish Influenza in the United States was reported on 4 March 1918 in Kansas, and by April the disease had spread to most American cities and Europe. This spring wave of the epidemic was serious, but not disastrous, and by midsummer it had subsided. Within two months, however, Spanish Influenza resurfaced, but the virus had mutated and now become a killer. Physicians recorded the first case of the second wave on 22 August, and from that time it spread like a wildfire throughout every city, town, and village in the world. By the end of the Spanish Influenza pandemic in 1919, it is estimated that the disease had infected 525 million people and killed 21 million throughout the world. It infected one-quarter of all Americans, and by early December of 1918, 450,000 Americans had died.[40]

A party of four boys traveling from Arizona to Sherman Institute brought Spanish Influenza to the school during the first week of October. They rode in a train compartment with a person infected with Spanish Influenza, and by the time the boys arrived at the school, they had each contracted the disease. Although Roblee immediately quarantined the boys in the Sherman Institute hospital, the virus proved so powerful as to infect almost everyone with whom the boys came into contact. These students then infected others.

Conser and Roblee established a strict quarantine for the school to prevent the spread of the disease to the community. Since at the time no Spanish Influenza cases had been reported in Riverside, the citizens were understandably concerned. To ease their fears and possible panic, Riverside Mayor Horace Porter and Health Officer W. B. Wells issued a statement regarding the epidemic, published on the front page of the *Arlington Times* newspaper. They assured local citizens that they had nothing to fear, that as a result of their quarantine the epidemic had been totally confined to Sherman Institute, and that everything possible was being done to prevent its spread.[41] Unbeknownst to Porter and Wells, Riverside's respite was to be short-lived. On 10 October, the first known Spanish Influenza victim in the area entered Riverside General Hospital, and by 15 October, that patient had died and six more had entered the hospital.[42] By the middle of October, the epidemic had spread throughout Riverside, Arlington, and Alvord, resulting in over four hundred cases in Riverside and two hundred at March Field, a United States Aviation Camp near Riverside.[43]

As of 25 October 1918, the Spanish Influenza virus had attacked 517 students, 24 employees, and 9 members of employees' families at Sherman Institute. The most critical period of the epidemic fell between 9 October and 14 October, with the largest number of students confined to bed at one time on 10 October, when 422 students and 18 employees were ill. Conser suspended all school activities, and every student and employee not yet infected helped care for the sick.[44] Since the school hospital had only a one-hundred-bed capacity, dormitories with screen porches housed the patients. As employees and students became ill, other employees and students took their places. Obtaining the services of trained nurses proved virtually impossible, due to competing demands in local communities, and Conser could hire only one trained nurse, one practical nurse, and three employees to help in departments with ill staff members. In conjunction with the school's resident nurse, employees, student nurses, and healthy students, they provided the best medical care possible, under the circumstances. Dr. Roblee visited the school at least once daily, and his associate made yet another daily visit.

The Spanish Influenza virus that attacked Sherman Institute was swift and powerful, but not particularly lethal. The 569 students stricken with the virus represented an incredible 65 percent of the 879-student enrollment, yet the resultant mortality was only 1.4 percent of those infected. The low mortality rate was primarily due to the level of medical care provided, but it also reflected the relative virulence of the viral strain. Between 1 October 1918 and 31 March 1919, the Public Health Service recorded a total Indian population of 304,854, with 24 percent, or 73,651 Indians, stricken with Spanish Influenza. Of those stricken, 6,270 Indians died, representing a 9 percent mortality rate.[45] Thus, while the Sherman Institute morbidity rate far exceeded the national average, the mortality rate was significantly less than the national average.

Conser attributed student mortality not to the Spanish Influenza epidemic itself, but to pneumonia. Fifty-two students acquired pneumonia as a secondary infection, eight of whom subsequently died. In recognition of these students' lives, they are as follows: Santiago Pacheco (Pueblo), Fred Smith (Navajo), Faith Dickerman (Mojave), Joe Linton (Mission), Byazza Jones (Navajo), Lucy Antone (Pima), Edward Capon (Papago), and Felipe Magee (Mission).

ACCIDENTS

Over the course of twenty years, a number of accidents occurred at Sherman Institute. With the emphasis placed on industrial training, farming, and sports, it is not surprising that accidents happened periodically. Though accidents are generally not discussed in terms of student health at nonreservation boarding schools, they nonetheless contributed to the health environment. Most of the accidents that occurred at Sherman Institute were minor, but more than a few had fatal consequences. With the exception of occasional notices published in the *Sherman Bulletin*, medical care personnel did not usually record minor accidents in available documents. Unfortunately, they recorded in detail only particularly serious accidents, or those that resulted in death, and these are included in the following discussion. In general, documented accidents fall into three categories: industrial, sports, and vehicular.

The first accident recorded at Sherman Institute happened in 1904, and fortunately it was not serious. A boy walking in his sleep at the farm fell from the second floor of the barn to the ground, breaking his arm.[46] Since it was midnight and impossible to secure the services of Dr. Parker, who lived twelve miles distant and surprisingly had no telephone connection, Hall had to take the boy to a nearby physician, who set the fracture for a fee of $20.00. Of interest in this case is what the boy was doing sleeping in the barn instead of in one of the dormitory rooms located in the farmhouse. In twenty years, this is the only mention of alternate sleeping quarters at the farm, so an explanation is not readily forthcoming.

Within a two-month period in 1907, two Sherman Institute students were injured in sports-related accidents, one of them fatally. During the last week in September, Wallace Singleton was injured so seriously on the school's recreation fields that Dr. Roblee was forced to operate on the wound, and Wallace retained partial paralysis of the left hand and arm as a result of the accident.[47] What caused the wound is unknown. It is interesting that Dr. Roblee performed the operation, since at the time Dr. Parker was the school's contract physician. Since Roblee and Parker were associates, it is probable that Roblee filled in for Parker in the emergency.

Two months later, eighteen-year-old John Pablo, a popular Pima boy from Blackwater, Arizona, was killed during a recreational game of football between Pima and Hopi boys at the school.[48] A boy on the opposite side of the field had the ball, and when John tackled him, he landed on his neck and could not get up. According to witnesses, John said he had no pain, but immediately thereafter he lapsed into unconsciousness and employees removed him to the hospital. Doctors Roblee and Dickson came to the hospital and administered restoratives, but to no avail. The physicians could not establish an exact cause of death without a post-mortem examination, but since John's family requested that his body be sent home for burial, this was not possible. Hall sent a telegram to the Sacaton Reservation superintendent, notifying him of John's death: "John Pablo of Blackwater dead accident in play. Shall I send body. If so will arrive Casa Grande Monday morning."[49] The manner and brevity of Hall's notification were quite unusual, as he usually spent considerable time writing to family members in such cases, providing details of the accident or illness and describing the child's life at school and how much the child would be missed.

The first industrial accident at Sherman Institute occurred in 1909. Bennie Pahseah, a fifteen-year-old Navajo boy, caught his arm in the centrifugal wringer in the laundry. The arm was so badly mangled that Dr. Roblee recommended amputation. However, Conser interceded and asked that everything possible be done to save the arm. Roblee succeeded in saving the arm, but the hand and lower arm were lifeless and required daily care. After one and a half years, the arm had become a major source of annoyance, and Conser permitted Roblee to amputate the arm between the shoulder and the elbow.[50]

Conser made a critical mistake in not obtaining permission from Bernie's parents prior to the amputation. Since a year and a half had elapsed since the accident, this was not an emergency situation and he could easily have notified them of his intent. Instead, Bernie's parents found out about the amputation after the fact, and understandably, were greatly distressed, demanding that he be sent home immediately. Conser implored the reservation day school superintendent to explain the situation to Bernie's parents, telling them that everything possible had been done, including electrical treatment, to bring life back into the arm.[51] Apparently, the superintendent placated Bernie's parents, since they allowed him to complete an additional year at Sherman Institute before returning home.

A third sports-related accident happened on the Sherman Institute athletic fields on 14 May 1915. Seventeen-year-old Robert More, a Mono boy from Northfork, California, was accidentally hit on the head with an athletic hammer, resulting in death from a brain concussion.[52] Depositions taken from students witnessing the accident stated that Charlie Goode had been throwing the hammer during track and field practice and had walked away, at which time, Robert More called out, "Throw the hammer back." Robert and Shay Etsitty had their backs toward each other, Shay picked up the hammer and cried, "Watch out," then threw the hammer, striking Robert in the head.[53] Conser had the school disciplinarian accompany Robert's body home and explain the details of the accident to his parents.

One of the saddest accidents at Sherman Institute occurred on the evening of 9 October 1915.[54] The school disciplinarian gave Ignacio Mariano, a fifteen-year-old Tohono O'odham (Papago) boy, permission to attend the County Fair. Not having any money left for carfare, he started walking back to the school about 7:30 P.M. along the trestle of the Pacific Electric Railway that was sixty to seventy feet long and twelve to fifteen feet above the public road. The motorman did not see Ignacio until he was too close to stop the car. He hit the boy, throwing him to the street below. Ignacio never regained consciousness and died on the operating table of either a brain concussion or a fractured skull. Witnesses testifying at the coroner's inquest stated that the boy, who was lame from an old tubercular infection and walked with a crutch, was in a leaning position when the car was approximately fifty feet away, holding his hand up as if signaling for the car to stop. When the car came close to him, Ignacio apparently became confused, dropped his crutch, and subsequently lost his balance, at which time the car hit him.

Interestingly, upon learning of Ignacio's death, his cousin Jose Lewis of Sasabe, Arizona, wrote to the commissioner of Indian affairs claiming that Ignacio's parents should collect damages from the Pacific Electric Railroad.[55] The commissioner of Indian affairs ordered an investigation into the matter. Officials determined that since the boy had been trespassing on the railway's property, no damages were due.

The second industrial accident at Sherman Institute occurred on 23 June 1919, when an explosion in the school bakery killed James Sousea, a seventeen-year-old Pueblo boy.[56] The school baker and one of the bakery students became ill and were unable to continue their duties. Conser sent one of the teachers to take charge of the bakery and temporarily detailed James Sousea, who was normally in the blacksmith shop but had bakery experience, to help out. James lit the oven burner. After it burned for an hour and the oven was hot enough for baking, he then turned the oil off. After the oil was turned off, James either accidentally or carelessly turned the oil back on again, which caused the formation of gas. He then lit a match, apparently to ignite the oil. This caused an immediate explosion, and since James was standing directly in front of the oven door, the flame that shot out from the door struck him. Fire burned the boy severely, and school officials took him to the hospital. Conser called Dr. Roblee, who came immediately, bringing his associate to help care for James's injuries. Although the doctors did everything possible to save his life, James died two days later.

Tragically, two fifteen-year-old friends who came to Sherman Institute together from the Papago Reservation died on the night of 23 June 1920.[57] José Juan Francisco and Salvador Lopez lived at the school farm and had been quarantined due to a reported case of measles. The boys, however, left the farm on the evening of 23 June to come to Sherman Institute, approximately four miles distant. The streetcar line passed in front of the school, and they apparently were walking along the tracks when they stopped to rest. Evidently, they lay back on the ground with their legs across the tracks and fell asleep. The streetcar ran over their legs, severing the limbs from the boys' bodies, and causing them to bleed to death. The accident occurred at eleven or twelve o'clock at night, but neither the conductor nor the motorman made a report of the accident until the next morning. Conser immediately went to the scene and took charge of the remains. A coroner's inquest was held, with a verdict of accidental death. However, Conser felt that even though the boys were technically trespassing, the motorman should have been more watchful and noticed the rather large objects laying on the tracks, enabling him to slow down before reaching them. The motorman "claimed that he did not see them on the track and that he did not know he had run over two human beings when he claims to have noticed a slight jar of the car at that place. Neither did he stop to investigate."[58]

The last accident between 1902 and 1922 that involved a Sherman Institute student also happened away from the school. Olin Zhebe Nolli, a nineteen-year-old Navajo boy from Keams Canyon, Arizona, ran away from Sherman Institute and jumped a Santa Fe Railroad train.[59] The train crew discovered him, unconscious, near a place called Helendale, California. They took him to the San Bernardino County Hospital at about 11:30 A.M. on 7 July 1921, but he died that evening at 5:00 P.M. The coroner's inquest ruled the cause of death a brain concussion caused by accidentally falling off the train. Since the train crew found him in the train, how they determined the cause of death was falling off the train is questionable, particularly since there were no witnesses. If Olin had fallen off the train hard enough to get a brain concussion, how could he have gotten up and back onto the train? Alternately, if the train crew had found Olin stealing a ride on the train and thrown him off, why would they have taken him to the hospital instead of leaving the Indian boy on the side of the tracks? It is likely that either a train police officer or a bum hit Olin over the head while he rode the train, leaving his body for discovery by others.

ILLNESSES

A variety of illnesses occurred at Sherman Institute between 1902 and 1922. Some of these appeared periodically, some regularly, and some only once. In general, illnesses are differentiated from epidemic diseases not necessarily by their level of severity but by the degree to which they taxed available medical care facilities and personnel.

Scabies

Sherman Institute students frequently suffered from scabies, or "itch," between 1902 and 1922, particularly until 1909.[60] The disease most frequently affected new students and those residing at the school farm. Hall attributed the high incidence of scabies among farming students to the fact that "the condition at the farm as far as cleanliness is concerned is not first class."[61] The standard procedure for eradicating the infestations involved fumigating the bedding and clothes of infected students. Dr. Parker instructed matrons and disciplinarians to send these items to the laundry for boiling, "to the end that the bedding, bed clothes, and clothing may not continually serve as centers of infection for other children."[62] During a particularly bad infestation at the Sherman Institute farm, Hall not only had the bedding collected for fumigation but ordered that all mattresses be removed and piled up somewhere in the barn where they could not be used. New mattresses replaced all the infested ones. Since students did not share beds at the school, it is difficult to understand how Parker thought the bedding of an infected child could spread the ailment to other children. Further, the single laundering ordered in each case would have been ineffective in eradicating the scabies mites—if they actually lived in the bedding. Interestingly, we now know that extensive fumigating or cleaning of clothing and bedding is unwarranted because the scabies mite does not live long off the human body. Contagion occurs primarily through direct skin-to-skin contact with an infected individual. An incomplete knowledge of the transmission mechanism resulted in continuing difficulty in eradicating scabies.

On the recommendation of Medical Inspector Murphy during his 1909 inspection of Sherman Institute, the direction taken against scabies changed markedly. Instead of simply treating existing infestations, preventive measures were implemented in an attempt to curtail the continuing problem. Murphy instructed matrons and disciplinarians to examine each student during bathing for evidence of scabies.[63] This demeaning and very time-consuming practice was designed to identify students with scabies and institute treatment, which was sulfur ointment, before other students could become infected. Apparently, Murphy did not believe the Indian students would seek treatment on their own, despite the fact that the papules accompanying the scabies mite burrows itched intensely, causing great discomfort. The bathing inspections actually were effective in decreasing the prevalence of scabies, although small epidemics of "itch" continued to occur periodically.

Spinal Meningitis

Two cases of spinal meningitis occurred at Sherman Institute between 1902 and 1922.[64] Julia Antonio, a sixteen-year-old Tohono O'odham (Papago) girl, became ill during the first week of February in 1912. Her case did not seem serious until 6 February, when she took a turn for the worse and Roblee diagnosed spinal meningitis. Although Conser's clerk notified her family of the seriousness of Julia's illness immediately, they had no time to take action, for she died on 8 February. Conser sent Julia's body, accompanied by Miss Jewett, a teacher at the school, to Tucson for burial. Julia's minister at Sherman Institute, Rev. Macquarrie, and her school friends held a funeral service prior to her departure for Tucson. Roblee never discovered the source of Julia's spinal meningitis.

The second case of spinal meningitis proved even more mysterious. On 17 February 1916, Conser wrote to the father of Lady Jamison, an eighteen-year-old Paiute girl, telling him that his daughter had symptoms of spinal meningitis, although a definite diagnosis had not yet been made. He strongly suggested that if at all possible, Mr. Jamison come to see Lady. On 21 February, Mr. Jamison telegraphed Conser, saying he could not come, due to the snow, but asking Conser to wire him Lady's condition. Lady's father was clearly distressed to hear of his daughter's serious condition and very worried that if she died, Conser would bury her at the Sherman Institute cemetery instead of sending her home. To that end, he telegraphed Conser on 23 February, "If Lady dies, send body to Mono Lake accompanied by sister."[65] He also sent a letter reiterating his desire to have Lady's body sent home, accompanied by her sister, Alice:

> Be sure and send my Daughter home when she is died all we folks are like to see the died body befor they burried her. They can come right to home by the Parcel Post. Be sure and send Alice to she can take care of her on coming.[66]

On 25 February, Jamison sent yet another letter to Conser, reminding him once again that Lady was not to be buried in Riverside, but to be sent home with her sister Alice. If Lady died, he wanted Alice sent home, but if she lived, they could both remain at Sherman Institute. Unfortunately, Lady Jamison died on 2 March 1916, and as promised, Conser sent her father a telegram apprising him of her death.

Henry Jamison sent a letter to Conser on 11 March, thanking him for sending Alice with Lady's body: "thanking you for good helping with them, that is alright, we see only one girl arrive at our home and I thought that be proper."[67] He noted that since Alice would be staying home, he did not think, "we folks are see you again there," closing with, "Good By. Very Truly. I am Your Friend."[68]

Interestingly, the letter did not end there. Perhaps as an afterthought, Jamison added two more pages, and these pages reflect the anguish of a father who believed that his child had died at the hands of another. According to Jamison, Alice told him that Lady had not died of spinal meningitis. Before she died Alice visited Lady, who told her that, "she is not sick in her body not in her back bone, she telling her that she only had head aches and she says she may get better when taken syrup or cough syrup." Alice believed that Lady died not of spinal meningitis, but because, "the Indian Lady work in hospital she may give Lydia my daughter that not right kind of remedy. She may give bad poison remedy to Lydia."[69] Jamison said that they had heard of this type of thing happening a great many times at the Stewart Indian School, and the family believed it had happened to Lydia (Lady).

Acknowledging that Conser probably had not seen or known when they gave his daughter, "internal the remedy. But the body get up here, they smell awful bad it smells they had been pour some medecine on all over the body." In conclusion, Jamison stated that the family did not believe that Lydia died of spinal meningitis, but of bad medicine given to her by the hospital girls. Inferring that he did not blame Conser for his daughter's death, he again wrote, "I am your friend," but added, "I think I will not going sent Alice to any United States Indian school any more. Good By Sir."[70]

Pneumonia

According to Dr. Parker, pneumonia was a disease far more prevalent among Sherman Institute students than among "other classes of the population in this section."[71] He did not explain why he believed this to be the case. Parker considered pneumonia, as contracted by Sherman Institute students, an infectious disease; when one case occurred, several occurred.[72] To prevent pneumonia, he recommended that matrons promptly send any child exhibiting a fever and headache to the hospital, though several other illnesses exhibited the same symptoms. In addition, he believed that alleviating overcrowding in the dormitories, providing adequate ventilation, sprinkling dormitory floors and mopping them instead of "stirring up the dust," and not rustling bed clothes enough to propagate dust would protect students from pneumonia.[73] Parker clearly did not understand the etiology of pneumonia.

At Sherman Institute, the reason pneumonia appeared to be an infectious disease ("when one case occurred, several occurred") is that it usually followed an epidemic of an infectious disease such as measles or typhoid fever. It was not that pneumonia represented an infectious disease in and of itself, but that it was a secondary bacterial infection that followed true infectious diseases. The primary infection rendered students' lungs vulnerable to the pneumococcus bacilli, which often proved far more deadly than the original disease. Very few students died from typhoid fever or measles, but several died from the pneumonia which followed. An explanation for this was that by the time the children had already been ravaged by one disease, they were immunologically, physically, and mentally weakened, unable to successfully fight the secondary pneumonia infection.

Acute Nephritis

On 11 April 1917, a sixteen-year-old Pomo girl named Isabel Luff died of uremic poisoning due to renal failure, the result of acute nephritis.[74] She had not been feeling well for some time and wrote her sister, asking for money so that she could come home. Upon receiving Isabel's letter, her sister wrote to Conser on 8 April, requesting that Isabel be permitted to return home,

> She said is sick and not going school anymore. So look to me it she like to come. Why not let her come home. Now please don't delay to long. I am her garding.[75]

On 10 April, before receiving the letter, Conser wrote to Isabel's sister, apprising her of Isabel's rapidly failing health:

> I regret to inform you that your sister Isabel Luff has rapidly developed kidney failure. She was up and around a couple days ago but her condition developed for the worse suddenly and the doctor says that her recovery is impossible and will probably pass away today.[76]

Conser noted that Isabel had been ailing for some time but nothing seemed of a serious nature until the very recent development. He had attempted to telegraph the sister, to no avail, and had only been able to find an address for her by going through Isabel's letters. Since Conser had been unable to telegraph Isabel's sister regarding her dire condition, he telegraphed Sister Benedicta, a nun at the Catholic Mission in Ukiah, asking her to advise Mr. Vaughn, the day school teacher at Ukiah, of Isabel's imminent demise, and to ask him to find and notify Isabel's father and sister. This rather convoluted situation provides a vivid illustration of the problems frequently encountered by Sherman Institute superintendents in notifying families of their children's health problems. Many families lived on remote, essentially inaccessible, reservations, such that it was almost impossible to contact them in a timely manner in case of a health emergency. Superintendents often had to go through many contact layers in order to finally reach students' families.

Isabel died the day after Conser sent his letter and telegram and before her family could be notified of her grave condition. On 12 April, Conser sent a telegram to Mr. Vaughn informing him that Isabel had died the previous day and that she would be buried at the Sherman Institute cemetery the next day. Although Isabel had requested burial at the cemetery, her family insisted her body be sent home. After a funeral service conducted by Isabel's priest at Sherman Institute, Conser sent her remains to Ukiah.

What is of particular interest in this case is the probable cause of Isabel Luff's acute nephritis. Apparently, she had been intimate with a boy several months prior to her illness and feared pregnancy. She requested assistance in alleviating the potential problem from a cousin in Ukiah, who subsequently sent her some traditional medicine wrapped in a Christmas package. Dr. Roblee did not find out about the medicine, probably used for abortions, until a short time before Isabel died, so he was not able to determine whether the action of the medicine was in fact responsible for her death.[77]

As discussed in note 74, the most common cause of acute nephritis is toxicity from hypersensitivity to drug therapy. The specific traditional medicine sent to Isabel is unknown, as is whether she actually ingested the drug. However, modern medicines such as those that commonly result in acute nephritis often contain extracts of traditional, plant-based Native American medicines. Consequently, it is possible that the medicine Isabel's cousin sent, if ingested, could have caused toxicity from a hypersensitivity to the medicine.

Systemic Blastomycosis

One of the most unusual cases at Sherman Institute occurred in the early months of 1914.[78] On 4 December 1913, an eighteen-year old Mojave boy named Billy Poor complained that his leg had been troubling him for some time and checked into the hospital for treatment. Dr. Roblee diagnosed Billy with tuberculosis of the knee and glands and operated on his leg by scraping to the bone.[79] After he had recuperated in the hospital for one month, Roblee recommended that Billy be sent home once he had sufficiently recovered enough to travel. By the beginning of February, Billy's condition had not improved, and in studying the case, Roblee conducted a number of microscopic tests on the secretions draining from Billy's leg. The tests determined that Billy definitely did not have tuberculosis, although the clinical symptoms indicated that was the case. On the basis of microscopic tests, Roblee diagnosed Billy with a rare disease called "Systemic Blastomycosis." Roblee advised that Billy remain at the hospital until he could consult with a reliable authority relative to treatment.[80] Recommended treatment for Billy consisted of ten cubic centimeters of Autogenous Vaccine prepared especially for him by Dr. Lorena Breed of Pomona, California. On 17 February 1914, the day following completion of his treatment, Billy went home to Yuma, Arizona. He died one month later.

Roblee never discovered the source of Billy's illness, although it is probable he acquired it when he ran away from school in September 1913. Billy did not feel well when he returned to Sherman Institute in November, and his condition continued to worsen, finally giving the appearance of tuberculosis. Of particular interest is the fact that Southern California is not an endemic area for blastomycosis.[81] Where Billy's travels took him is unknown, but he may have been exposed to *Blastomyces dermatitidis* mold on a farm. This is not the natural site for the mold, but since it generally is not found farther west than the northern Midwest, it is the only reasonable explanation.

Homesickness

Though not technically an illness, homesickness is included in this discussion for two reasons. First, it offers the only information available in
Sherman Institute documents that specifically addresses mental health,
and second, because evidence indicates homesickness may have
increased students' vulnerability to disease. Hall first mentioned the
prevalence of homesickness, though usually in regard to children who
had run away from the school, noting, "most children are homesick for
a time."[82] In 1909 Conser verbalized a connection between homesickness
and illness, although he probably did not realize he was doing so.
Responding to Indian Office Circular No. 311, which questioned differences between older and younger children, Conser remarked,

> Smaller pupils are more demonstrative than older ones and show more signs
> of homesickness on arrival but recover more quickly. *If* there is any differ-
> ence, *probably* the smaller pupils suffer most on arrival.[83]

Although he did not make a direct connection between homesickness
and illness, Conser continued, "There is more sickness among the younger
pupils. There are about three young pupils sick to one older pupil."[84]

Student morbidity and mortality statistics do not necessarily support
Conser's statement, at least not for serious illness and disease. Conser's
response specified that younger children were those up to and including
third grade (generally up to nine years old) and older children were those
in fourth grade and higher (generally ten years of age and older). Between
1902 and 1922, out of 240 students ill enough to be sent home, 13 students age nine and younger were sent home, compared to 227 students
ten years of age and older. In all probability, Conser's statement referred
to the frequency of common ailments and health complaints, the cases of
which are, unfortunately, not available for comparative analysis.

Conser was not alone in connecting homesickness to health. In 1908,
Dr. Aleŝ Hrdlička addressed the influence of students' mental health on
their resultant vulnerability to tuberculosis. In considering his very profound discourse, one clearly recognizes that the same factors apply not

only to tuberculosis but also to every epidemic, accident, and illness experienced by nonreservation boarding school students, including those at Sherman Institute.

"In the nonreservation boarding schools," he wrote, "a factor of importance is the depressing effect on the newly-arrived student of a radically different environment." He accurately determined that, "a child taken from a reservation where it has become accustomed to almost unrestricted freedom of will and motion, is subjected to discipline for at least four-fifths of its waking hours." For the first time in their lives, children at boarding schools experience, "the exertion of studying in a strange language, the change of associations, and homesickness, the lack of sufficient diversified exercise out of doors, and (to it), unusual food." All of these factors have a "depressing and physically exhausting effect" on Indian children, making "the pupil an easier prey to consumption."[85]

Hrdlička's observations regarding the connection between depression and vulnerability to disease proved incredibly astute. Unlike many individuals in the Indian Service, he recognized that Indian students at nonreservation boarding schools were not just pawns in some grand assimilationist scheme. Instead, they were children who missed their families, who were lonely and scared, and who were literally surrounded by foreign smells, tastes, and sounds. Boarding schools denied Indian children the familial comfort and support system integral to every growing child, the very mechanism that helps children deal with change. Loss of the familiar, coupled with immersion in a strange new world, often led to depression. The depression may have been short-lived, as in the homesickness felt by every child, at least fleetingly, or it may have become a chronic condition that impacted a child's mental and physical health.

According to Hrdlička, coping with the radically different environment of nonreservation boarding schools physically exhausted students, leading to an increased vulnerability to disease. While most medical authorities now recognize the existence of childhood depression and its impact on physical health, such was not the case in the early years of the twentieth century, rendering Hrdlička's proposal somewhat unique. We now know that childhood depression can cause somatic complaints such as headaches, abdominal pain, and insomnia.[86] If these symptoms continue, appetite loss and fatigue may result, ultimately weakening children's immunological defenses and making them more vulnerable to disease. Hrdlička's assessment of the connection between the depressing effect of nonreservation boarding schools and students' vulnerability to tuberculosis clearly had a strong basis in fact. Unfortunately, his perceptions were not universally shared, and as a result, the "radically different environment" of the schools remained unchanged and student morbidity and mortality, particularly from tuberculosis, continued to rise.

CHAPTER 6

Tuberculosis: Policy and Practice

TUBERCULOSIS IS A UNIVERSAL DISEASE SPANNING GEOGRAPHICAL, CUL-
tural, and temporal boundaries. Yet there is scant evidence of its presence among indigenous people of the Americas prior to the European
invasion in 1492.[1] During the early years of European occupation, a variety of epidemic diseases decimated native populations, but tuberculosis
did not have a significant effect, primarily because traditional lifeways
remained dominant. Not until the nineteenth century did this disease
pose a critical threat to Native American health. Tuberculosis fed on people confined to reservations, living in crowded and unsanitary conditions, with minimal health care available to prevent and treat the disease.
By the time the first nonreservation Indian boarding school opened in
Carlisle, Pennsylvania, in 1879, tuberculosis had reached epidemic proportions on some reservations, and Indian youth often carried this disease into the schools. The living environment in these schools further
exacerbated the health crisis.

For almost one hundred years tuberculosis preyed upon Indian children in nonreservation boarding schools, resulting in higher morbidity
and mortality rates than any other single disease. Sherman Institute was
no exception. Yet according to available Indian Office statistics, this
school had a consistently lower incidence of tuberculosis than almost
every other nonreservation boarding school, than the Indian population
of Southern California, and in some cases, than the white population of

the region. While many factors contributed to the relatively low incidence of tuberculosis at Sherman Institute, the manner in which Superintendents Hall and Conser chose to implement Indian Office policies
pertaining to tuberculosis proved the most important.

Tuberculosis is a chronic, recurrent, infectious disease caused by the
Mycobacterium tuberculosis (tubercle bacillus).[2] Mere contact is not sufficient to spread the disease. Human tuberculosis occurs almost exclusively
as the result of inhalation of organisms dispersed as droplet nuclei from
a person with pulmonary tuberculosis. The *M. tuberculosis* may float in
the air for several hours, greatly increasing the chance of spread.[3] Tuberculosis can infect many parts of the body, but the most common site of
infection is the lung, with resultant pulmonary tuberculosis. Upon entering the body of a healthy person, the tubercle bacillus may become
encapsulated, then either break out during a period of stress or ill health,
or remain dormant indefinitely. In others, the bacilli immediately initi-
ate a slow process toward debilitation, usually running its course in two
to five months, although acute cases may take only weeks.

In the early stages of tuberculosis, there are often no symptoms, or
symptoms that resemble influenza. Ninety to 95 percent of tuberculosis
infections go unrecognized, producing only a positive tuberculin skin test
and a latent infection.[4] Low fever, weight loss, chronic fatigue, and heavy
sweating, particularly at night, characterize the secondary stage of tuberculosis. Patients in the later stages of the disease typically have a cough
with sputum that becomes progressively bloody, yellow, thick, or gray;
chest pain; shortness of breath; and sometimes, reddish or cloudy urine.
In most cases a tubercular person recovers without treatment before the
disease progresses. However, when an individual whose health is already
compromised becomes infected, the disease often progresses rapidly, and
recovery is no longer a viable option, even with appropriate treatment.

Tuberculosis is one of the so-called filth diseases, named for their ability to thrive in unsanitary, crowded living conditions.[5] Filth diseases are
generally considered to be diseases of the urban poor; individuals forced
to live in crowded small spaces with inadequate sanitation facilities,
places seemingly impossible to keep clean. This was the type of living

environment that bred tuberculosis, and it was the reason indigenous peoples had virtually no exposure to tuberculosis prior to the nineteenth century. Although traditional Native American lifeways varied greatly, they generally did not include occupation of closely confined spaces over long periods of time. Instead, movement over large expanses of land, coupled with fresh air and water, characterized their living environment. Few opportunities for contagion existed, particularly from filth diseases.

Not until the removal of Native Americans to reservations began in the 1850s did filth diseases, particularly tuberculosis, become a significant health problem. Often an entire family occupied a single room with a dirt floor, little ventilation, and wholly inadequate sanitation. Some individuals expectorated freely on the dirt floors.[6] Limited access to fresh water and a diet significantly different from that traditionally consumed exacerbated the unhealthy living environment forced upon displaced Native Americans of this era. In consequence, what had always been a disease of the urban poor visited native peoples with a vengeance. Indians had become the poorest of the rural poor in the United States. Tuberculosis soon became the predominant disease on reservations, in many cases striking at least one member of every family.[7] Few Native Americans escaped the ravages of this disease.

Prior to Robert Koch's discovery of the tubercle bacillus in 1882, the three most widely held medical explanations for tuberculosis were heredity, unfavorable climate, and sedentary living. The latter explanation included conditions that encouraged the onset of the disease: lack of exercise, poor ventilation, and defective lighting.[8] Yet even after discovery of the causative agent, belief in the old medical explanations prevailed, particularly that of heredity when it concerned Indians with tuberculosis. During the late nineteenth and early twentieth centuries, the most popular explanation for the high incidence of tuberculosis among native peoples was that of lack of natural immunity, related to their history of exposure; since the Indians had no history of exposure, they also had no natural immunity.[9] Many researchers measured ethnicity and the incidence of tuberculosis against the prevailing industrial work ethic: the closer a group was to being assimilated into industrial capitalism, the more "civilized" it was perceived to be and the greater its immunity to tuberculosis.[10] The general perception of Native Americans as being "uncivilized" explained their high incidence of tuberculosis. Many considered acculturation and assimilation crucial to reducing tuberculosis, adding impetus to the role of nonreservation boarding schools in saving Indians from the horrors of this most dread disease.[11] The more quickly Indians could be assimilated into white society, it was believed, the more quickly their incidence of tuberculosis could be reduced.

Despite the fact that nonreservation boarding schools supposedly offered a mechanism by which Indian children could be released from the "natural" inevitability of contracting tuberculosis, the schools were, instead, virtual hotbeds of the disease. By the time Captain Richard Pratt established Carlisle Indian School in 1879, rampant tuberculosis existed on most reservations, reaching near-epidemic levels on many. Children coming from the reservations to the schools often carried incipient tuberculosis with them, unknowingly sharing the infection with all those with whom they came into contact. Crowded dormitories, with two or three children sleeping in each bed, coupled with often inadequate nutrition, poor sanitary conditions, and the tremendous stress of living in an unfamiliar environment, not only exacerbated the potential for latent tuberculosis to become active but greatly increased the possibilities for transmittal of the disease. Further, at some boarding schools that had trouble filling high enrollment quotas, such as Crow Creek in South Dakota, the superintendents regularly admitted children with unmistakable signs of tuberculosis to the schools, letting them mingle freely with the general student population. In explaining his admissions policy, Supt. Frank Avery at the Crow Creek boarding school noted, "We also enroll many who are conspicuously scrofulous, and others who at least very quickly develop tubercular lung trouble." Avery claimed that only by enrolling tubercular children could he reach enrollment quotas set by the Indian Office. Further, because of limited school facilities, "we necessarily put these pupils, sound and unsound, into dormitories and classrooms together. Nothing else is possible."[12]

The Indian Office evidenced an ignorance of the disease's etiology that prevented them from taking decisive action to control and eradicate the disease. Commissioner of Indian Affairs William Jones (1897–1904) maintained a firm belief that tuberculosis was hereditary and that Indians were simply predisposed to succumb to the disease, a belief shared by many Indian Service physicians and school superintendents. As far as he was concerned, there was little the Indian Office could do either to prevent or to eradicate the disease. Some school superintendents considered military drills to be an effective tuberculosis combatant because the drills provided students with fresh air, exercise, and discipline. Still others viewed dried sputa as the principal cause of tuberculosis, with spittoons and frequent wet mopping of floors the best mode of prevention. At least one school inspector thought scrofula was a form of an inherited venereal disease.

The 1901 *Course of Study for the Indian Schools of the United States* correctly, if simplistically, described tuberculosis as being "due to a living germ (something like a seed)" that is coughed up by people with tuberculosis, and "when this gets dry it will float in the air," to be breathed in by any man, woman, or child.[13] Yet in describing who was most at risk for the disease, the *Course of Study* erroneously stated that only in students with unhealthy lungs due to "sleeping with head under the bedclothes or by bad air from neglect day or night" would the germ live and develop. The Indian Office document further noted, "There is little danger to a healthy person, even in the near presence of the germ, because the lungs of a healthy person do not offer the right conditions for the seed or germ to develop in."[14] In closing, the *Course of Study* sweetly proclaimed, "Sunshine will kill the germs of disease and make plants and children grow in health."[15]

No one in the Indian Office or Indian School Service seemed able to agree on precisely how tuberculosis was transmitted, so they could not agree on the most effective preventative measures. Few would agree that mere sunshine would do the trick, although interestingly, ultraviolet light actually does kill the tubercle bacillus. Consequently, during most of Jones's term in office, official policies concerning tuberculosis in the nonreservation boarding schools were neither dictated nor enforced.

In 1901, the year Sherman Institute broke ground, the secretary of the interior directed Commissioner Jones to respond to reports made by Indian service physicians and Indian School Inspector William McConnell that tuberculosis was prevalent in the schools. While Jones could not deny the truth of these reports, he explained his tolerance of the contagion and his inaction in controlling it by appealing to the "tendency theory" of the disease. According to his theory,

> The transfer of an Indian boy from the free, active life, in which his ancestors have for generations lived, to confinement of the school room and regular duties, has a tendency to develop this disease.[16]

Jones's uneducated response served only to add credence to the claims of McConnell and the Indian service physicians; the nature of nonreservation boarding schools necessarily resulted in a high incidence of tuberculosis. This admission was far removed from the early argument that the civilizing effect of such schools would serve to reduce the number of tubercular Indian children.

Few accepted Jones' response to the tuberculosis crisis as satisfactory, and concerned members of both the public and the Indian Office put increasing pressure on him for further action. Reacting to this pressure, in July 1903, Jones ordered Indian Service physicians to conduct a health survey of the Indian population, with special emphasis on the health of Indian students. This survey represented the first comprehensive study of Indian morbidity in the United States.[17] Jones asked physicians to take special note of tuberculosis, scrofula, and syphilis.

The Indian Office completed its evaluation of the physicians' survey in March 1904. Relating to tuberculosis, the survey concluded that tuberculosis was more widespread among Indians than among an equal number of whites, with the greatest prevalence being among Indians due to:

- Failure to disinfect tubercular sputum.
- Poor sanitation and lack of cleanliness.
- Improper and poorly prepared food.

- Intermarriage of Indians of the same tribe.
- Intermarriage of Indians and whites.
- Taking pupils predisposed to tuberculosis from camp life and confining them in school.
- Overcrowding in dormitories.
- Lack of proper medical attention after infection.
- The use of alcohol.[18]

In perusing these stated causes of tuberculosis among the Indian population, two things are evident. First, Indian Office physicians remained uncertain about the etiology of tuberculosis, and second, racialist attitudes clearly influenced their evaluation of the causative factors involved in the disease. Instead of correctly ascribing tuberculosis to bacteria found on reservations and in boarding schools, the prevailing racialist view attributed the high incidence of tuberculosis among Indians to their "uncivilized" state, with its concomitant filthy habits, loose morals, and alcoholism. Neither the medical uncertainty nor the racialist attitude were exclusive to the Indian Office, but instead reflected the general demeanor of the era. This was a period of discovery in medicine, as well as a period in which physicians and other professionals sought to explain conditions in American society by reproducing racialist doctrines under the aegis of objective science.

Regardless of the misguided health survey evaluation, it succeeded in forcing enactment of the first official Indian Office policies relating to tuberculosis in nonreservation boarding schools. In the first of several directives, Jones forbade school superintendents to enroll students who lacked a medical certificate attesting to their physical and mental soundness. Whenever physicians observed signs of tuberculosis during the enrollment examination, they were to send the child home. Jones directed school physicians to reexamine students periodically, and if they observed signs of tuberculosis, to send the student home. If any doubt existed as to the tubercular condition of a student at a nonreservation boarding school, the commissioner directed physicians to place the student under special surveillance, reducing the student's workload and enriching his or her diet. School superintendents were to send students home if even faint signs of tuberculosis persisted. Unfortunately, these policies contained no mention of the surveillance period's length or how quickly a tubercular student was to be sent home after receiving a positive diagnosis.

Under the guise of prevention, Jones ordered school superintendents to provide each building with metal cuspidors, partially filled with disinfectants, to eliminate the chance of contagion from uncontained expectoration or sputum given an opportunity to dry and become airborne.[19] Jones directed school superintendents to keep all dormitories dust free, well ventilated, and as much as possible, flooded with sunlight, measures curiously consistent with the "sedentary living" theory of tuberculosis causation espoused prior to Koch's discovery of the tubercle bacillus in 1882.

The school physician's role in tuberculosis prevention expanded greatly. In addition to conducting enrollment examinations and periodic reexaminations throughout the year, physicians' job duties included inspecting the school grounds, making suggestions for sanitary improvements, and lecturing on the topic of hygiene, all on a weekly basis.

Commissioner Jones's tuberculosis policies, while of noble intent, were nonetheless ineffectual. He disseminated policy information through circular letters to school superintendents, even though the effectiveness of circulars was notoriously suspect. Many Indian Office field service employees never read the established service rules, let alone the numerous circulars sent out on a regular basis. Jones relied solely on school superintendents to comply with his directives, despite the fact that Indian school service inspectors did not enforce them. As a result, the tuberculosis problem in nonreservation boarding schools continued unabated during the remainder of Jones's tenure.

Indian Office policies enacted during Jones's tenure had little impact on tuberculosis morbidity and mortality at Sherman Institute. This was not because Superintendent Harwood Hall chose not to implement them, or because they were ineffective, but because Hall had already established similar practices at the school prior to Jones's weak edicts. Hall was not a visionary, and he evidenced little more concern for the health of students than many other superintendents. Rather, Hall's predecessors at Perris Indian School had established most of the tuberculosis practices. Hall simply inherited and continued to implement the policies after the move to Sherman Institute.

The most critical practice in tuberculosis prevention at Sherman Institute had actually been established in 1891, prior to the opening of Perris Indian School, and thirteen years before the enactment of Jones's policy. Perris Indian School's first superintendent, W. H. Savage, and the Mission-Tule Agency physician, Dr. C. C. Wainwright, had established and enforced a policy requiring that every potential student at the school undergo a rigorous physical examination before being permitted to enroll. Savage and Wainwright accepted only children evidencing perfect health at Perris Indian School. If a significant period of time elapsed before an accepted student arrived at the school, or if a physician other than Wainwright had given the initial examination, Wainwright reexamined the child at Perris Indian School. Any signs of tuberculosis automatically negated the child's enrollment at the school, and he was sent home immediately. Signs of tuberculosis in students already boarding at the school were also grounds for an immediate return home.

Hall proved to be less diligent in enforcing these policies at Sherman Institute, although the rules remained at the core of his tuberculosis prevention program. Hall required each student seeking enrollment to have a physicians' certification of sound health, although some notable exceptions were made, particularly for trachomatous students. The school's contract physician, Dr. A. S. Parker, examined entering students, and as before, signs of tuberculosis resulted in the student being denied enrollment and being sent home. Yet as far as sending tubercular students home who were already in residence at the school, Hall's record was inconsistent and his practices sometimes contradictory.

In most cases, when Parker diagnosed an enrolled student with tuberculosis, Hall sent the child home immediately, especially before 1905, when a hospital was finally constructed. In the spirit of prevention, he even sent some children home, such as Bessie Johnson and Jessie Masten in 1904, prior to an actual diagnosis of tuberculosis:

Both girls are not well. They are in no serious condition, but as the physician pronounces a slight trouble of the lungs, I am sending them home to live—not to die. I have seen so many pupils kept until so late, and it is my intention to do otherwise.[20]

In sending Lulu Kisto and Hannah Roberts home to Casa Grande that same year, Hall emphasized his belief in early intervention, an adherence to Indian Office policy, and criticism of other nonreservation boarding schools. Hall wrote that the "Doctor has made no adverse report as to their health, but I believe they ought to go home. I think both of the girls have weak lungs, and while not in an alarming condition, yet in view of the strong circular letters relative to the pupil's health from the Office, I think it wise to send them home." Hall understood the implications of his action, saying, "You know how it is with most schools; children are kept oftentimes until they are beyond recovery and I want to do otherwise." [21] He emphasized again that he sent the girls home to live, not die.

Despite Hall's stated belief in sending tubercular children home in a timely manner, not every case received this consideration. In some instances, he did not send students home at all, but treated them at the school until they died, then had their bodies buried in the school cemetery or shipped home. These cases, such as that of Lizzie Edwards, occurred when an acute case of tuberculosis rendered the student too ill to travel, when adverse environmental conditions precluded safe travel, or when the student had no family to which he or she could be returned.

Your niece, Lizzie Edwards, has been sick for quite a long while, as you are aware, with consumption. I would have sent her home months ago, but owing to high waters and bad weather, it was impossible. She is now too weak to stand a trip and I am afraid she will pass away at any time. She has had the very best medical care and nursing, and every thing done for her possible. She will not be with us very long, poor child.[22]

Yet these were not the only cases in which children evidencing tubercular symptoms were not sent home until, to use Hall's own words, they were "beyond recovery."

In an unpublished article about the horrors of nonreservation boarding schools, Edward Davis of Mesa Grande Reservation claimed that Hall refused to allow sisters Camilia and Flavia Ruiz to return home. The girls entered the school healthy and strong but developed coughs and complained of feeling sick over a period of time. Camilia, the first to become ill, and her father asked Hall numerous times to allow her to go home, but it was no use.

> The superintendent kept refusing, that she could get better medical attention up there than down here and no doubt she could, but it was her heart that was sick as well as her body and all the doctors in the world couldn't heal that.[23]

Camilia finally became so ill that she was confined to her bed, and according to her father, even then the family was not notified of her condition. A family friend finally drove from the Mesa Grande Reservation to Riverside, loaded Camilia into a wagon, and traveled two days to bring her home, where she died five minutes after arriving. Flavia suffered a similar fate, dying four days after being brought home.[24] It is important to note that Davis's narrative is not substantiated by available documents. Flavia Ruiz (San Diegueño) attended Sherman Institute and returned home twice, the last time six months prior to her death. There is no record of a Camilia Ruiz attending Sherman Institute, only a Camilia Stokes (Luiseño) of Mesa Grande Reservation. Although this is probably the same person, it is curious that, as sisters, Flavia and Camilia had different last names and different tribal affiliations. Camilia returned home two weeks before Flavia, and subsequently died at an unknown date.[25]

Hall's decision to keep the Ruiz sisters at Sherman Institute for treatment, if in fact he did so, is inexplicable, clearly contradicting his stated beliefs and both previous and subsequent actions. Evidence has not been discovered that indicates Hall's alleged behavior in the case of the Ruiz sisters was common or that it happened at any other time. The question is why, in the same year, would Hall send girls home to the Hoopa and Sacaton reservations before Parker had actually diagnosed them with tuberculosis, yet deny the Ruiz girls such a right. If anything, the living environment on Mesa Grande was more favorable to recovery than that at either of the other reservations. In fact, in 1904 the Hoopa Reservation possessed the highest tuberculosis morbidity rate of any other reservation in the United States, with 277.8 cases per 1,000.[26] Sending Bessie Johnson and Jessie Masten home to such an environment effectively signed their death certificates, though Hall could not have known this at the time. Hall's reasoning for retaining the Ruiz sisters remains elusive, but available documentation does not indicate that this represented a common practice at Sherman Institute.

Physical examinations and removal of tubercular students from the school formed the core of Sherman Institute's existing tuberculosis practices that preceded official Indian Office policies. In addition, every other policy dictated by Jones in 1904, with the possible exception of placing metal cuspidors in every building, had also been put into practice at Sherman Institute before becoming official, and in several cases the practices at Sherman Institute exceeded policy requirements.

Francis E. Leupp became the next commissioner of Indian affairs in 1905. Yet it would be three years before the Indian Office enacted any additional tuberculosis policies for the nonreservation boarding schools. During those three years, tuberculosis morbidity and mortality among Indian populations worsened markedly. Leupp knew even less about tuberculosis than had Jones, even subscribing to the very incorrect notion that scrofula (glandular tuberculosis) was a venereal disease that could be eradicated by moral correctives and the cessation of liquor traffic among Indians.[27]

Leupp did not take action against tuberculosis until 1908, after finally being convinced of its tremendous threat to Indian health. In what was to be one of his more important moves, Leupp appointed Special Agent Elsie Newton to cooperate with the Smithsonian Institution in preparing an exhibit on Indian morbidity for the Sixth International Congress on Tuberculosis. Elsie Newton had long identified Indian health as a crucial issue, and as such, put tremendous effort into the exhibit. The Smithsonian Institution provided accurate and current data obtained by Drs. Aleŝ Hrdliĉka and Paul Johnson during a research trip investigating tuberculosis among five Indian tribes and at the Phoenix Indian School. Hrdliĉka and Johnson's report convinced Leupp that tuberculosis was "the greatest single menace to the future of the red race."[28]

Once Leupp experienced the tuberculosis epiphany, he acted quickly and decisively. Leupp appointed three Indian Service physicians, with Elsie Newton, to a committee designed to study the ways and means of controlling and ultimately eradicating tuberculosis among Indian populations. The committee made a number of recommendations, including establishing sanatarium camps on reservations and at nonreservation boarding schools, monthly weighing of students in nonreservation boarding schools, and urging school physicians to adopt an index card record-keeping system. After receiving the committee's recommendations, Leupp appointed Newton to the position of supervisor of schools, so that she would be in a position to oversee compliance with the recommendations. Finally, the most important action taken by Leupp in his campaign against tuberculosis was inviting Dr. Joseph A. Murphy, an expert on tuberculosis, to join the Indian Service as medical supervisor of schools.

In addition to these appointments, Leupp established a number of important tuberculosis policies for nonreservation boarding schools during the remainder of his tenure as commissioner. These policies, which have been detailed in previous chapters, included the immediate dismissal of all tubercular children from nonreservation boarding schools; disinfection of school supplies, books, and wind instruments; and construction of sleeping porches at hospitals.

Commissioner Valentine succeeded Leupp in 1909, and for the most part, continued his tuberculosis policies, particularly that requiring immediate dismissal of tubercular children. The fact eluded Valentine, as it had Leupp, that this policy not only exacerbated the spread of tuberculosis to reservation populations but also virtually guaranteed the child's death, since few reservations had adequate medical facilities or personnel to care for tuberculosis patients. Health policies specific to Valentine's administration, and Sherman Institute's compliance with said policies have been thoroughly discussed in the first three chapters of this book and do not require further elucidation. However, in addition to these health policies, Valentine initiated a number of innovative programs designed to rid nonreservation boarding schools of tuberculosis. Valentine, who taught at the Massachusetts Institute of Technology prior to joining the Indian Office, had a decidedly different perspective on fighting tuberculosis than had his predecessors. He believed that education offered the key to eradication.

At Commissioner Valentine's request, in 1910 Dr. Murphy prepared a short book called *Manual on Tuberculosis: Its Causes, Prevention, and Treatment* that Valentine required all teachers and students to read. The Indian Office supposedly sent copies of the book to all school employees and students. However, Sherman Institute received only sixty-seven copies of the book, enough for distribution only to selected students.

In conjunction with the distribution of Murphy's book, Valentine sponsored an essay contest for all Indian students on "The Causes, Prevention, and Treatment of Tuberculosis."[29] In 1912, approximately twenty thousand students from the second grade up competed for prizes, spending seven and one-half hours over a three-day period writing their essays without the aid of books or notes. Teachers, superintendents, and doctors judged the essays and awarded 561 prizes—gold, silver, and bronze buttons—and the Indian Office wrote personal letters to each winner.[30] Students at Sherman Institute successfully competed, with twelve winning prizes. The students' work so impressed Dr. Roblee that he showed several of the essays to noted tuberculosis expert Dr. Tucker. Dr. Tucker enthusiastically praised the essays and requested permission from Conser to publish one of them in pamphlet form to be distributed throughout the state.[31]

As part of Valentine's educational crusade against tuberculosis in nonreservation boarding schools, he sent instructional posters to all school superintendents on the hygienic handling of dairy herds, because cows could transmit tuberculosis through unpasteurized milk. Despite Valentine's concern and laudable efforts to eliminate at least one source of tuberculosis, as late as 1928 no nonreservation boarding schools pasteurized milk, but instead brought it in pitchers directly from the farm to the dining room table.[32] The instructions included directions for keeping milk rooms clean and screened, sterilizing pails and cans with live steam or boiling water, and allowing at least five hundred cubic feet of air inside the barn for each cow. To keep cows healthy, the Indian Office directed that they were to be given only pure running water to drink, be kept clean, and have good feed, and employees were to immediately separate any unhealthy cow from the rest of the herd. Before milking any cow, the milker had to thoroughly wash his or her hands, including under the nails, wear a special suit of clothes, and use neither tobacco nor chew while milking.[33] Valentine directed inspectors to check for compliance with these hygiene instructions while on their tours of duty.

Sherman Institute complied with the poster instructions as much as possible, but this proved difficult in many aspects. The dairy barn located at the school farm had been one of the first buildings constructed and had not been modernized or expanded, despite the extensive use it had received over the more than ten-year period since the school's opening. Keeping the barn clean and providing adequate air space for the dairy herd was especially difficult as the dairy herd expanded but the barn did not. The school was most successful in attempting to keep the cows and their milkers reasonably sanitary.

Upon assuming office in 1913, Cato Sells continued the educational health programs developed by Valentine. In addition, he directed school superintendents to actively participate in the "Tuberculosis Day" program sponsored by the National Association for the Study and Prevention of Tuberculosis. A week before the designated day, students prepared papers on tuberculosis, with the best ones read during special school programs. The following year, Sells increased the perceived effectiveness of "Tuberculosis Day" by providing superintendents with the addresses of tuberculosis associations that could provide free lecture outlines, speeches, and supplementary materials.[34] In 1916, Sells expanded the program to a "Tuberculosis Week" during the month of December and literally inundated students with information regarding the causes, prevention, and treatment of tuberculosis. The timing of Sells's program is interesting because it occurred shortly before many students returned home for Christmas vacation. Since one of the main goals of tuberculosis education programs was to have students teach their parents, the timing of Sells's "Tuberculosis Week" was clearly fortuitous. Information would still be freshly imprinted on the students' brains when they journeyed home, and they would be far more likely to transmit it to their families than if a considerable period of time had elapsed.

In 1914, Sells increased the sizes of dairy herds at schools to augment dairy products in students' diets. In addition, he supplied each school with milk sediment testers to test the purity of milk. If tests found unclean milk, steps to find the source of the dirt were to be taken immediately. Unfortunately, the sediment testers did not detect the presence of the tubercle bacillus, though that was the main reason for enforcing dairy herd hygiene.

The Indian Office recognized a connection between cows and tuberculosis as early as 1898, but no official policies emerged regulating the testing of dairy herds for tuberculosis. Sporadic testing of cows between 1906 and 1908 detected a high incidence of tubercular cows at nonreservation boarding schools. Since this clearly represented a serious health threat, the Bureau of Animal Industry offered to systematically test dairy herds at every boarding school. Sells accepted the offer, but the planned testing program did not commence until the 1910–11 school year. After that, the Bureau of Animal Industry performed the tuberculin testing on boarding school dairy herds only by special request.

Tubercular cows posed a serious health threat throughout the nation, and especially at nonreservation boarding schools after Sells increased the size of dairy herds. By 1917, the national situation warranted creation of a special tuberculosis eradication unit within the Bureau of Animal Industry, and in July, Sells arranged for systematic testing to again be conducted for school dairy herds.

Interestingly, on 2 December 1916 Conser requested that the Indian Office make arrangements for tuberculin testing of Sherman Institute's dairy herd as soon as possible.[35] What led to this request is not known, but it proved fortuitous. When the Bureau of Animal Industry finally tested the herd on 23 March 1917, the inspector found that thirteen cows and five heifers had tuberculosis. At the recommendation of the inspector, Conser arranged for the immediate sale of the animals to a slaughterhouse, with inspection to be made by a bureau representative to ensure against the improper use of the meat.[36]

Throughout the remainder of his term in office, Sells continued to actively pursue avenues of educating Indian students about tuberculosis. At the end of his administration in 1920, Sells remarked that, "During my administration, Indian school children have been so thoroughly drilled in the causes and prevention of tuberculosis that I have no hesitancy in saying that they have a greater familiarity with this essential knowledge than have the same number of children among any other people."[37] Sells's assessment was undoubtedly correct, and his focus on education contributed to a decline in tuberculosis in the following decades.

From the ineffective circulars issued by Jones in 1903 to the aggressive directives of the Sells administration, virtually every Indian Office preventive health program focused on the eradication of tuberculosis. These programs have been exhaustively discussed in the first three chapters of this dissertation. In every case, superintendents at Sherman Institute strictly complied with the official policies and implemented school-specific practices based on personal experience with health issues.

The question that must now be addressed is whether implementation of these policies and practices was effective in eradicating tuberculosis at Sherman Institute. If preventive policies and practices did not eradicate tuberculosis, did they have a significant impact on the morbidity and mortality rates at the school? Were there mitigating factors that affected the policies and practices? Finally, how did tuberculosis morbidity and mortality rates at Sherman Institute compare to those at other nonreservation boarding schools?

TABLE 6.1

TUBERCULOSIS MORBIDITY, SHERMAN INSTITUTE,

1902–1922

School Year	Enrollment	Number of Confirmed Cases*	Percentage of Enrolled Population
1902–03	389	2	0.51
1903–04	638	9	1.14
1904–05	722	1	0.14
1905–06	596	4	0.67
1906–07	687	1	0.15
1907–08	699	7	1.00
1908–09	672	10	1.48
1909–10	555	11	1.98
1910–11	712	13	1.82
1911–12	631	18	2.85
1912–13	639	11	1.72
1913–14	690	12	1.74
1914–15	744	16	2.15
1915–16	790	21	2.66
1916–17	787	22	2.80
1917–18	802	18	2.24
1918–19	879	30	3.41
1919–20	974	11	1.13
1920–21	1030	13	1.26
1921–22	1059	20	1.89

* Does not include cases of "weak lungs" or "tubercular tendencies," etc.

Policies and practices implemented by the Indian Office and school superintendents did not eradicate tuberculosis at Sherman Institute. In fact, as may be seen in Table 6.1 and Figure 6.1, tuberculosis morbidity increased substantially between 1902 and 1922, peaking during the 1918–19 school year at 3.41 percent of the enrolled student population. Conversely, during the early years of the school, when few preventive policies existed, tuberculosis at Sherman Institute was at its lowest point. A number of factors explain this phenomenon.

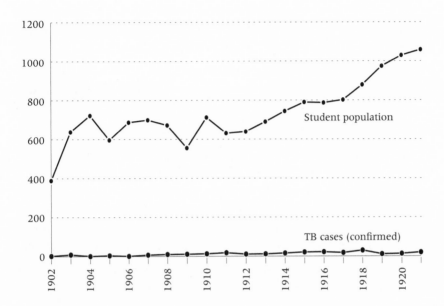

Figure 6.1. Tuberculosis Morbidity, 1902–22.

The most important reason for the low tuberculosis morbidity rates during the early years is that the founding student population was very healthy. The majority of students were those transferred from Perris Indian School, where they had been under the care of the Mission-Tule Agency physician, Dr. Wainwright. Beginning in 1891, Wainwright had actively selected only the healthiest students from Southern California Indian populations to attend the school. Reservation Indians in this area already had a very low incidence of tuberculosis, so it was not particularly difficult to select nontubercular children. If any child at the school showed signs of tuberculosis, he or she was immediately sent home, thus limiting contagion potential.

With the transfer to Sherman Institute in Riverside and the enrollment expansion, the largest number of students continued to be drawn from Southern California reservations for several years. Not until the student population became more diverse culturally and geographically did the incidence of tuberculosis increase measurably. By the end of the research period, students representing thirty-nine tribes from around the United States attended Sherman Institute, and Mission Indians from Southern California were no longer the majority. As the diversity of Indian students increased, tuberculosis morbidity increased. This trend continued until the 1919–20 to 1921–22 school years, when morbidity decreased dramatically. Interestingly, this coincides with a large infusion of Navajo students into the Sherman Institute population.

Until the 1919–20 school year, the maximum number of Navajo students at Sherman Institute had been 65 (in 1918–19). In 1919–20, this jumped to 189 students, in 1920–21 it jumped to 261 students, and in the 1921–22 school year, the Navajo population increased to 337 students. In each of the latter three school years, there were significantly more Navajo students than students from any other tribe. Unfortunately, many of the students diagnosed with tuberculosis during these three years were Navajo, especially in 1921–22, when tubercular Navajo children were the majority.

Why would a substantial increase in Navajo students result in a substantial decrease in tuberculosis morbidity? Was this inverse relationship coincidental—did it actually reflect the cumulative effectiveness of the numerous preventive tuberculosis policies and practices? Or was there a direct correlation between Navajo children and tuberculosis?

Historically, the Navajo have been reported as having a very low incidence of tuberculosis, though this data is suspect. In their 1908 study, *Tuberculosis among Certain Indian Tribes,* Hrdlička and Johnson reported that, "The natives most free from tuberculosis—the Navajo—occupy an extensive and naturally healthful region, where they live under conditions more nearly aboriginal than those found in any other locality north of Mexico." Yet they qualified this conclusion by noting that, "The tribe no doubt suffers more from tuberculosis than is indicated in the reports of the Indian Office."[38] The size of the Navajo territory and the number of people living there made it impossible, in their opinion, to obtain exact data on tuberculosis morbidity and mortality.

Regardless of the inadequacy of data, Hrdlička and Johnson reported that Indians living at the Navajo Agency in New Mexico had a morbidity rate of 1.7 cases of tuberculosis per 1,000 people and the lowest mortality rate (45.7/1,000) of all tribes included in the study. Navajos living at the San Juan Agency had a morbidity rate of only 0.7 cases per 1,000 people.[39] Inexplicably, Hrdlička and Johnson did not include any Southern California Indians in their study, so a comparison is not possible. The 1912 Public Health Services report, *Contagious and Infectious Diseases among Indians,* found significantly higher tuberculosis morbidity among Navajos, at 8.3 percent of the population, in fact representing the second-highest morbidity rate in Arizona. Despite this increase, Navajo morbidity was still lower than that of many tribes throughout the United States. Southern California Indians were not included in this study, either. Further, Navajo children transferring to Sherman Institute from reservation boarding or day schools had already been preselected out for tuberculosis, so they would have represented a healthy population.

As Sherman Institute was infused with low-tuberculosis-risk Navajo children, who, in fact, formed the majority of the student population, the incidence of tuberculosis at the school decreased to approximately one-third the level it had been in previous years. The mechanism that permitted this decrease was twofold: first, few Navajo children had incipient tuberculosis, coming into the school, and second, the relatively low-risk Navajo reservation population lessened the probability of students becoming infected while home on vacation and transmitting the disease to others upon their return to school. While the cumulative effect of preventive policies and practices undoubtedly impacted tuberculosis morbidity and mortality, it was not until Navajo children entered Sherman Institute in such large numbers that a significant decrease in tuberculosis rates occurred. Unfortunately, while the increased number of Navajo students effectively decreased tuberculosis morbidity and mortality rates at Sherman Institute, it probably increased the incidence of tuberculosis among the reservation populations.[40]

Another explanation for the very low tuberculosis morbidity rates during the early years at Sherman Institute can be attributed to record

keeping. Before 1909, a mechanism for accurately recording tuberculosis morbidity and mortality rates did not exist. Superintendents submitted monthly reports that included information about enrollment,
attendance, hospital admittance, and deaths, but these forms did not ask
for specific information regarding tuberculosis or any other disease.
Annual reports were narratives summarizing activities at schools and
reservations, with health information generally relegated to qualitative
statements such as, "the students' health was excellent this year." In
1909, Commissioner Valentine developed the first standardized forms for
reporting specific details of tuberculosis and trachoma, by then considered the two greatest threats to Indian health. Analysis of data contained
on the forms allowed the Indian Office to determine the actual extent of
these diseases, compare equivalent data from all the nonreservation
boarding schools, and determine whether their preventive programs
were working. Tuberculosis morbidity and mortality data from Sherman
Institute is consequently far more complete for the years after 1909 than
for those before. Data for the years between 1902 and 1909 has been
culled from a variety of sources and hence lacks some specificity.

With the introduction of standardized, detailed reporting, it became
possible for the Indian Office to track the incidence of tuberculosis across
the country, and its distribution by type and gender. These particular statistics were used primarily in ethnic comparisons to support the premise
that tuberculosis among Indians was somehow different than that among
white or black Americans. For example, Hrdlička and Johnson noted that
among Indians, pulmonary tuberculosis involved both sexes in nearly
equal proportion, with a slightly greater frequency of infection in
females. In contrast, white males had the highest incidence of pulmonary
tuberculosis.[41] Interestingly, as evident in Table 6.2, the tuberculosis distribution by gender at Sherman Institute more closely followed that
described for white populations than that for Indians. Since available
data is incomplete in regard to differentiating types of tuberculosis prior
to 1910–11, only tabulated data for subsequent years is presented.

As is evident in the following table, pulmonary tuberculosis was by far
the most common type of tuberculosis found at Sherman Institute, at 59.5

TABLE 6.2

TUBERCULOSIS DISTRIBUTION BY TYPE AND GENDER,
SHERMAN INSTITUTE, 1910–1922

School Year	Pulmonary		Glandular		Bone		Other	
	Male	Female	Male	Female	Male	Female	Male	Female
1910–11	5	6	0	0	1	0	0	1
1911–12	7	6	2	0	0	0	0	3
1912–13	1	6	2	1	0	1	0	0
1913–14	6	5	0	0	0	0	1	0
1914–15	3	5	5	3	0	0	0	0
1915–16	6	5	4	3	0	1	0	2
1916–17	11	5	1	4	0	0	0	1
1917–18	5	4	0	5	0	0	1	3
1918–19	9	8	6	4	1	0	1	1
1919–20	1	3	2	1	1	1	2	0
1920–21	3	1	2	1	0	0	3	3
1921–22	8	3	4	2	1	0	2	0
TOTAL	65	57	28	24	4	3	10	14
CUMULATIVE TOTAL	122		52		7		24	

perecent of the total, followed by glandular (25.4 percent), other (11.7 percent), and finally, bone tuberculosis (3.4 percent). Included in the "Other" category were tubercular meningitis, tubercular peritonitis, and tubercular laryngitis. In every type of tuberculosis, males and females had approximately the same number of cases, averaged over the twelve-year period. The distribution of tuberculosis by type at Sherman Institute is consistent with the distribution among other populations during that period.

One of the most critical factors in analyzing tuberculosis among non-reservation boarding school students was the method of diagnosis used to determine: (1) that tuberculosis was present, and (2) what type of tuberculosis the child contracted. The first consideration was extremely important because the efficacy of a particular diagnostic method could make a considerable difference in morbidity statistics. More important, however, was that inadequate diagnostic procedures permitted some children to remain in the general school population because of a false negative diagnosis, yet forced other children to be sent home because of a false positive diagnosis. The second consideration was equally important because Indian Office policy generally excluded only children with pulmonary tuberculosis from the schools.

In determining whether a student had pulmonary tuberculosis, Sherman Institute physicians relied most heavily upon patients' reports of their symptoms. Common complaints included chest pains, shortness of breath, fatigue, troubled breathing, sleeplessness, and loss of appetite. In the early stages of the disease, many of these symptoms went unnoticed and unconnected because they were common to a plethora of other illnesses. Individuals might have also complained of simply not feeling well, but essentially been asymptomatic. The fact that weight loss was one of the earliest symptoms of tuberculosis, yet usually not noticed by students, led the Indian Office to first recommend, then mandate in 1909, the monthly weighing of every student in an attempt to identify the disease before it could progress appreciably. Once students reported the initial symptoms, however, the physicians had a number of diagnostic options available, though the efficacy of many was questionable.

Spirometry represented one of the most common diagnostic tools used by physicians in the late nineteenth century and at least through the early 1900s.[42] A spirometer measured pulmonary function, considered an important factor in many illnesses. Both physicians and patients believed that small lung capacity always preceded the onset of tuberculosis.[43] Consequently, if a student exhibited diminished pulmonary function in addition to the stated symptoms, the physician usually diagnosed tuberculosis. There is evidence that as part of the yearly physical examination at Perris Indian School, Dr. Wainwright screened students for tuberculosis using a spirometer, which may partially account for the very low incidence of the disease. Neither Dr. Parker nor Dr. Roblee continued the practice at Sherman Institute. Despite the fact that spirometry offered an accepted diagnostic and screening tool at the time and that spirometers were readily available at an average cost of ten dollars, the Indian Office apparently did not recommend their use, especially if diagnosis could be made by other procedures at no cost.

The most common procedures utilized by both physicians at Sherman Institute for diagnosing tuberculosis were simple palpation (touching) and percussion (tapping) of the chest wall. Employing these methods allowed a physician to detect diminished lung capacity, because palpation or percussion of the chest wall over a diseased lung presented a different sensation than that over a healthy lung. In numerous cases, both Parker and Roblee diagnosed students with "weak lungs," or "tubercular tendencies," on the basis of these examinations. The student may not have presented all the classic symptoms of tuberculosis, but the diminished lung capacity evidenced by sensation proved adequate cause to send the student home, or, at the very least, to have him or her placed in observation.

There is no evidence that Parker attempted to confirm preliminary diagnoses of tuberculosis. If palpation and percussion indicated a student had tuberculosis, he sent the student home. However, these clinical procedures were not specific to tuberculosis, and as a result, Parker probably sent children home who did not have tuberculosis, but other lung diseases, such as bronchitis. Alternately, if a student presented other symptoms, but no lung deficiency, Parker had no way to ascertain whether that student had tuberculosis. Consequently, tubercular student were sometimes allowed to remain in school until the disease worsened and more severe symptoms appeared.

Unlike Parker, Roblee regularly confirmed suspected cases of tuberculosis by examining patients' sputum for evidence of the tubercle bacillus. If a student exhibited signs of tuberculosis, Roblee performed both a manual and a sputum examination. He isolated suspected cases of tuberculosis until he received the sputum results, then sent the student home upon confirmation of diagnoses. Roblee felt a high level of comfort and trust in microscopic examination, since he had undergone extensive postgraduate training in bacteriology and microscopy at clinics in Vienna and Heidelberg. He developed a modern, fully equipped laboratory in his private practice, which he freely utilized in his work at Sherman Institute.

Interestingly, neither Parker nor Roblee made use of the subcutaneous tuberculin test in diagnosing tuberculosis. The tuberculin test involved applying a small amount of tuberculin on a scarified area of the skin of the arm. A red papillar eruption at the site of inoculation indicated a positive reaction.[44] Since the test revealed active cases of tuberculosis and evidence of tubercular infection, either remotely or recently, it served as an invaluable screening tool. Yet, despite the fact that tuberculin testing offered an accepted and effective method of tuberculosis testing, there is no evidence that any nonreservation boarding school physicians utilized the test, or that the Indian Office encouraged, recommended, or funded the use of tuberculin testing.[45]

In addition to not making use of tuberculin testing, neither Parker nor Roblee used X-rays for diagnosing tuberculosis. The X-ray machine had been invented in 1895 and was adopted almost immediately for use in diagnosing tuberculosis. By 1900, most tuberculosis specialists agreed that X-rays were essential for diagnosis of the disease.[46] Many physicians in the early 1900s embraced this important new diagnostic tool and taught themselves to use the machines. Roblee actually had an X-ray machine in his private practice laboratory. Yet there exists no evidence that Roblee or Parker ever used an X-ray to diagnosis tuberculosis among Sherman Institute students. The school hospital did not possess an X-ray machine, and it is highly unlikely that the physicians would have taken students to their private offices to X-ray their chests. Apparently, despite a recognition among tuberculosis specialists and general physicians alike that X-ray machines proved invaluable in diagnosing tuberculosis, the Indian Office did not authorize their purchase for nonreservation boarding schools. By not requiring the regular use of either tuberculin skin tests or X-rays, the Indian Office significantly impacted the ability of school physicians to accurately diagnose tubercular Indian students in a timely manner. Instead, they were left to cruder, less efficacious, and of course, less costly, methods of diagnosis.

In later stages of pulmonary tuberculosis, symptoms became more obvious, and Sherman Institute physicians did not focus as much on diagnosing the disease as on determining how far it had progressed and what form it took. Second-stage symptoms include fever, sore throat, night sweats, cough, hemorrhage, expectoration, menstrual disruption, painful swallowing, and hoarseness. Although few Sherman Institute students reached this stage while still attending school, occasionally a student was not diagnosed until hemorrhaging occurred. While the combined presence of fever, sore throat, cough, painful swallowing, and hoarseness might easily have been incorrectly diagnosed as any number of upper-respiratory infections, physicians and nurses could mistake pulmonary hemorrhaging for little else than tuberculosis. In these cases, superintendents sent the children home immediately, but by then, many other students had undoubtedly been exposed to the tuberculin bacillus.

In attempting to determine the degree of pulmonary tubercular advancement, percussion and palpation provided little definitive information. Auscultation (listening to the chest), either by ear (immediate) or stethoscope (mediate) allowed Sherman Institute physicians to detect chest sounds indicative of various degrees of lung conversion. Once this level of examination became necessary, the diagnosis offered little hope for recovery, and the student was essentially sent home to die.

The procedures used to diagnose other types of tuberculosis varied. Glandular tuberculosis (scrofula) generally presented easily discernable symptoms. The disease is marked by ulcers that usually result from a tuberculous sinus, occurring commonly on the chest, neck, axillae, and groin, especially in children and adolescents. Even if confined to the groin, matrons and disciplinarians could easily observe the ulcers during bathing time. Diagnosis of bone tuberculosis, the most rare type of tuberculosis at Sherman Institute, was considerably more difficult, and precisely how physicians made this diagnosis is unknown. Tubercle bacilli usually attack the vertebrae and the ends of long bones. Symptoms of localized back or joint pain are common, but are not specific to tuberculosis. Diagnosis is best confirmed by biopsy of either bone or synovial tissue, and it is highly unlikely Parker or Roblee performed this test.[47] It is far more probable that the doctors diagnosed bone tuberculosis when a bone injury, particularly to a joint, failed to heal properly and perhaps worsened. They assumed that the bone had become tubercular, whether it actually had or not, partly because they had no other explanation, but also because in dealing with Indians, almost any physical ailment that did not quickly heal was considered vulnerable to tuberculosis.

The "Other"' category of tuberculosis at Sherman Institute included tuberculous meningitis, tuberculous peritonitis, and tuberculous laryngitis. These types of tuberculosis are very difficult to accurately diagnose without a biopsy or examining cerebrospinal fluid microscopically. Though Roblee had expertise in microscopy, it is doubtful that he performed either of these procedures to confirm his diagnoses. Consequently, the diagnoses made for Sherman Institute students are suspect, and students may have instead had other infections resembling tuberculosis.

The possibility of suspect diagnosis is especially relevant in considering tuberculous meningitis, alternately listed as meningeal tuberculosis, which was the most frequent diagnosis for "Other" types of tuberculosis. Tuberculous meningitis was most common among children between the ages of birth and five years old, yet none of the students at Sherman Institute diagnosed with this disease fell into that age category. Instead, the students ranged in age from ten to twenty-two, with an average age of seventeen years old. Common symptoms include fever, unremitting headache, nausea, and extreme drowsiness, but these are generally the same symptoms presented for other forms of meningitis. A stiff neck and straight leg raising are more clearly indicative of tuberculous meningitis, but these are inconstant symptoms.[48] What caused Roblee to diagnose tuberculous meningitis instead of simply meningitis is inexplicable, since without the use of modern diagnostic tests they would have been extremely difficult to differentiate.

A similar diagnostic problem is evidenced in tuberculous peritonitis, which is tuberculosis of the peritoneum (lining of the abdominal cavity). Symptoms may be mild, with fatigue, abdominal pain, and tenderness, or acute enough to mimic bacterial peritonitis.[49] The most reliable diagnostic procedure, and one probably not used by Roblee, is paracentesis and peritoneal needle biopsy with microscopic examination of the fluid for tuberculosis bacilli. Without using these procedures, it would have been extremely difficult to diagnose tuberculous peritonitis. What particular symptoms did the Sherman Institute students present that led Roblee to believe they suffered from tuberculous peritonitis? Available records offer no insight into Roblee's diagnosis rationale. In almost every case, both tuberculous meningitis and tuberculous peritonitis represented secondary infections in students who had been ill with either measles or typhoid fever. These secondary infections usually took an acute form, and as a result of their virulence, seven students died in the Sherman Institute hospital. Postmortem examinations were not performed on any of the students, so it was impossible for Roblee to confirm his diagnoses that the students had died from tuberculous forms of the disease.

Finally, a single student, fifteen-year-old Chester Denetclaw (Navajo), was diagnosed with tuberculous laryngitis in 1921 and subsequently died from the infection. This diagnosis is curious. A virus typically causes laryngitis, and while it may also occur in bronchitis, pneumonia, influenza, pertussis, measles, and diphtheria, laryngitis is not generally associated with tuberculosis. In fact, tuberculous laryngitis is not listed as a form of tuberculosis in modern medical reference texts.[50]

In considering the tuberculosis diagnoses of Drs. Parker and Roblee, it becomes increasingly evident that even prominent, highly qualified physicians possessed an incomplete knowledge of the etiology and pathology of tuberculosis. Although physicians understood the clinical manifestations of pulmonary and glandular tuberculosis relatively well by the early twentieth century, it is apparent that they knew far less about other types of tuberculosis. Precisely how Sherman Institute physicians identified the more obscure types of tuberculosis without the benefit of advanced diagnostic procedures remains a mystery. In addition, physicians did not seem to have a firm grasp on how tuberculosis was transmitted. In one case, Roblee believed that operating on a student diagnosed with tuberculous peritonitis would ultimately result in the student acquiring pulmonary tuberculosis, as if opening the peritoneum spread tuberculosis bacilli to the lungs.[51]

Over the twenty-year period between 1902 and 1922, there were 250 confirmed cases of tuberculosis in its various forms among students at Sherman Institute. In addition, there were many probable cases of tuberculosis that were simply noted as "weak lungs" or "tubercular tendencies," but for which a confirmed diagnosis was never made. Since the latter children were sent home immediately upon discovery of their possible condition, there is no way of knowing whether they actually were tubercular or not. Once Parker or Roblee sent a child home because of sickness, rarely did a parent allow the child to return to school. Consequently, it is not possible to conclusively determine how many cases of tuberculosis occurred at the school over the twenty-year research period.

The policy of sending tubercular children home, whether with a confirmed or a possible diagnosis, also renders a determination of actual tuberculosis mortality impossible. Mortality figures are available only for students suffering from an acute form of tuberculosis or who could not be sent home for a variety of reasons and who subsequently died at the school. This clearly skews the data to the point of irrelevance. Extrapolation based on available mortality figures is also infeasible, since the actual number of children who may or may not have had tuberculosis, but were sent home, is an unknown variable. Since possible case, and actual mortality, data is incomplete, tuberculosis at Sherman Institute can be evaluated only by using confirmed morbidity figures, particularly those recorded after the advent of standardized forms in 1909.

Even a single case of tuberculosis proved terrifying and onerous to the parents of Sherman Institute students, and this was as it should be. Yet the incidence of tuberculosis at Sherman Institute should also be judged in the context of other nonreservation boarding schools in order to understand whether preventive measures implemented by Hall and Conser were effective in minimizing tuberculosis. How did Sherman Institute compare in tuberculosis morbidity to other schools that were under the same mandated Indian Office policies? Did strict compliance with official policies and implementation of school-specific practices help protect Sherman Institute students from tuberculosis?

TABLE 6.3

COMPARISON OF TUBERCULOSIS MORBIDITY,

NONRESERVATION BOARDING SCHOOLS, 1911–1912

Nonreservation Boarding School	Students Examined	Students Afflicted	Percentage of Examined Population
Carlisle	1031	54	5.24
Salem	325	45	13.85
Chilocco	536	12	2.24
Genoa	340	1	0.29
Albuquerque	332	11	3.31
Haskell	719	11	1.53
Grand Junction	–	–	–
Carson	318	31	9.75
Fort Mojave	400	18	4.50
Pierre	149	4	2.68
Phoenix	808	125	15.47
Fort Lewis	–	–	–
Fort Shaw	–	–	–
Mt. Pleasant	306	22	7.19
Tomah	–	–	–
Pipestone	212	8	3.77
Flandreau	445	12	2.70
Wittenberg	–	–	–
Greenville (CA)	125	18	14.40
Morris	–	–	–
Chamberlain	–	–	–
Fort Bidwell (CA)	126	19	15.08
Rapid City	–	–	–
Sherman (CA)	631	18	2.85
Wahpeton	76	4	5.26
Bismarck	72	4	5.56

– No examinations made

Table 6.3 presents comparative tuberculosis morbidity data for all nonreservation boarding schools in the 1911–12 school year. As previously noted in chapter 4 of this book, the 1911–12 school year was chosen for comparison for a number of reasons. First, because it is the first year for which comparative figures are available for nonreservation boarding schools without accessing primary source material. It also represents the midpoint of the research period, as well as the era prior to the reforms of the 1920s. Finally, utilizing data from the same school year for all health issues contributes to analytical consistency.

In comparing the preceding tuberculosis morbidity figures, it is apparent that Sherman Institute students fared very well in comparison to other nonreservation boarding schools, particularly those in California. Greenville and Fort Bidwell, both California boarding schools, had one-fifth the enrollment of Sherman Institute, yet their tuberculosis morbidity rates were five times higher than those at Sherman Institute, despite the fact that they drew students from essentially the same Indian population. Since research has not yet been conducted for these schools, it is not possible to compare their implementation of preventive health policies and practices with those of Sherman Institute, or to determine how this impacted tuberculosis morbidity.

Sherman Institute also compares favorably with similarly sized nonreservation boarding schools, such as Carlisle, Chilocco, Haskell, and Flandreau. Of this group, Carlisle had the highest tuberculosis morbidity rate and Haskell had the lowest, with Sherman Institute ranking in the approximate middle, with Chilocco and Flandreau. Little is known of the preventive health policies and practices at these schools, because research regarding these schools, though published, does not focus on health issues. Surprisingly, the data for Phoenix Indian School reflects their general hospital, not the sanatorium, and this school, otherwise similar in many ways, had a tuberculosis morbidity rate over five times higher than that at Sherman Institute.[52]

It is also possible to compare the tuberculosis morbidity at Sherman Institute with that of Southern California reservation Indians and Indians throughout the nation, albeit on a generalized basis for the purposes of this study. In 1912, the Indian Office estimated that at least 10 percent of all Indians living on reservations in Southern California had tuberculosis.[53] Nationwide, of 42,645 Indians examined for tuberculosis in 1912, 16.11 percent (6,870) tested positive for tuberculosis.[54] With a tuberculosis morbidity rate of 2.85 percent in 1912, Sherman Institute offered a healthier environment for students than did reservation living, at least in terms of tuberculosis incidence.

It is not possible to make direct comparisons between tuberculosis morbidity rates at Sherman Institute and within the white population of Southern California because the biennial reports of the California State Board of Health offer only mortality figures. However, in 1910, the Board of Health reported, "Southern California leads decidedly in the proportions for tuberculosis."[55] The report continued, "The proportions per 1,000 total deaths for tuberculosis of the lungs were no less than 175.9 and 176.8 for this main division against only 131.0 and 126.1 for the entire state." To put this in perspective, while tuberculosis mortality in 1910 at Sherman Institute cannot be confirmed, the morbidity rate for pulmonary tuberculosis equaled 18.26 per 1,000 cases. Clearly, the mortality rate at Sherman Institute would have been significantly less than that of the Southern California white population.

In addressing tuberculosis morbidity and mortality at Sherman Institute, it soon becomes apparent that in spite of the availability of relatively abundant data, a great deal of important information will never be known or understood. Some questions can be answered. Were the preventive policies and practices implemented at Sherman Institute effective in minimizing tuberculosis? Certainly. Did actions taken by the Indian Office, or by superintendents and physicians, successfully stop the flow of tuberculosis into and out of Sherman Institute? No. What we cannot answer is why, despite the implementation of many policies and practices designed to eradicate tuberculosis, children at Sherman Institute, like those at other nonreservation boarding schools, continued to acquire this most devastating of diseases and were sent home to die. The parents of these children most certainly asked the same question.

CHAPTER 7

Sore Eyes

TRACHOMA CAUSED HIGHER MORBIDITY AT SHERMAN INSTITUTE THAN ALL other diseases combined, including tuberculosis. The disease did not cause death, only terrible pain, suffering, and potential blindness. Trachoma had long been a part of many Native Americans' lives, but by the early twentieth century it had reached near-epidemic proportions, particularly in nonreservation boarding schools and on Southwestern Indian reservations. By 1908, the Indian Office recognized trachoma as a significant health threat to all Indians, second only to tuberculosis. Implementation of numerous preventive and treatment programs partially mitigated the threat posed by trachoma, though it continued to wreak havoc on Indian eyes well into the twentieth century. In large part, the ineffectiveness of the programs was due to only minimal understanding of the etiology and pathology of the disease. At Sherman Institute, preventive and treatment programs had little direct impact on trachoma morbidity, and the disease incidence actually increased over time. Interestingly, although trachoma continued its course unabated at Sherman Institute through 1922, the morbidity rate was lower there than at almost every other nonreservation boarding school throughout this period.

Trachoma has often been called "sore eyes" because of its characteristic symptoms that cause great irritation and pain to the sufferer's eyes. Evidence indicates that trachoma may have been endemic to indigenous peoples of North America. Meriwether Lewis first recorded the incidence of what appears to be trachoma in 1806:

> they have almost invariably soar [*sic*] eyes at all stages of life. the loss of an eye is very common among them; blindness in perdsons of middle age is by no means uncommon, and it is almost invariably a concomitant of old age.[1]

Though Lewis did not know what caused the condition, he ascribed it to "their exposure to the reflection of the sun on the water to which they are constantly exposed in the occupation of fishing."[2]

In reality, a microorganism called *Chlamydia trachomitis* causes trachoma. The disease is evidenced by the growth of granules on the inner surfaces of the eyelids, giving the lids a rough appearance and causing considerable irritation and pain. Typically, the granules are found only on the upper eyelids, but in severe cases, cover the lower eyelids as well. If left untreated, the disease causes blindness, and in extreme cases, loss of the affected eye.

Trachoma progresses in stages.[3] After an incubation period of approximately seven days, conjunctival hyperemia, eyelid edema, photophobia, and lacrimation gradually appear. Seven to ten days later, small follicles develop in the upper tarsal conjunctiva, which is the clear layer of tissue lining the inside of the eyelids and the surface of the whites of the eyes. The follicles gradually increase in size and number over a period of three to four weeks. During this stage, inflammatory papillae appear on the upper tarsal conjunctiva and new blood vessels begin to grow on the cornea. This stage of follicular/papillary hypertrophy may last from several months to over one year and ultimately involve the entire cornea, significantly reducing vision.

Unless adequate treatment is given, scarring occurs. Follicles and papillae gradually shrink and are replaced by scar tissue that causes inward turning of the eyelid and lashes (entropion) and lacrimal (tear) duct obstruction.[4] The lashes continually rub against the eye, causing considerable irritation and discomfort. Entropion leads to further corneal scarring and neovascularization. When the diseased tissue infolds on itself, it carries infecting and irritating materials further into the eyelid, often causing secondary bacterial infections. These infections result in further scarring and are responsible for the chronicity of trachoma.

Scar tissue produces an opaque obstruction on the cornea that causes partial or complete blindness. Scarring also creates a reduction in lacrimation, impairing the eye's cleansing ability. Any debris remaining in the conjunctiva hardens, leaving the victim with a feeling of always having a foreign body trapped under the eyelid.

Trachoma is most contagious in its early stages. It may be transmitted by eye-to-eye contact, eye-to-hand contact, and eye-seeking flies. Most commonly, the sharing of contaminated articles such as towels, handkerchiefs, and bedding transmits the disease. Development of the stages of trachoma depends on the virulence of the chlamydia microorganism. Genuine trachoma (exempt from secondary infections) often has a benign course, with clinical manifestations so imperceptible that they sometimes pass unobserved.[5] Thus, many victims do not know they have the disease until examined by a physician. Trachoma imparts no immunity to its victims and offers equal opportunity for infection to all, regardless of age or gender.

Reports of trachomatous conditions among Indians surfaced periodically after Lewis's initial report in 1806. Descriptions such as "sore eyes," "weeping eyes," "drooping eyes," "granulated lids," and "conjunctivitis" all noted characteristic symptoms of trachoma, but may equally have applied to a variety of other eye disorders common to Indians. Consequently, the true prevalence of trachoma among native peoples during most of the nineteenth century is unknown.

With the establishment of nonreservation boarding schools, beginning in 1879, reports indicating the presence of trachoma among students appeared with increasing frequency. In large part this was due to the fact that to boost enrollment, even students clearly evidencing a trachomatous condition were brought into the schools. Once there, living conditions conducive to the spread of trachoma abounded. This is particularly significant considering the fact that trachoma was widely recognized as posing such a large threat to community health that immigrants with trachoma were denied entry to the United States as early as 1891.

The etiology of trachoma was not understood in the late nineteenth century. Though Indian Service physicians and administrators recognized the presence of trachomatous eyes among the students, they did not know what caused the condition, or how to effectively treat it. Proposed causes of trachoma ranged from syphilis to tuberculosis to low light, with prescribed treatment fashioned accordingly. The first official recognition of trachoma's prevalence at nonreservation boarding schools appeared in the 1901 *Course of Study for the Indian Schools of the United States*. Directing that, "The children should be taught a few general rules for the treatment of sore eyes, fever, and emergency cases," the *Course of Study* noted, "Sore eyes, being prevalent in the schools, is the first malady to which the attention of pupils should be directed."[6] Interestingly, every student was to be taught the recommended treatment for sore eyes, apparently for use on each other or on family members when they returned home. The treatment was not specific for trachoma, but instead based on general medical practices for any eye disorder:

> When inflamed, teach always to bathe in hot water. Boric acid, one-half level teaspoonful to the pint, added is good. Apply to the eyes and bandage. Caution against rubbing the eyes. Isolate the sore-eye patients. Guard against infection. It may be necessary to keep in a darkened room or have a shade put over the eyes as a last resort.[7]

The directive did not stipulate that children with sore eyes were to use faucets and running water instead of washbasins for bathing the eyes. Nor did it mandate the distribution of individual towels to each student, despite the fact that such precautions had been recommended as early as 1898 at an Indian Service physicians' conference.

At the time Sherman Institute was built in 1902, Hall made no special accommodations for the prevention of trachoma among students. This is probably due to the fact that trachoma had not been a problem at Perris Indian School, and since its student population transferred en masse to Sherman Institute, he had no reason to believe trachoma would be a health issue at the new school. Further, trachoma did not generally pose a problem among Southern California Indians, and it was from this population that the founding student population had been drawn. As previously discussed, Hall implemented strict sanitation policies and no-sharing rules, both of which served to lessen the incidence of trachoma during the early years at Sherman Institute.

Such was not the case at other nonreservation boarding schools. The 1903 Indian Service physicians' survey noted that, after tuberculosis, trachoma was the most serious malady afflicting Indians throughout the United States. In 1904, evidencing a decidedly imperfect understanding of the etiology of trachoma, Commissioner Jones issued a lame response to the physicians' pronouncement:

> Eye diseases are to receive proper attention and no children should be required to do schoolroom or other work whose eyes are likely to be injured thereby. It must be borne in mind that many of these diseases are contagious, and precautions such as furnishing of individual towels, etc. should be taken to prevent their spread.[8]

Neither formal policy nor guidelines for protecting students from trachoma accompanied Jones's feeble edict. Procedures necessary for the control of trachoma, such as the use of faucets and running water, individual beds, quarantine of students with eye secretions, and disinfection of school supplies used by afflicted children, were neither mandated nor funded. Unless a school superintendent truly prioritized student health, he or she generally made no changes and trachoma morbidity rates continued to climb.

The Indian Office did not address the issue of trachoma again until 1906, and by this time, their orientation had clearly changed. The high incidence of trachoma among boarding school children was now attributed to the "tendency to weak eyes on the part of Indian children."[9] To avoid exacerbating this tendency, pupils affected with eye problems, "should not be allowed to concentrate their eyes for long periods upon fine print, small stitches, etc., in dimly lighted rooms."[10] Instead of accepting blame for the boarding schools' inability to curb trachoma, the Indian Office placed the blame on the implied inherent weakness of the Indian children.

The first recorded cases of trachoma at Sherman Institute occurred in 1907, although some cases undoubtedly existed well before that time. During the early years, Hall depended on a healthy founding student population, as well as strict school sanitation, to avoid a high trachoma morbidity rate. As the student population expanded and students came from more diverse cultural and geographical areas, the potential for trachoma increased. Though every student remained subject to a rigid physical examination prior to enrollment, students afflicted with trachoma were not denied entrance to Sherman Institute. As a result, trachoma became a serious and prevalent health problem.

Students evidencing symptoms of "sore eyes" at Sherman Institute were immediately separated from the general population and placed in the school hospital for treatment. However, the efficacy of treatment provided during this period is definitely questionable. Upon the arrival of Mary Israel at Sherman Institute as resident nurse, Hall communicated his extreme displeasure with the previous record of trachoma treatment at the hospital and implored that she, using her training as a physician, institute considerable change. Apparently, the length of treatment at Sherman Institute's hospital extended for a far longer time than Hall, in his twenty-two years' experience in Indian schools, had previously experienced. Not willing to cast aspersions on the school's level of medical care, Hall noted the possibility that the sore eyes at Sherman Institute were somehow different than the usual type of sore eyes:

> The sore eyes we have at present may be something different from the usual sore eyes among Indian pupils and I do not pretend to know in regard to this matter, but it seems to me that the treatment received by these pupils in the last four months has certainly been very incomplete, some of them remaining in the hospital for three months with sore eyes.[11]

Hall noted that, in his experience, if treatment for sore eyes was provided promptly and energetically, and looked after constantly, the condition could be cured within five to ten days. Further, treatment for sore eyes had been successfully accomplished thousands of times by "the ordinary Assistant Matrons" at reservation schools. Yet at Sherman Institute, a child sent to the hospital for sore eyes and treated by medical professionals could be expected to remain hospitalized throughout the school term. Hall asked Israel to "use your very best endeavors and energy to cure them up."

Hall worried that students did not receive the right treatment for sore eyes at Sherman Institute. Not only did this hinder the process of assimilation, as students spent months in the hospital instead of the classroom, but it also adversely impacted the school's reputation:

> The reputation of our school is hinged, to a large extent, upon the treatment of the sick at the hospital. Oftentimes pupils call upon physicians from the outside for treatment with the statement that the treatment received at the school does not seem to do them any good. Employees also go outside for their medical advice in many instances. All of this should not be for I can see no reason why we cannot look after our sick as well as they can at the city hospitals.[12]

Hall's mention of dissatisfaction among students and employees with the medical care provided at Sherman Institute is curious. At no other time during the twenty-year research period is such a complaint made, and it is probable that Hall's claims were somewhat exaggerated. Employee salaries were so low that they would seemingly preclude consultation with an outside physician. Further, of particular relevance is the fact that the school's physician, Dr. A. S. Parker, was the preeminent physician in Riverside, with a large and successful private practice. The insular medical community that existed at the turn of the century in Riverside would have made it difficult to find a physician willing to accede that Parker had not provided adequate medical care at the school.

In addition, students generally did not have money to pay for anything, let alone outside medical care. If a student did have sufficient money, he or she would still have to be taken to a Riverside physician by a school employee, an improbable situation, at best.

It is likely that Hall's tirade had more to do with the failings of the previous resident nurse than with the actual conditions at Sherman Institute. In correspondence with the concerned father of a trachoma patient, Hall noted, "We have a most excellent Nurse now, the best, I think, we have ever had, and the best care is given to any child who is sick. The one whom I made to resign was a perfect failure and the children got in bad shape during her stay here."[13] Since morbidity for other diseases at the school was low at this time, the nurse's failings presumably were limited to trachoma treatment.

Francis E. Leupp was the first commissioner of Indian affairs to take substantive action against the Indian trachoma problem. Leupp became interested in trachoma after receiving startling data in 1908 regarding the high incidence of the disease at Phoenix Indian School. Joining forces with Indian School Supervisor Elsie Newton and Surgeon General Walter Wyman of the Public Health and Marine Hospital Service, Leupp successfully lobbied Congress to provide funding for the fight against trachoma. Their most effective argument was one commonly used by the Indian Office in seeking additional health appropriations: the abysmal health of Indians posed a serious threat to the white populations near reservations. On 20 February 1909, Congress appropriated $12,000, "to investigate, treat, and prevent the spread of trachoma among the Indian population."[14]

The Indian Office's first task in the war on trachoma was to investigate the incidence of trachoma among Indians, particularly at nonreservation boarding schools. On 20 March 1909, Leupp sent a circular entitled "Trachoma Hospital for Indians" to every boarding school, directing that physicians carefully examine all enrolled pupils to discover whether any of them had trachoma. In response to this communiqué, within a few days Dr. Roblee conducted the first comprehensive trachoma examinations at Sherman Institute, aided by Dr. J. A. Murphy, medical supervisor of the Indian Office. The results of the examinations revealed that of the 672 students examined at Sherman Institute, 125, or 19 percent, exhibited symptoms of trachoma.[15] The results of examinations at other schools were similar and even worse.

In 1910, buoyed by the first reasonably accurate statistics of trachoma morbidity, the Indian Office launched a trachoma "campaign." A girls' cottage at Phoenix Indian School was transformed into a trachoma hospital, and the Indian Office hired well-known Southwestern ophthalmologist Dr. Ancil Martin to treat children at the school, as well as Indians from the surrounding region. Two other noted ophthalmologists, Drs. William H. Harrison and Daniel W. White, traveled to reservations and schools in the Southwest, treating trachoma victims. A third ophthalmologist treated patients in the Northwest. During the first year of the campaign, the doctors examined twenty thousand Indians, 20 percent of which had trachoma.[16] Interestingly, the Indian Service ophthalmologists never visited Sherman Institute, apparently trusting the skills of Dr. Roblee to treat trachomatous students. Unfortunately, in the 1910–11 school year the trachoma morbidity rate at Sherman Institute more than doubled from the previous year, so, clearly, Roblee could have used some help in caring for the afflicted students.

Reports of the Indian Service ophthalmologists indicated that trachoma posed a far greater health threat to Indians than previously imagined, particularly to those in the Southwest. The original $12,000 appropriation would not even scratch the surface of treating and ultimately alleviating the Indian trachoma problem. In response to the urgency of the situation, CIA Valentine requested additional appropriations to quell the scourge, noting that Indian trachoma was "simply beyond belief."[17]

Near-epidemic trachoma at Sherman Institute led Superintendent Conser to implement more aggressive preventive measures than had previously been employed. Shortly after discovering the high incidence of trachomatous patients at the school in 1909, Conser requested authorization from the Indian Office to hire a nurse for three months to provide special care for trachoma patients. Conser proposed paying the

temporary nurse $75.00 per month from the $12,000 Indian Office trachoma fund, instead of from his regular school fund. Apparently, Dr.
Roblee had been operating on students with trachoma, but because of
the inefficiency of the temporary nurses Conser was able to hire for the
salary allowed from regular school funds, Roblee had declined to continue the operations. With as many as seventy-five patients needing
daily attention over a period of time, the need for a trained medical care
professional was evident, even to the commissioner of Indian affairs.
Conser received authorization for a temporary trachoma nurse within
two weeks of his request. Funding for an additional three months' nursing service was also authorized.

Due to the large number of trachoma cases at Sherman Institute during the 1909–10 school year, Dr. Roblee wanted to visit the Phoenix
Indian School trachoma hospital in order to learn what was being done
there and to acquire additional knowledge regarding the treatment of
trachoma. Conser strongly supported Roblee's desire and requested
authorization for his visit, with payment for his expenses to be made
from the appropriation for "Preventing the Spread of Trachoma among
the Indians," an amount estimated to be $50.00. Unfortunately, Valen-
tine declined authorization for Roblee to visit Phoenix or any other place
for the purpose of informing himself regarding the treatment of trachoma. Valentine's response made Conser livid.

In a tersely worded response, Conser reminded Valentine that Roblee
was a very busy man with a large practice in Riverside, and he had far
better things to do with his time than travel anyplace to gather information about trachoma, particularly since this information did not benefit
his private practice. In his private practice he had had only one case of
trachoma during the last five years, and he turned any case affecting the
eyes over to a specialist.[18]

Conser further noted that Roblee had been giving trachomatous
patients special attention, sometimes coming every day to operate or otherwise provide treatment. On at least one occasion, Roblee came at 7:30
A.M., bringing two other physicians with him, to perform an operation
on one of the students. Conser reminded the commissioner that all of

this went well beyond Roblee's contractual obligations, yet he received no additional compensation. Since Sherman Institute had seen 200 cases of trachoma in the preceding twelve months and Roblee had operated on 125 of the cases, Conser felt that Roblee's extra training at minimal expense to the Indian Office was clearly warranted. Fifty of the students had been operated on at least twice, and a number of them had been operated on three times, leading both Roblee and Conser to consider that perhaps Roblee's trachoma treatment skills could be honed.[19] Unfortunately for Roblee and the Sherman Institute students, the Indian Office did not concur.

The situation faced by Conser and Roblee was not unusual, but common. The Indian Office encouraged school physicians to train themselves in trachoma treatment, but did not restrain them from operating on patients if they had little or no previous training or experience. This was a potentially serious problem, since Medical Inspector Murphy recommended that physicians operate on all cases requiring it, though he did not state what criteria they were to use in determining which cases required surgery. To an inexperienced physician faced with the horrors of trachoma, the choice was probably always in favor of surgery instead of the slower medicinal treatment option. Murphy gave inexperienced physicians the option of requesting expert assistance for a short time, provided a suitable expert lived in the vicinity of the school or reservation. If an ophthalmologist experienced in trachoma treatment was not locally accessible, a regular physician could request a special visit from one employed by the Indian Office. Unfortunately, the waiting list was long.

Indian Service and contract physicians had long been expected to train themselves in trachoma treatment, but in 1911 the Indian Office finally published a booklet to standardize the physicians' training. Entitled "Management and Treatment of Trachoma among Indians," the booklet was authored by two Indian Service physicians, Dr. W. H. Harrison and Dr. Daniel W. White. The authors advocated operating on all trachoma cases using the expression technique, which was the most common trachoma operation at the time.[20] The operation consisted of everting (turning inside out) the eyelid, applying cocaine as an anesthetic, then expressing the granules on the underside of the eyelid with a forceps, preferably the Knapp roller forceps. Following expression of the granules, the debris and blood were washed from the eye with boric acid or a bichloride of mercury solution. The Indian patient was to be placed in a darkened room for a few hours after the operation, with ice compresses placed over the eyelids to reduce swelling. Upon awakening in the morning, for several days after the operation, secretions emanating from the ruptured granules would stick the patient's eyelids together. The physician or nurse repeated the flushing procedure until all secretions ceased. Over the next few days, the treatment expanded to include brushing the eyelids with a solution of nitrate of silver and flushing with an argyol solution until the acute inflammation subsided. Postoperative treatment began at this point.[21]

The expression technique was not the only method of trachoma treatment during the early years of the twentieth century. Other operations included grattage, electrolysis, galvano-cautery, X ray, and excision of the tarsal plate.[22] Grattage, an operation that was to gain great popularity after 1924, was generally used only when granules had been covered over by a layer of epithelium and were not accessible to the pincer action of the forceps.[23] This operation proved even more painful than the expression technique, with sandpaper or a toothbrush dipped in boric acid provided the grating action. The Indian Office neither ordered nor prohibited any particular operation for the treatment of trachoma, although the expression method continued to be recommended as the operation of choice until well after 1914.

Evidence has not been found that Dr. Parker performed any trachoma operations at Sherman Institute between 1902 and 1909. Indeed, this may have been the primary reason treatment continued for months. Since Hall blamed the resident nurse for inadequate care, and Parker rarely visited the hospital, it may be that trachoma was treated only by the method prescribed by the Indian Office in 1901—flushing with a boric acid solution and bandaging. Between 1909 and 1922, Dr. Roblee treated trachomatous Sherman Institute students with the expression technique. However, contrary to Indian Office recommendations, he did not operate on every case of trachoma. In fact, in ten out of the twelve years for which statistics are available, far more students were treated, but not operated on, than those operated on, at a ratio of more than three to one.

This situation was not unique to Sherman Institute, however. At all nonreservation boarding schools reporting at the end of the 1911–12 school year, the number of students operated on for trachoma was half that for students treated for trachoma without an operation. The fact that so many boarding school physicians chose a more conservative method of treatment in spite of Indian Office regulations may reflect a general hesitancy on their part to operate without sufficient training and experience. Unfortunately, data does not exist that suggests which type of treatment proved most efficacious in curing trachoma.

The reasons that Roblee chose not to operate on every student are uncertain. One obvious reason may be that without advanced training and without the continued assistance of a skilled nurse, he simply did not feel confident in his surgical skills and thus chose more conservative treatment whenever possible. Conceivably, screening caught most students at an early stage of the disease, thus rendering radical treatment unnecessary. Patients with early-stage trachoma were usually treated with boric acid in various forms. According to prevailing medical opinions of the time, afflicted patients were not to use their eyes to a great extent, so classroom work was dispensed with in most cases for a considerable portion of the year.[24] In a number of cases, Conser purchased dark glasses for trachomatous students, but there is no evidence that this type of prophylactic measure would have been effective in treating the disease.

There is evidence that trachoma patients not operated on were treated with copper sulfate pencils at Sherman Institute.[25] This would have been highly unusual, since copper sulfate was commonly used only as a postoperative treatment. After the initial inflammation from the operation subsided, frequent rubbings of a copper sulfate pencil were made over the inner eyelids. Advocates viewed the copper sulfate as a curative, while the rubbing action stimulated blood flow in the eyelids and aided healing.[26]

During the 1914–15 school year, only nineteen students were operated on for trachoma, while sixty-six were treated but not operated on. Yet, between 14 January 1915 and 1 April 1915, Conser ordered twenty-two dozen copper sulfate pencils. Twelve dozen pencils were ordered in January, then Conser ordered an additional ten dozen pencils on 1 April 1915, all for use during the 1914–15 school year. It would have been virtually impossible to use the 264 copper sulfate pencils ordered in January and April for postoperative treatment of nineteen patients. Considering how late in the school year the pencils were ordered, it is probable that most of the operations had already been performed prior to the orders.

The question, then, is why Conser would need to order 264 copper sulfate pencils if not to use them in the treatment of trachomatous students who had not been operated on? In April, Conser claimed that the hospital had only enough copper sulfate pencils for thirty days' use, meaning that most of the twelve dozen pencils ordered in January had already been used by 1 April.[27] Exactly how copper sulfate pencils would have been used in nonpostoperative trachoma treatment is unknown, but from the available data, it is apparent that such was the case at Sherman Institute. In justifying his 14 January order, Conser stated that the copper sulfate pencils were, "used in treating eyes for trachoma."[28] Conser did not specify whether the pencils were for nonoperative treatment or postoperative treatment. Yet the use of copper sulfate even in postoperative treatment was not without controversy because of the intense pain it caused patients. It is difficult to understand why Dr. Roblee, by all reports a kind and compassionate physician, would have utilized such a painful procedure in the nonoperative treatment of students he genuinely seemed to care for. It is possible that another explanation exists for the large number of copper sulfate pencils ordered, but what that might be is not immediately forthcoming.

The most controversial issue of the Indian Office's trachoma campaign was whether trachomatous children should be admitted to schools. As early as 1894, regulations stipulated that children with contagious diseases should be barred from the schools in order to protect the health of other children.[29] Trachoma certainly qualified as a contagious disease, but even children with obvious symptoms were not prohibited from enrolling in nonreservation boarding schools. The principle reason for this alteration of policy is that Medical Supervisor Murphy strongly favored keeping trachomatous children in the schools, where they could receive prolonged treatment on a daily basis and also be able to continue their education.[30] Murphy based his recommendations on his belief that trachoma progressed in stages and that not all stages were contagious, so summarily dismissing all trachomatous children was unnecessary.

Conser and Roblee apparently concurred with Murphy's beliefs and recommendations regarding trachoma. Throughout the research period, many children admitted to Sherman Institute showed obvious signs of trachoma. The condition and its severity were duly noted on the "Physician Certification" section of the student's enrollment application, but in no case was enrollment denied because of trachoma. Afflicted children were sent immediately to the hospital for treatment, and once they were considered no longer contagious they were allowed back into the general student population. Similarly, children who acquired trachoma while at school were never sent home because of the disease, as was common with tuberculosis. Conser typically notified the child's parents or reservation day school teacher of the child's condition, and he or she received treatment at the Sherman Institute hospital until a cure was affected. In fact, Conser did not permit children to return home until completely cured of trachoma. After receiving parents' requests that trachomatous children come home for vacation, Conser typically responded, "I have to advise you that at present their eyes are not in good condition and I wish to hold them until they are entirely cured."[31] This policy benefited not only the children's families, but ultimately Sherman Institute as well. By retaining trachomatous students until they were cured, it insured that the students could not infect family members back home on the reservations or other children that would potentially be seeking enrollment at the school. Further, allowing trachomatous students to interrupt their treatment and return home temporarily exacerbated the eyes' already fragile condition, requiring more radical treatment upon the student's return to school.

In February 1912, CIA Valentine formalized the Indian Office's trachoma policy with the issuance of Circular 602. As discussed in previous chapters, Circular 602 set forth specific preventive health measures to be implemented at all nonreservation boarding schools. These regulations formed the basis for the Indian Office's claim that with proper school management, trachomatous children would not spread the disease to their classmates.

An integral element of Circular 602 was the required quarantine of all children in the contagious stage (inflammation and purulent secretions) of trachoma. The secretions were considered to contain the infectious agent, and any time trachomatous children in this stage touched their eyes, then any other object or person, they were spreading the disease. Children in this acute stage were to be treated by the school physician, and only after the physician determined that they were no longer contagious could the children be returned to the general student population.

Preventive measures designed to stem the spread of trachoma were essentially the same as for any other disease: individual beds, towels, and brushes; disinfection of school supplies, boiling of clothing during laundering; and frequent eye examinations. By enforcing quarantine and implementing these preventive measures, Valentine and his supporters were confident that allowing the enrollment and retention of trachomatous students would not adversely impact the nonreservation boarding school student populations.

As previously discussed, Superintendent Conser concurred with the official Indian Office stance regarding trachoma. He felt that strict compliance with the mandated preventive measures and the addition of certain school-specific practices would mitigate the health threat posed by trachomatous students and enable him to maintain a healthy student population.

Not everyone agreed with the trachoma policy espoused by Supervisor Murphy and Commissioner Valentine. In 1912, physicians of the Public Health and Marine Hospital Service studied the incidence of trachoma and various other diseases among Indians throughout the United States. The results of their trachoma research, published in *Contagious and Infectious Diseases among the Indians,* suggested that trachoma was generally more prevalent in boarding schools than in the reservations from which the students were drawn.[32] Further, groups of students in nonreservation boarding schools from areas where trachoma was absent or only slightly prevalent presented a high percentage of infection. This inferred that students contracted trachoma in the nonreservation boarding schools, and upon their return home, were actually the means for introducing trachoma in a territory where it was previously absent or at least uncommon.[33] To illustrate this situation, the reporting physicians used Sherman Institute as an example.

At the time of the field research in 1912, Dr. R. A. Herring examined 536 students at Sherman Institute for trachoma, diagnosing 137 with the disease, for a 25 percent morbidity rate.[34] This represented one of the highest morbidity rates of any nonreservation boarding school studied. Sherman Institute trachoma morbidity also ranked higher than the national average of 22.7 percent for all Indians examined. Yet the trachoma incidence among Indians in California, from which most Sherman Institute students were drawn, equaled only 15.3 percent, considerably less than the national average. Even more significant, 133 students at Sherman Institute were members of Mission Indian tribes in Southern California, where trachoma afflicted very few Indians, and of these students, 25 had trachoma. Based on this information, Dr. Herring concluded that the students did not acquire the infection at home, and that this offered convincing proof of the ease with which trachoma could be disseminated through the agency of the schools.[35] Trachomatous students returning to their Southern California reservation homes also concerned Dr. Herring because he feared that they would introduce the disease into a previously uninfected territory. Since people living on these reservations were generally bereft of regular medical care, and over 75 percent of untreated trachoma cases result in permanently impaired vision, the potential impact to their health and vision was obvious.

Despite the Public Health Service's findings that nonreservation boarding schools fostered the spread of trachoma, the report failed to recommend that the Indian Office change its policy of enrolling trachomatous students in nonreservation boarding schools. Only schools uninfected with trachoma could prohibit the enrollment of trachomatous children. The report recommended that the Indian Office simply enforce its existing health regulations at all other schools. Regulations considered particularly important to stemming the spread of trachoma were that all schools should at all times be under competent medical and sanitary supervision, that all boarding schools with trachomatous students should be provided with adequate facilities for the care and treatment of the disease, including the permanent services of a trained nurse, and that systematic medical examinations should be made regularly of all children.[36] The Public Health Service recommended separate schools for trachomatous children where practicable, and whenever it was impracticable, the strict segregation of trachomatous children from healthy ones in separate dormitories, classrooms, dining rooms, and playgrounds. Unfortunately, the Indian Office never found the recommendation for separate schools practicable, and in fact, strict segregation of trachomatous children in separate facilities in existing schools rarely occurred. They did, however, find the preventive and mitigative measures for trachoma recommended by the Public Health Services report practicable, and incorporated them into the 1913 *Rules for the Indian School Service*, which remained in effect at least through 1922.

The Public Health Service's study made two very important points. It recognized the inherently flawed logic of permitting trachomatous children to enroll in nonreservation boarding schools. Since at the time physicians did not understand trachoma's etiology and pathology, they could not accurately assess the level of contagion. There existed no guaranteed "safe" time for allowing afflicted children to mingle with healthy ones. Further, absolute enforcement of even the most elemental sanitary procedures meant to curtail trachoma transmission proved impossible, given the ages of students at the schools. Children and adolescents generally do not do everything they are told to do, and in many cases rebel

by not doing any of it. The employee-to-student ratios at the schools precluded complete supervision and enforcement. Consequently, the mere
presence of trachomatous students in a school would necessarily result
in the spread of the disease, regardless of regulations. Sherman Institute
offers a perfect example of this premise. Despite strict compliance with
Indian Office health regulations and diligent enforcement of school-
specific trachoma policies, the trachoma morbidity rate continued to be
excessive throughout the research period. As long as nonreservation
boarding schools continued to admit trachomatous students, trachoma
continued to pose a significant health threat to the students—period.

The Public Health Service offered one of its most important contributions in providing actual trachoma data for nonreservation boarding
schools. Table 7.1 illustrates the number and percentage of afflicted students, as recorded by the research physicians. In most cases, these figures
are considerably higher than those reported by individual school physicians to the Indian Office. Both sets of data reflect trachoma examinations made in 1912, with the school data compiled over the course of the
1911–12 school year and that of the Public Health Service collected
between 28 September and 30 December 1912.[37] Therefore, Public
Health Service physicians collected data contained within *Contagious and
Infectious Diseases among the Indians* six months after the school physicians
collected their last data.

Additionally, of some importance is the fact that historically, more illness occurred at every nonreservation boarding school during the
autumn than at any other time of the year. School superintendents
attributed this to children going home for summer vacation and bringing various diseases back to school with them. However, even considering these issues, the difference between the number of trachoma cases
recorded by the Public Health Service and those reported by school physicians is in many cases extraordinary.

A number of factors influenced the disparity in trachoma case reporting. The primary reason for the underreporting of trachoma by school
physicians is undoubtedly that most Indian Service physicians and contract physicians were not specially trained in the diagnosis or treatment

TABLE 7.1

COMPARISON OF RECORDED TRACHOMA CASES, 1911–1912 ANNUAL REPORT AND 1912 PUBLIC HEALTH SERVICES REPORT

Nonreservation Boarding School	Enrollment AR/PHS	Afflicted with Trachoma AR/PHS	Percent of Enrollment AR/PHS
Carlisle	1031 / 552	145 / 76	14.06 / 13.76
Salem	325 / 316	20 / 29	6.15 / 9.17
Chilocco	536 / 509	44 / 334	8.20 / 65.61
Genoa	340 / 227	108 / 98	31.76 / 43.17
Albuquerque	332 / 339	55 / 75	16.56 / 22.12
Haskell	719 / 700	139 / 111	19.33 / 15.85
Grand Junction	–/–	–/–	–/–
Carson	318 / 200	80 / 24	25.15 / 12.00 '
Fort Mojave	496 / 244	22 / 69	5.50 / 28.27
Pierre	149 / 164	9 / 57	6.04 / 34.76
Phoenix	808 / 410	94 / 59	11.63 / 14.00
Fort Lewis	–/–	–/–	–/–
Fort Shaw	–/–	–/–	–/–
Mt. Pleasant	306 / 298	38 / 45	12.41 / 15.10
Tomah	–/ 237	–/ 16	–/ 6.74
Pipestone	212 / 187	23 / 42	10.89 / 22.46
Flandreau	445 / 350	9 / 68	2.02 / 19.43
Wittenberg	–/–	–/–	–/–
Greenville	125 /–	1 /–	.80 /–
Morris	–/–	–/–	–/–
Chamberlain	–/–	–/–	–/–
Fort Bidwell	126 /–	*481 /–	76.43 /–
Rapid City	–/ 236	–/ 40	–/ 17.00
Sherman	631 / 536	36 / 137	5.70 / 25.55
Wahpeton	–/ 108	–/ 18	–/ 16.60
Bismarck	–/ 71	–/ 19	–/ 26.70

AR = 1911–12 Annual Report (Table 20, pp. 168–172)

PHS = 1912 Public Health Service Report (*Contagious and Infectious Diseases among the Indians*, Table III, pp. 29–31.

* This figure represents recurring cases.

– No examinations made

of trachoma. Some physicians may not have recognized symptoms that an experienced Public Health Service physician easily noted. Trachoma screening was not typically part of the requisite yearly physical examination, and unless the symptoms of trachoma were clear-cut and obvious to even an inexperienced physician or nurse, a trachomatous child could have avoided detection and early treatment. In addition, benign trachoma often has so few symptoms that without a competent physician specifically examining the patient for trachoma, the trachoma may go undetected until well into the contagious stage of the disease. In the meantime, any number of healthy children could be exposed to the disease.

Underreporting of trachoma cases may also have been intentional on the part of school physicians and superintendents. To admit to a high morbidity rate for any disease would essentially be admitting to noncompliance with Indian Office health regulations. Further, a high morbidity rate for a disease on which so much preventive emphasis had been placed would infer a disregard for student health, inadequate school management, and incompetent medical care. All of these factors would be potential grounds for Indian Office intervention.

On the other hand, school superintendents and physicians would have little fiscal incentive for intentionally underreporting trachoma cases. School administrators constantly sought additional appropriations for nonreservation boarding schools, many of which were for health-related purposes. After 1909, when the Indian Office began to aggressively prioritize health issues at boarding schools, increased funding was available for the purpose of improving and maintaining health. To claim that a school had less disease than it actually had, particularly such a high-profile disease as trachoma, would have been fiscally counterproductive. This would mean that the Indian Office would channel available funds to schools with seemingly greater health problems.

Of interest in analyzing disparate trachoma statistics is that those schools with the largest differences in case reporting are those schools whose physicians treated most trachomatous students with means other than operations. In fact, at four of the schools—Chilocco, Pierre,

Pipestone, and Flandreau—physicians performed no trachoma operations. Since the Public Health Service physicians conducting the research examinations generally favored more radical means of treatment, their perceptions of what constituted a total cure may have differed from that held by the school physicians. Thus, a student considered cured by the school physician may have instead been counted as afflicted with trachoma by the research physician.

The Public Health Services study had little lasting impact on the Indian Office trachoma campaign, other than incorporation of recommended preventive and mitigative measures in the *Rules*. The Indian Office disregarded the study's research results that indicated trachoma represented an even greater problem in the nonreservation boarding schools than had been previously apparent. They also ignored the study's conclusion that boarding schools exacerbated the spread of trachoma, and the policy of admitting trachomatous students continued, as did trachoma morbidity. Interestingly, in 1916 Commissioner Cato Sells announced the success of the Indian Office's trachoma campaign and claimed that the old-time virulence of the disease was gone. "The treatment of trachoma is difficult," he reported, "but the problem in the schools is nearly solved."[38] Unfortunately, Sells's claims proved premature. Trachoma continued to threaten the health of boarding school children throughout much of the following two decades.

Despite the disparate findings of the Public Health Services report, trachoma morbidity at Sherman Institute between 1902 and 1922 must be viewed in terms of official statistics recorded by Sherman Institute physicians and compared to those submitted by physicians at other nonreservation boarding schools. Trachoma morbidity recorded in the autumn of 1912 by Public Health Services physicians is roughly five times higher than that recorded by Dr. Roblee for both the previous year and the subsequent year. The possible reasons for this significant disparity have been discussed, but an explanation based on anything more than speculation is not attainable. Therefore, it is not possible to establish an appropriate context within which to analyze trachoma morbidity over time based on this single set of data. Was trachoma morbidity always higher than reported? Was it sometimes higher and sometimes lower? Was it higher only under specific examination circumstances? The answers to these questions do not exist. All that does exist in a concrete form are the statistics recorded and submitted each year by school officials to the Indian Office. Since all nonreservation boarding schools had the same forms and the same recording parameters, these data offer the only consistent method of evaluating trachoma morbidity over time at Sherman Institute, and of comparing it to similar institutions.

Reliable data regarding trachoma morbidity at Sherman Institute between 1902 and 1908 does not exist. The Indian Office did not require boarding schools to record this information prior to the 1910–11 school year, and archival research found only two documents noting individual cases of trachoma prior to 1908, the year the first comprehensive examination for trachoma was conducted. More than two trachoma cases undoubtedly occurred between 1902 and 1908, but there is no evidence to indicate trachoma posed a substantial health threat to students at the school.

Such was not the case between 1908 and 1922. As shown in Table 7.2, trachoma remained an ongoing health problem at Sherman Institute throughout the remainder of the research period. Trachoma afflicted no less than 5 percent of enrolled students during this period, and during the 1921–22 school year, almost one-third of the student population exhibited symptoms of trachoma.

What could explain the high incidence of trachoma morbidity, particularly in the latter years, when seemingly every preventive health measure had been implemented? Perhaps the most relevant factor is the change in student demography at Sherman Institute. The founding population of the school had been comprised almost exclusively of children from Southern California reservations. As noted in the Public Health Services report, trachoma was virtually nonexistent in this territory. Consequently, children coming to Sherman Institute had not been exposed to the disease, and due to the geographic homogeneity of the student population, they were not exposed to trachoma at the school, either. As the years passed and the school expanded, the student population

TABLE 7.2
TRACHOMA MORBIDITY AND TREATMENT,
SHERMAN INSTITUTE, 1908–1922

School Year	Enrollment	Afflicted with Trachoma	Percent Enrolled Population	Cases Operated Upon	Cases Treated but Not Operated Upon
1908–09	672	125	18.60	U	U
1909–10	656	270	41.20	U	U
1910–11	670	152	22.69	64	88
1911–12	631	36	5.71	12	24
1912–13	639	36	5.63	15	73
1913–14	690	35	5.07	13	41
1914–15	744	85	11.42	19	66
1915–16	790	64	8.10	4	60
1916–17	787	65	8.26	41	24
1917–18	862	53	6.15	22	31
1918–19	879	56	6.37	5	51
1919–20	974	129	13.24	33	96
1920–21	1030	96	9.32	66	30
1921–22	1059	327	30.88	0	327

U = unknown

Some cases required more than one course of treatment

became more diverse, both culturally and geographically. Many of the areas from which most of the new students came, particularly Arizona and New Mexico, had a considerably higher incidence of trachoma than did the Indians of Southern California. For example, as recorded in 1912 by Public Health Services physicians, the trachoma rates for reservation Indians in Arizona and New Mexico were 19.00 percent and 22.24 percent, respectively. In comparison, the rate for all California reservation Indians was 8.52 percent, and in Southern California, trachoma was essentially nonexistent. By the 1911–12 school year, the number of children at Sherman Institute from Arizona and New Mexico exceeded those from Southern California, counterbalancing the low trachoma rate inherent in children from the latter reservations. Many of these children came to school afflicted with trachoma, and Conser enrolled all of them, despite clear evidence of the disease. As the percentage of students from Arizona and New Mexico grew, the trachoma morbidity rate increased. Although the Sherman Institute policy stipulated that trachomatous children be separated from the general population immediately and sent to the hospital for treatment, this did not always happen, particularly during periods of limited hospital bed availability.

In some cases demographic change does not fully explain the extent of the trachoma morbidity rate. Morbidity decreased substantially in the years following commencement of the Indian Office trachoma campaign in 1910, despite the infusion of students from high-trachoma regions. An increased focus on early detection and treatment effectively limited contagion opportunities. Implementation of preventive measures such as quarantine, individual towels, and running water also decreased trachoma transmission to healthy students, as well as reinfection of those previously afflicted.

Yet, during the 1914–15 school year, the trachoma incidence at Sherman Institute more than doubled. Analysis of available documents and statistics unfortunately provides no substantive information as to the reason for this dramatic jump. A measles epidemic affecting 122 students occurred the same year. Attention to the large number of ill students, several of whom contracted pneumonia, may partially explain the increase in trachoma, in that medical personnel were not as diligent in examining and treating trachomatous students. The epidemic also limited opportunities for quarantine of trachomatous students, because Roblee allocated all available hospital beds to measles patients. However, the measles epidemic was short-lived and probably does not represent a key factor in the trachoma morbidity increase. Unfortunately, no other explanatory factors have been discovered.

After 1914–15, the morbidity rate at Sherman Institute declined considerably for the next four years until the 1919–20 school year, when it more than doubled. This time, no epidemics occurred, and with the exception of trachoma, the student population was healthy. In this case, however, a significant change in student demography may fully explain the increase. Beginning in 1919 and continuing at least through 1922, the number of students from Arizona and New Mexico, particularly Navajo students, increased significantly. The reason for this increase is unknown, but the infusion of these children had a tremendous impact not only on trachoma morbidity but on tuberculosis morbidity as well. Coincidentally, the number of trachomatous students during the 1921–22 school year (327) almost exactly equaled the number of Navajo students enrolled that year (337). This represented the highest trachoma morbidity rate in twenty years at Sherman Institute, as well as the highest enrollment of Navajo students. While the exact number of trachomatous Navajo children is unknown, based on the incidence of Navajo students afflicted with tuberculosis that year, it is probable that the majority of trachoma patients were Navajo.

Despite the high trachoma morbidity rate at Sherman Institute throughout the research period, this rate was lower than that at almost every other nonreservation boarding school, most years. This is clearly illustrated for the 1911–12 school year in Table 7.3.[39] Although many factors influenced trachoma morbidity at the schools, the most relevant included homogeneity of student population, trachoma incidence on reservations from which students were drawn, and the consistency with which superintendents and physicians enforced preventive health measures.

During the early years at Sherman Institute, the key factors in the comparatively low trachoma morbidity rates were the relatively homogenous population and the low incidence of trachoma on Southern California reservations from which most students came. However, once the student population became more heterogeneous, the morbidity rate continued to be comparatively low because Superintendent Conser strictly enforced both Indian Office–mandated and self-imposed, school-specific preventive and mitigative health measures. Schools with historically unsanitary conditions and high-risk populations, such as Genoa Indian School, had correspondingly high trachoma morbidity rates. Enforcement of sanitary conditions and preventive health measures at Sherman Institute did not completely alleviate trachoma, but served to keep the morbidity rate lower than it would have been without these practices.

TABLE 7.3

COMPARISON OF TRACHOMA MORBIDITY AND
TREATMENT, NONRESERVATION BOARDING SCHOOLS,
1911–1912

School	Enrollment	Afflicted with Trachoma	Percent Enrolled Population	Cases Operated Upon	Cases Treated but Not Operated Upon
Carlisle	1031	145	14.06	37	108
Salem	325	20	6.15	5	14
Chilocco	536	44	8.20	0	44
Genoa	340	108	31.76	24	84
Albuquerque	332	55	16.56	18	37
Haskell	719	139	19.33	1	60
Grand Junction	–	–	–	–	–
Carson	318	80	25.15	57	23
Fort Mojave	496	22	5.50	6	16
Pierre	149	9	6.04	0	9
Phoenix	808	94	11.63	94	0
Fort Lewis	–	–	–	–	–
Fort Shaw	–	–	–	–	–
Mt. Pleasant	306	38	12.41	0	56**
Tomah	–	–	–	–	–
Pipestone	212	23	10.89	0	12
Flandreau	445	9	2.02	0	9
Wittenberg	–	–	–	–	–
Greenville	125	1	0.80	0	1
Morris	–	–	–	–	–
Chamberlain	–	–	–	–	–
Fort Bidwell	126	481*	76.43	0	75
Rapid City	–	–	–	35	–
Sherman	631	36	5.70	12	24
Wahpeton	76	0	0	0	6
Bismarck	72	0	0	0	0

Source: 1911–1912 *CIA Annual Report*, Table 20, pp. 168–72.

* This figure represents recurring cases; 76.43% of the population was afflicted with trachoma.

** Some cases required more than one course of treatment

– No examinations made

In 1922, a committee of ophthalmologists appointed by the American Medical Association visited three boarding schools—Albuquerque, Fort Defiance, and Sherman Institute—for the purpose of studying trachoma. The committee reported that each of the schools was housed in large buildings provided with spacious playgrounds. Each child housed in the roomy and airy dormitories slept in a separate bed with clean linen. The children washed under running water and dried their hands and faces on individual towels. Children observed by the committee appeared well nourished, active, and happy. Yet many children had trachoma. The committee concluded,

> From our investigations it was apparent that, notwithstanding the sanitation of the schools, the disease is propagated there and that some of the pupils who enter in the autumn with unaffected eyes return to their homes in the summer with trachoma.[40]

Both the 1913 Public Health Services report and the 1922 American Medical Association report correctly concluded that nonreservation boarding schools exacerbated the spread of trachoma, and as proof of that premise, both offered Sherman Institute as an example. Students from Southern California reservations, which had virtually no trachoma, acquired the disease while at school and transferred it to previously healthy reservation populations. What the studies did not consider is that the most critical factor in trachoma morbidity rates in nonreservation boarding schools was not the conditions at the school itself, but instead, the population demographics of the school, especially when they included large numbers of students from areas such as Arizona and New Mexico. When trachomatous students were enrolled in Sherman Institute, particularly from the Navajo Reservation, students from low-trachoma-incidence areas, such as Southern California reservations, contracted the disease. Upon their return home, Southern California Indian children then spread trachoma to previously unaffected populations. Thus, the problem was not so much that nonreservation boarding schools exacerbated the spread of this heinous disease, but that the Indian Office

not only allowed but mandated the continued enrollment of trachomatous students in the schools. The fact that Sherman Institute strictly
enforced all preventive measures possible, yet still had a high incidence
of trachomatous students clearly indicates the critical impact of these
outside factors.

———

Conclusion

AS ONE OF THE LAST NONRESERVATION BOARDING SCHOOLS ESTABLISHED in the United States, Sherman Institute benefited from lessons learned at other schools regarding the issue of student health. The earliest schools, such as Carlisle and Salem, at first gave little consideration to student health, instead focusing on the rapid assimilation of as many Indian children as possible. However, student morbidity and mortality at nonreservation boarding schools rose exponentially at these and subsequent schools, creating concern among Indian populations, Indian Office officials, and Progressive Era reformers. In addition to the inherent tragedy of so many sick and dying Indian children, it soon became evident that maintaining student health was integral to the education and "civilization" of Indian children.

As a consequence of the emerging recognition that health played a vital role in Indian education, the Indian Office issued a number of preventive health policies for implementation at nonreservation boarding schools. During the late nineteenth century, most of these policies dealt with design elements for the schools, such as providing adequate light and ventilation. Due to chronically penurious government appropriations, however, the policies were frequently not implemented or enforced. Preventive health measures generally were effective only when boarding school superintendents prioritized student health and acted accordingly.

By the time the federal government provided funding for Sherman Institute in 1901, the Indian Office had evidenced a stronger emphasis on health issues at nonreservation boarding schools. The *Course of Study for the Indian Schools of the United States,* issued in 1901, included guidelines for school design, as well as physical plant sanitation, curriculum, and personal hygiene, all intended to decrease the rising student morbidity and mortality. However, in considering the establishment of Sherman Institute, the most important factor in relation to health was the personal orientation of its first superintendent, Harwood Hall (1902–9).

As an experienced nonreservation boarding school administrator, Hall recognized the importance of student health in the successful assimilation and education of Indian children. He also recognized that a school full of sick and dying children would not be attractive to tourists or to facilitating a thriving outing program, both of which were critical factors in his drive to develop the quintessential Indian school of the West. Further, since Hall and his family lived at the school, illness among Indian students presented a viable threat to his own family's health.

These considerations led to Hall's strict compliance with Indian Office preventive health polices, as well as to his implementation of school-specific policies that he knew from experience at other schools would maintain and improve student health at Sherman Institute. Actions taken by Hall in furtherance of good student health included school design, pre-enrollment health screening procedures, sewage treatment, establishment of a nurse's training program, and most important, rigorously enforced school sanitation. Hall's prioritization of student health, beginning with the opening of Sherman Institute in 1902 and continuing throughout his administration, laid the foundation for a healthy school environment that subsequent superintendents could build upon.

Sherman Institute's second superintendent, Frank Conser (1909–22), continued Hall's tradition of strict compliance with Indian Office health policies and implementation of school-specific health practices learned from experience. In many ways, Conser proved even more diligent in prioritizing student health at Sherman Institute. School sanitation, diet, exercise, and the creation of a state-of-the-art school hospital marked his particular contributions to the maintenance and improvement of student health at the school.

Conser's term at Sherman Institute coincided with important changes in Indian Office ideology regarding health in relation to Indian education. These changes are reflected in Commissioner of Indian Affairs William Jones's statement in 1903, "Indian children should be educated, but should not be destroyed in the process. Health is the greatest consideration."[1] The emphasis placed on student health at nonreservation boarding schools increased significantly over the next two decades, resulting in more effective preventive health policies, as well as more funding for their implementation. Conser took full advantage of the expanded appropriations available for health issues, lobbying relentlessly for improvements to Sherman Institute, most of which he argued as being necessary for student health. As a result, the healthy living environment established at the school by Harwood Hall in 1902 continued throughout the administration of Frank Conser, and beyond.

Despite compliance with Indian Office health policies and implementation of school-specific health practices, however, epidemics, accidents, and illnesses regularly occurred among the student population at Sherman Institute. In large part, this was due to the fact that hundreds of children and young adults lived together in a relatively closed space. In any environment such as this, there will be sickness and accidents. Furthermore individuals in the school age cohorts are generally more susceptible to disease pathogens, for a number of reasons, among which are lack of proper personal hygiene and immature immunological systems. In the case of Indian students, traditional sharing practices contributed to the transmission of disease. Children and young adults also have accidents, perhaps because of a certain amount of fearlessness, or a lack of wisdom, but certainly also because their active lifestyles provide them with opportunities for accidents.

The expansion of the school's outing program brought more students into contact with the outside community, increasing the potential for contagion. During the late nineteenth and early twentieth centuries, the temperate climate brought thousands of tubercular patients to Southern

California for a cure. As more Sherman Institute students ventured out into the community, their opportunities for exposure to tuberculosis from this transient population increased.

Exposure to tuberculosis also occurred when students returned to their reservation homes for vacation, since the incidence of tuberculosis among reservation Indians of Southern California alone exceeded 10 percent between 1902 and 1922. Unfortunately, a child could be infected with tuberculosis while on vacation or outing, then return to school and transmit the disease to innumerable other students before it could be detected. The lack of efficacious screening techniques for tuberculosis at Sherman Institute and other nonreservation boarding schools guaranteed the continuance of this cycle of contagion.

The historiography of student health at nonreservation boarding schools is essentially nonexistent, with only cursory, qualitative references available. Consequently, direct quantitative or procedural comparisons are not possible. However, available Indian Office statistics enable placement of Sherman Institute student health in a comparative context with other nonreservation boarding schools, as well as with reservation Indian populations. On the basis of these statistical comparisons, student health at Sherman Institute fared very well. Sherman Institute students consistently had lower morbidity and mortality rates than did those at the majority of nonreservation boarding schools between 1902 and 1922. They also appeared to have lower morbidity and mortality rates than did Indians living on reservations from which students came, although available statistics are inadequate for direct comparisons.

Most nonreservation boarding schools continued to evidence poor health at least through 1928, as detailed in the Meriam report.[2] Several critical factors resulting from a prioritization of health issues kept the same from being said about Sherman Institute. This is not to say that there weren't far too many cases of illness and death among Sherman Institute students, for in the heart of a parent, even one case is too many. Yet, compared to the common perception of nonreservation boarding schools as death factories for Indian children, and to the available morbidity and mortality figures for school and reservation Indians, Sherman

Institute students would be considered a relatively healthy population. Whether the good health of Sherman Institute students actually represents an exception to the case of all other nonreservation boarding school populations is not known at this time.

In general, parents did not blame Sherman Institute for their children's illnesses or even for their deaths. They did, however, worry about their children's health while they lived at the school. Between 1902 and 1922, many parents of Sherman Institute students wrote to the superintendents asking about their children's health. In fact, Superintendent Harwood Hall once noted that he received letters from concerned parents every day, asking about their children's health.[3] Some of these letters were in response to rumors of illness at the school or to letters received from children, telling of personal illness. Other letters reflected parents' need for reassurance that their children, living so far away, actually were healthy and doing well at the school. Most Indian families knew of the reputation long held by nonreservation boarding schools as unhealthy places for Indian children, and they needed to know that their children were safe at Sherman Institute. In each case, Hall or Conser responded, typically within one day of receiving the parent's letter, apprising the parent of their child's condition. Since both superintendents already sent letters and telegrams to parents of ill children, the letters sent in response to parent inquiries usually served only to reassure parents that their children were fine.

The prompt, consistent responses to parents' letters of concern and the timely notification of student illness contributed greatly to parents' confidence in the ability of Sherman Institute to keep their children healthy. The open-door policy of the school, whereby Hall and Conser encouraged parents to visit their children and tour the school at any time, added to the sense that the superintendents were not trying to hide unhealthy living conditions and sick children. The fact that the Sherman Institute hospital also served the reservation Indian community of Southern California further reinforced parents' perception that the school offered a healthy place for their children to live, and that in the event they became ill, the children would be well taken care of. "Mother and I will now tell you how thankness we are to you and your nurses for your great patience and care for our boy," wrote the brother of John Wellington in 1912. "Our feeling toward you is more than these words, we cannot express it."[4]

Since many reservations did not have hospitals or regular medical care, the facilities and personnel at Sherman Institute represented a positive resource to many families. However, in some cases, parents believed that sending their children to Sherman Institute would keep them healthier than if they stayed at home, and when this did not happen, the parents became angry and embittered. In 1909, a number of children from the Round Valley Reservation went to Sherman Institute, only to be sent home a short time later with tuberculosis. In this case, the parents blamed the school for their children's illness.[5] Unfortunately, Round Valley had the highest incidence of tuberculosis in California, and it is probable that the children had incipient tuberculosis when they arrived at Sherman Institute. When they sent their children to Sherman Institute and away from the pervasive disease on the reservation, the Round Valley parents expected that their children would be safer at school than at home. When this did not happen, some Round Valley Reservation parents refused to send children to Sherman Institute.

Most reservations had traditional medicine men or women through the beginning of the twentieth century, and although they provided care for many ailments, they were often unsuccessful in treating diseases such as tuberculosis, smallpox, and measles. These diseases of Euro-American culture had no known cures in traditional medicine because they had not existed prior to contact. In these cases, parents had no choice but to trust in white medicine, and when that failed them, their frustration turned to anger and mistrust. At Sherman Institute, this fortunately proved to be the exception, not the rule.

Little evidence exists that tells us how Sherman Institute students felt about their illnesses. However, based on the few available letters, they did not blame the school, its superintendents, or medical personnel for poor health, even when it meant being sent home from school. Students sent home sick wanted to return to school as soon as they became well: "I am going to tell you, that my health have improved a great deal," wrote Sara Patton (Pima) in 1911, "I will be back to Sherman about the 4th of October."[6] Another Pima girl, Hannah Roberts, who had been sent home in 1904 for "weak lungs," wrote to Harwood Hall saying that she was "now well and anxious to return to school at once."[7] Whether these examples are actually representative of the way the majority of students felt is unknown. However, according to Michael Coleman, Indian students at other boarding schools shared the same sentiments: "La Fleshe, Chris (Mescalero), and others generally did not blame the schools for the sickness which struck them or kin or schoolmates." Coleman notes that Native American narrators, "specifically noted the concern and dedication of teaching and medical staff during such crises."[8]

Perhaps the most important evidence regarding the way students felt about their health in relation to Sherman Institute comes not from archival documents, but from the students' actions and memories. Registration records at what is now Sherman Indian High School indicate that scores of students who went to Sherman Institute between 1902 and 1922 sent their children to school there, when the time came. In turn, those children sent their children to Sherman Institute, a tradition that continues to this day. Participants in Alumni Day celebrations and correspondents with the Sherman Indian Museum website relate their own positive experiences, as well as those passed down through the generations. Clearly, not every child who attended Sherman Institute had a positive experience, and the information provided by those who did is skewed by their willingness to share memories and participate in celebrations of the school. However, what is also clear is that between 1902 and 1922, Sherman Institute offered a healthy living environment to Indian children, and because of that, successive generations of parents have continued to send their children to the school for the past one hundred years.

———————

Notes

INTRODUCTION

1. Scott Riney, *The Rapid City Indian School, 1898–1933* (Norman: University of Oklahoma Press, 1999), 44–71.

2. Michael C. Coleman, *American Indian Children at School, 1850–1930* (Jackson: University Press of Mississippi, 1993), 163–64.

3. Examples of this sentiment may be found in the following correspondence: Mr. Fred Long (for Hannah Roberts) to Harwood Hall, 8 July 1904; Sarah Patton to Frank Conser, 7 September 1911; Stella Bellas to Conser, 1 May 1922. All letters: NARA, Record Group 75, LR.

4. K. Tsianina Lomawaima, *They Called It Prairie Light: The Story of Chilocco Indian School* (Lincoln: University of Nebraska Press, 1994), 23–26. In this section about students at Chilocco Indian School prior to the 1920s, Lomawaima's only reference to health is that "Parents in El Paso heard in 1905 that diphtheria had struck the school and children had died." (24).

5. Robert A. Trennert Jr., *The Phoenix Indian School, Forced Assimilation in Arizona, 1891–1935* (Norman: University of Oklahoma Press, 1988), 101–9.

6. Brenda J. Child, *Boarding School Seasons: American Indian Families, 1900–1940* (Lincoln: University of Nebraska Press, 1998), 55–60.

7. Lewis Meriam, *The Problem of Indian Administration* (Baltimore: Johns Hopkins University Press, 1928).

8. David Wallace Adams, *Education for Extinction: American Indians and the Boarding School Experience, 1875–1928* (Lawrence: University Press of Kansas, 1995), 124–35.

9. Email message to Sherman Indian Museum website from James Ruiz, 27 April 2001.

CHAPTER ONE

1. The Office of Indian Affairs was alternately referred to as the Indian Office until the 1930s, when the designation was changed to Bureau of Indian Affairs. Since Indian Office is the term used in the majority of primary source documents from 1902 to 1922, it is used throughout this book instead of the more formal Office of Indian Affairs.

2. Dr. Martha Waldron, "The Indian in Relation to Health," *Sanitarian* 37:304–5. Though voiced by many, an example of the perceived inherent weakness of Indian children is vividly illustrated by the following statement of Dr. Martha Waldron, resident physician of Hampton Institute: "the hygiene of the school room, the dormitory, and the workshop is of more vital importance to the Indian child than to the child of any race further advanced in civilization, and hence of greater physical stamina."

3. Commissioner Thomas J. Morgan, "Health of Indian Pupils," *Sixtieth ARCIA* (Washington D.C.: Government Printing Office, 1891), 72.

4. W. N. Hailmann, *Circular Letter of Instruction* (Washington, D.C.: Government Printing Office, 1895).

5. Diane Therese Putney, "Fighting the Scourge: American Indian Morbidity and Federal Indian Policy, 1897–1928," (Ph.D diss., Marquette University, 1980), 8–9.

6. Putney, "Fighting the Scourge," 8–9.

7. CIA to Secretary of the Interior, 25 January 1898, LS, Education, BIA.

8. *Course of Study for the Indian Schools of the United States* (Washington, D.C.: Government Printing Office, 1901), 199.

9. Ibid.

10. Ibid., 196.

11. Since the days of Socrates, many European doctors had held the belief that a miasma (filth) emerging from corpses or other rotting matter in the earth caused sudden outbreaks of disease. When these emanations were brought forth under certain meteorological conditions and encountered individuals with appropriately weakened constitutions, these theorists believed that epidemics resulted. Since the miasma itself was a potent form of filth, it was generally considered that only by maintaining cleanliness in one's living environment would it be possible to keep the miasma, and thus disease, at bay. For most of the nineteenth century, the public health movement had been based on the valid assumption that cleanliness, fresh air, and pure water were essential to community health, and on the less valid assumption that epidemic diseases were caused by an indefinable

substance called miasma. However, as early as 1860, some attention had been given to the then unpopular "germ [or contagionist] theory."

12. Sister Kathleen Savani, "The Last Song: History of Sherman Institute, Riverside, California," unpublished manuscript (1966), 29–30, Local History Collection, Riverside Public Library, Riverside, Calif.

13. The availability of ample water from local artesian wells, the existence of a modern sewer system, and the fact that electricity had already been run to the site were undoubtedly some of the selling points for this particular piece of land. It is not known who instructed Conser to investigate this specific site, but it is interesting that the site was adjacent to Frank Miller's streetcar company in Chemawa Park, and owned by Miller's sister and brother-in-law, and that apparently no other sites were offered for consideration. Frank Miller, who also owned the popular Glenwood Hotel, had been the strongest force in political machinations involved in bringing the new school to Riverside.

14. Harwood Hall had previously been superintendent of Perris Indian School and Phoenix Indian School (both nonreservation boarding schools), and of reservation boarding schools at the Quapwa and Pine Ridge agencies.

15. Hall to Frank Kyselka (Supervising U.S. Indian Agent, Hupa, Calif.), 1 July 1902, SIMA, LPB, 1–2.

16. Hall to CIA, 1 August 1900, SIMA, LPB, 348–52.

17. In 1890, a similar configuration was proposed at Haskell Indian School, but it was not implemented until the 1920s. Dormitory rooms for two or three students were also utilized at Rapid City Indian School in the late 1920s. As far as can be ascertained from available secondary sources, Sherman Institute was the first nonreservation boarding school to utilize small dormitory rooms or individual rooms instead of large dormitory rooms.

18. Hall to CIA, 2 June 1902, SIMA, LPB, 321.

19. Ibid., 352.

20. Hall claimed that the water at Perris Indian School was inadequate in quantity to serve the student population. He argued that the lack of water would result in significant health problems because the children could not bathe properly, the school could not be cleaned, and the students would go hungry because there was insufficient water for irrigation. If the school was not closed and a new school built, Hall claimed that the children would suffer from a variety of diseases, and many would undoubtedly die. Many local citizens vehemently opposed Hall's claims of inadequate water, and this became a very controversial issue. For a complete discussion of approval for a new school based on claims of unhealthy water in Perris and healthy water in Riverside, see Jean A. Keller, "In the Fall of the Year

We Were Troubled with Some Sickness," in *Medicine Ways: Disease, Health, and Survival Among Native Americans,* ed. Clifford E. Trafzer and Diane Weiner (Walnut Creek, Calif.: Alta Mira Press, 2001), 32–51.

21. So-called filth diseases, such as cholera, typhoid, dysentery, and typhus are transmitted through bacteria found in contaminated water, food, and utensils, or through contact with an infected person. These diseases typically result from unfavorable environmental conditions such as polluted water, grossly inadequate sewage, and congested housing. Untreated sewage acts as a breeding ground for pathogenic bacteria, which can then contaminate groundwater.

22. Hall to CIA, 23 October 1902, NA, PSWR, SI, LS, LPB, 491.

23. Circular No. 99, 1 July 1903. Circulars issued by the Education Division, 1897–1909, BIA.

24. Ibid.

25. Ibid.

26. Hall to Mr. J. F. Singletary, Disciplinarian, 8 November 1904, SIMA, LPB, 101.

27. Putney, "Fighting the Scourge," 15–16.

28. Kalsomine was a trademarked variant of calcimine, a white or tinted liquid containing zinc oxide, water, glue, and a coloring matter, that was commonly used for washing walls and ceilings.

29. Hall to CIA, 18 September 1907, NA, PSWR, RG 75, LS, LPB, 81.

30. Acting CIA C. F. Larrabee to Hall, 11 April 1905 (Education 20626–1905), NA, PSWR, SI, LR.

31. Hall to CIA, 24 September 1906, SIMA, LPB, 189

32. Ibid.

33. Lewis Merriam, *The Problem of Indian Administration* (Baltimore: Johns Hopkins University Press, 1928), 321. After visiting Sherman Institute in 1928, Lewis Merriam remarked that unlike most kitchens at nonreservation boarding schools, the ones at Tulalip, Sherman Institute, and Warm Springs were not adequate in size, but were very small and crowded.

34. During the summer of 1908, Dr. Aleŝ Hrdliĉka, a physical anthropologist with formal medical training, and Dr. Paul Johnson, a bacteriologist, examined five Indian tribes and the students at the Phoenix Indian School for tuberculosis. The Indian tribes, who were all known to have high rates of tuberculosis, were the Oglala, Hoopa, Menominee, Quinaielt, and Mojave. The study found a tuberculosis morbidity rate of 3 to 5 percent among the five tribes and a mortality rate ranging between 80 and 125 per 10,000 people. The results of the study convinced Leupp that tuberculosis was the "greatest single menace to the future of the red race."

35. Francis Leupp, "Fighting Tuberculosis among the Indians," *Southern Workman* (November 1908): 588, in Records of the Board of Indian Commissioners, Reference Material, HEALTH BIA.

> I could, in short, have cited the opinions of physicians, missionaries, and others familiar with the subject through living among the Indians themselves, that this very class of schools, with their herding practice and their 'institutional' routine, their steam-heated buildings and their physical confinement, furnish ideal conditions for the development of germ diseases among a race put through the forcing process there. I could have added the testimony of experienced members of the field staff of our Indian Service to the effect that the greatest percentage of cases of tuberculosis on the reservations where they are respectively at work is to be found among pupils returned from the nonreservation boarding schools before graduation.
>
> The whole method of conducting these schools is conducive of unwholesome conditions for young people who have been accustomed themselves, and are descended from an ancestry always accustomed, to the freest open-air life.

36. *ARCIA,* 1910, 10, emphasis mine.

37. *Manual of Sherman Institute, 1912–13* (Riverside, Calif.: Institute Press, 1912), 4–5.

38. Putney, "Fighting the Scourge," 98.

39. *ARCIA,* 1910, 11.

40. *Annual Report* (narrative) 1912, Sherman Institute, 12 August 1912, NA, PSWR, SI.

41. *ARCIA,* 1909, 5.

42. Department of the Interior, United States Indian Service, *Rules for the Indian School Service* (Washington, D.C: Government Printing Office, 1913), sec. 44, p. 9.

43. Hall noted this fact as early as 1907 in his request for a sleeping porch to be built on his residence. Hall stated that due to Riverside's high temperatures during much of the year, it was impossible to sleep comfortably indoors. His request was denied. Modern spring, summer, and fall temperatures in Riverside are commonly in excess of one hundred degrees, while evening temperatures during the year often fall below freezing, making sleeping porch accommodations equally impossible.

44. Putney, "Fighting the Scourge," 102.

45. Ibid., 104.

46. Department of the Interior, *Rules for the Indian School Service,* sec. 44, p. 8.

47. *Annual Report* (narrative) 1916, Sherman Institute, NA, PSWR, SI.

48. *Annual Report* (narrative) 1912, Sherman Institute, NA, PSWR, SI.

49. Beginning with the first month of his superintendency and continuing through 1922, there are many letters from Conser to the CIA voicing concerns over the unsanitary condition of the toilets at Sherman Institute, particularly those in the dormitory basements. Due to poor ventilation, odors often emanated through the floors into the dormitory rooms above. Some examples of these letters are the following, all found in PSWR, SI, LS: Conser to CIA, 9 September 1909, LPB, 344–45; Conser to CIA, 26 April 1912, LPB, 129; Conser to CIA, 5 December 1916; Conser to CIA, 23 November 1922.

50. Ibid.

51. *ARCIA*, 1911, 5.

52. Ibid.

53. Dr. Newberne's first name not available.

54. Conser to CIA, 5 December 1916, Education-Schools 106429–1916, NA, PSWR, SI.

55. Conser to CIA, 23 November 1922, Education-Health 75427–22 W C, NA, PSWR, SI.

56. Putney, "Fighting the Scourge," 32.

57. *Report of the Superintendent of Indian Schools,* in CIA Report, 1897, 330–31; CIA Report, 1898, 20 .

58. Hall to CIA, 3 August 1906, NA, PSWR, SI, LS, LPB, 91.

59. Hall to CIA, 10 July 1907, NA, PSWR, RG 75, SI, LS, LPB, 24.

60. Meriam, *The Problem of Indian Administration,* 318.

CHAPTER TWO

1. These were not preventive programs specifically denoted as such by the Indian Office. Instead, they represent general categories of preventive programs, based on available documentation.

2. *Course of Study for the Indian Schools of the United States* (Washington, D.C.: Government Printing Office, 1901), 197.

3. Ibid.

4. Ibid.

5. Joseph F. Murphy, "The Prevention of Tuberculosis in the Indian Schools," *Journal of Proceedings and Addresses of the National Education Association* (1909): 920.

6. Polingaysi Qoyawayma (Elizabeth Q. White), *No Turning Back: A Hopi Indian Woman's Struggle to Live in Both Worlds* (1964; reprint, Albuquerque: University of New Mexico Press, 1992), 69.

7. Ibid. In response to Polingaysi's scolding, her father went to someone who

was building a house and got enough boards to build her a bed frame, on which he placed a ticking bag filled with cornhusks for a mattress. Later, he also built a table.

8. While there are no universal cultural traits among Native Americans, the sharing of personal goods with others, as a way of showing trust and friendship, is a common trait among many. Although not documented, it is probable that Indian children at Sherman Institute shared personal items as a way of making friends in a very foreign and lonely environment.

9. "Health," *Sherman Bulletin* 4, no. 14 (6 April 1910): 1.

10. *ARCIA,* 1911, 6–7.

11. In addition to the standard health topics generally covered in his lectures, while at Sherman Institute Shoemaker made note of the great dangers of pipe passing, alcohol use, and cigarettes.

12. *ARCIA,* 1911, 6–7.

13. Upon taking office in 1913, Sells read the results of the Public Health Services studies conducted in 1912 and publicly stated that Indian health was in a deplorable condition. He vowed to provide Indians with more hygienic homes, better school facilities, better medical attention, and a comprehensive program of disease prevention, particularly for trachoma and tuberculosis. Sells made health a priority of his administration and successfully convinced Congress to appropriate larger sums of money for Indian health every year, increasing from $90,000 in 1913 to $350,000 in 1917. A large portion of this money went to preventive health programs designed to eradicate tuberculosis and trachoma, since they represented the first- and second-greatest causes of Indian morbidity in the United States.

14. Putney, "Fighting the Scourge," 107.

15. These reprinted Public Health Service Bulletins generally included a number of shock-oriented items designed to catch the students' attention: "Do You Know That: Untreated pellagra ends in insanity? Bad temper is sometimes merely a symptom of bad health? Insanity costs every person in the United States $1 per year?" Often, the bulletins alluded to Indian students' future concerns: "Do You Know That: Intelligent motherhood conserves the nation's best crop? Sedentary habits shorten life? Heavy eating like heavy drinking shortens life?"

16. *Sherman Bulletin* 15, no. 32 (13 May 1921): 4.

17. Conser to CIA, 22 May 1917, NA, PSWR, SI, LS. Special "Baby Week" festivities included lectures given daily in all the girls' departments. The Sherman Institute seamstress gave instruction on the proper clothing for babies and how to make it, the domestic science teacher taught the proper

diet for babies, and the school laundress instructed girls on how to clean babies' clothes and diapers. The school nurse gave instruction on how to hold babies, how to keep them clean, and how to identify and treat various ailments. The *Sherman Bulletin* included articles regarding the special lectures.

18. Commissioner Jones, believing that it was his duty to educate Indian children for citizenship as quickly as possible, specifically instructed superintendents to fill their schools to capacity. School superintendents cooperated for a number of reasons, either from a shared sense of duty, for the additional $167 stipend available for each student, or out of fear of Jones.

19. Circular No. 102, 21 September 1903. Circulars issued by the Education Division, BIA.

20. Circular No. 106, 23 March 1904. Circulars issued by the Education Division, BIA.

21. Circular No. 127, 14 August 1905. Circulars issued by the Education Division, BIA.

22. Prior to any child being enrolled at Perris Indian School, they were required to undergo a rigorous physical examination by Dr. C. C. Wainwright, Mission-Tule Agency physician. Students were also given physical examinations before going home for vacation and upon returning to school from vacation or outing. While Wainwright ceased to be the agency physician before Sherman Institute opened, Harwood Hall, who had been the Perris Indian School superintendent, implemented the same procedures when Sherman Institute opened.

23. Dr. Joseph Murphy to Conser, 25 May 1909, NA, PSWR, SI, LR, LPB, 173.

24. Ibid.

25. Report by Committee on Measures for Combating Tuberculosis, 29 December 1908, Education Circular No. 266, NA, PSWR, SI.

26. *Rules for the Indian School Service* (Washington, D.C.: Government Printing Office, 1913), 8–9.

27. Ibid., 9.

28. *Manual of Sherman Institute*, 1.

29. Ibid., 2.

30. Ibid.

31. *Rules for the Indian School Service*, 28.

32. For one hundred rations, authorized subsistence rations in 1898 were: ninety pounds of flour or cornmeal; five pounds of rolled oats, ninety pounds of beef net (or eighty pounds of beef plus ten pounds of bacon); three pounds of coffee (or one pound of tea or two pounds of cocoa);

twelve pounds of sugar; twelve pounds of beans (or four pounds of rice, barley, or hominy); twelve pounds of dried fruit (or substituting fresh fruit, one bushel of apples, pears, or peaches and thirty pounds of grapes); one and one-half gallons of syrup or molasses; one bushel of potatoes; four pounds of salt; one-quarter pound of pepper or other spices; one pound of baking powder; and two pounds of lard.

33. CIA to Secretary of Agriculture, 5 January 1899, LS, Education, BIA.

34. Putney, "Fighting the Scourge," 35–36.

35. *Course of Study for the Indian Schools of the United States,* 198.

36. For example, in 1912, the student population of Sherman Institute was 631, while that of Chilocco was 536 and that of Chemawa (Salem) was 325.

37. *Annual Report* (narrative), Sherman Institute, 1 September 1906, NA, PSWR, SI, LPB, 313. *Annual Report* (narrative), Sherman Institute, 26 August 1907, NA, PSWR, SI, LPB, 206.

38. Scott Riney, *The Rapid City Indian School, 1898–1933* (Norman: University of Oklahoma Press, 1999), 54.

39. In addition to regular Indian Office inspector's reports, the Meriam Report of 1928, though somewhat after the research focus period of this dissertation, reported that, "Sherman Institute gave the greatest variety and spent more for food than any other school studied." (Lewis Meriam, *The Problem of Indian Administration* [Baltimore: Johns Hopkins University Press, 1928], 327).

40. Qoyawayma, *No Turning Back,* 63–64.

41. Medical Supervisor Joseph Murphy to Conser, 25 May 1909, NA, PSWR, SI, LR, 174.

42. Mark H. Beers and Robert Berkow, eds., *The Merck Manual of Diagnosis and Therapy* (Whitehouse Station, N.J.: Merck Research Laboratories, 1999), 298.

43. Milk production and consumption data, while varying somewhat each year, generally stayed within this range. In estimating the consumption rate, the figure was based on average annual attendance of 750 children over the twenty-year research period and a 365-day year, although the majority of students were at the school during only the nine-month school year. Consequently, this figure represents a worst-case scenario. The employee mess probably purchased the remaining milk for the consumption of faculty and staff, since the Indian Office required that the employee mess purchase all food separately.

44. While yearly milk consumption data for other schools is not available, in 1928 the Meriam report noted that as a rule, the number of fresh milk cows at nonreservation boarding schools was "insufficient to supply an

average of a pint of milk a day per child for cooking or drinking purposes," though in a few exceptional cases the supply averaged a quart a day (324).

45. Dr. Johnson G. McGahey, Standing Rock Agency, North Dakota, "Address to the Annual Physicians Conference," *ARCIA*, 1899, 462.

46. Ibid.

47. Major E. P. Grinstead, "The Value of Military Drills," from *The Native American*. Published in *Sherman Bulletin* 8, no. 14 (8 April 1914): 4.

48. *Course of Study for the Indian Schools of the United States*, 198.

49. Ibid., 197.

50. *ARCIA*, 1909, 5.

51. *Rules for the Indian School Service*, sec. 43, p. 8.

52. Ibid., sec. 44, p. 98.

53. *Annual Report* (narrative), Sherman Institute, 12 July 1913, NA, PSWR, SI.

54. Ibid.

55. *Annual Report* (narrative), Sherman Institute, 1919, NA, PSWR, SI.

56. *Annual Report* (narrative), Sherman Institute, 1922, NA, PSWR, SI.

57. *Course of Study for the Indian Schools of the United States*, 199.

58. Ibid., 200.

59. Ibid., 196.

60. Estelle Reel, Superintendent of Indian Schools, "Superintendent Circular No. 63, February 15, 1904," NA, PSWR, SI, LR.

61. Ibid.

62. Conser to CIA, 1 June 1912, NA, PSWR, RG 75, SI, LS.

63. *Rules for the Indian School Service*, sec. 61, p. 10.

64. Circular No. 602, 15 February 1912, Circulars, 1904–1934, BIA.

65. Crash is a coarse, plain linen, cotton, or similar fabric used for making towels.

66. Circular No. 825, 13 February 1914, Circulars, 1904–1934, BIA.

67. Conser to CIA, 24 February 1914, NA, PSWR, SI, LS.

68. Kalsomining as a method of disinfection is explained in note 28 in chapter 1.

69. Aleŝ Hrdliĉka, *Tuberculosis among Certain Tribes of the United States*, Smithsonian Institution Bureau of Ethnology Bulletin 42 (Washington, D.C.: Government Printing Office, 1909), 30.

70. Circular No. 242, 30 September 1908. Circulars issued by the Education Division, BIA.

71. Circular No. 246, 27 October 1908. Circulars issued by the Education Division, BIA.

72. Circular No. 254. "Disinfection of Indian Service Books, November 18, 1908," NA, PSWR, RG 75, SI, LR.

73. While formaldehyde is normally present at low levels (0.06 ppm) in both outdoor and indoor air, acute health effects can occur when present in the air at levels above 0.1 ppm, which would be possible, given the level of daily disinfecting necessary for a school the size of Sherman Institute. Symptoms could include burning sensations in the eyes, nose, and throat; nausea, coughing, chest tightness, wheezing, and skin rashes. Formaldehyde has also caused cancer in laboratory animals and may cause cancer in humans. The Indian Office recognized the irritating properties of formaldehyde and included appropriate health warnings on all instructions for formaldehyde disinfecting.

74. *Rules of the Indian School Service*, sec. 50, p. 9.

75. Circular Education-Schools, "Infection through use of books," 23 March 1913, SIMA, LR.

CHAPTER THREE

1. Hall to CIA, 1 August 1900, NA, PSWR, SI, LS.

2. Hall to CIA, 11 August 1905, NA, PSWR, SI, LS.

3. Ibid. To renovate Ramona Home after it had been used to house ill students, Hall requested an expenditure of $150 to pay for five hundred pounds of kalsomine, one hundred pounds of glue, two hundred pounds of Plaster of Paris, five pounds of Venetian Red, and five pounds of Venetian Lake. All of these materials were mixed together, then spread on the interior walls of the building in the process of "kalsomining" or disinfecting. Further, one of the first groups of patients cared for in Ramona Home was infected with bedbugs, and despite every endeavor to exterminate them, the bedbugs infested the walls of the dormitory through cracks in the plaster, remaining there for the next three years. The kalsomine mixture was used to seal the cracks, trapping the bedbugs inside the walls and alleviating the problem.

4. Jean A. Keller, "In the Fall of the Year We Were Troubled with Some Sickness," in *Medicine Ways: Disease, Health, and Survival Among Native Americans*, ed. Clifford E. Trafzer and Diane Weiner (Walnut Creek, Calif.: Alta Mira Press, 2001), 32–51.

5. Intense, uncontrollable vomiting and diarrhea characterize typhoid fever. Treatment requires that this material be continually disposed of so that well individuals do not come into contact with the bacteria contained within the vomit or fecal material. Also, prompt disposal prevents flies from landing on the material and potentially spreading the disease.

6. *Sherman Bulletin* 1, no. 2 (13 March 1907): 1

7. *Sherman Bulletin* 1, no. 28 (13 November 1907): 3; Conser to CIA, 18 October 1911, NA, PSWR, SI, LS, LPB, 242.

8. Conser to CIA, 15 November 1909, NA, PSWR, SI, LS, LPB, 41.

9. Francis E. Leupp, *The Indian and His Problem* (New York: Charles Scribner's Sons, 1910), 292–93.

10. Conser to CIA, 28 October 1910, NA, PSWR, SI, LS, LPB, 389.

11. Ibid., 389–90.

12. *Annual Report* (narrative), 12 August 1912, NA, PSWR, SI.

13. Conser to CIA, 31 July 1916, NA, PSWR, SI, LS.

14. Ibid.

15. Since Sherman Institute was one of the largest nonreservation boarding schools, most other schools without staff physicians had smaller student populations. For example, in 1912, the school population at Pipestone was 212, that at Fort Bidwell was 126, that at Rapid City was 150, and that at Pierre was 149. Schools of comparable size to Sherman Institute (631), such as Carlisle (1031), Haskell (719), and Phoenix (808), had full-time staff physicians.

16. Diane Therese Putney, "Fighting the Scourge: American Indian Morbidity and Federal Indian Policy, 1897–1928" (Ph.d. diss., Marquette University, 1980), 9.

17. Ibid., 61–62.

18. Ibid., 55. During the nineteenth century, Indian Service physicians gained a rather unfavorable reputation for a variety of reasons, including drinking, lechery, and laziness. In 1898, Dr. Joseph R. Finney of the Fort Berthold agency suggested that the physicians form a professional organization named the Association of Physicians of the United States Indian Service to help Indian Service physicians overcome a bad reputation, inculcate pride in their work, and improve the quality of service rendered to the Indians.

19. K. Tsianina Lomawaima, *They Called It Prairie Light: The Story of Chilocco Indian School* (Lincoln: University of Nebraska Press, 1994), 23.

20. Putney, "Fighting the Scourge," 9. Contract health care at Sherman Institute may also have had local political motivation. The school's first contract physician was a close friend of Frank Miller, who had been instrumental in bringing Sherman Institute to Riverside. In fact, he maintained a successful medical practice in the Glenwood Building, which was owned by Miller. A contact such as this would have been invaluable to Miller in keeping apprised of conditions at Sherman Institute; something unlikely had a staff physician been present. Miller had a vested interest in Sherman Institute as both a tourist attraction and an economic boon to the com-

munity, so he undoubtedly had an interest in prevailing conditions at the school. Making a strong recommendation to Hall to contract with a local, friendly physician would have had obvious benefits.

21. Hall to CIA, 16 July 1902, SIMA, LPB, 380.

22. "Ashley S. Parker, M.D., President 1901," *The Bulletin*, Riverside County Medical Association, October 1979, 25.

23. CIA to Hall, 16 July 1902, SIMA, LR, LPB, 380.

24. CIA to Hall, 23 June 1903, NA, PSWR, SI, LR.

25. CIA to Hall, 26 October 1903, NA, PSWR, SI, LR.

26. "Parker, A. S., Physician and Surgeon," advertisement in *Riverside City Directory* (Los Angeles: Riverside Directory Co., 1905), 206.

27. See chapter 5 for a discussion of Parker's conflicting theories of causation.

28. The position of Riverside County physician had been established in 1880, in conjunction with the first Riverside County Hospital. Responsibilities of the county physician included care of all patients at the county hospital, which provided medical care for indigent residents of Riverside County. The Riverside County physician was also permitted to care for private patients, as both Parker and Roblee continued to do during their joint tenure.

29. Whether Parker's ill health was actually the reason for his resignation is questionable, since he subsequently moved from Riverside to Needles, California, and accepted the position of physician and surgeon with the Santa Fe Railroad. In 1921, he moved to Merced, California, where he carried on a large industrial practice until 1950.

30. Roblee served as Sherman Institute's contract physician from 1909 until 1937, except for the two-year period between 31 December 1917 and 1 January 1919, when Roblee was appointed a major in the Medical Reserve Corps of the U.S. Army. He requested a furlough during this period, and his associate, Dr. C. Vanzwalenberg, filled the vacancy until Roblee returned.

31. "William Wallace Roblee, M.D., President 1905," *The Bulletin*, Riverside County Medical Association, November 1979, 25–27.

32. Contract physicians were not required to take the Civil Service test. Their contracts were subject to a fifteen-day notice of termination, they were paid on a quarterly basis after submitting an invoice to the Indian Office listing the hours worked, and they accrued no government benefits. If a contract physician wanted to go on vacation or was otherwise unable to perform his contractual duties, he was responsible for finding a suitable replacement to provide care to the nonreservation boarding school students or risked having his contract terminated.

33. *Rules for the Indian School Service* (Washington, D.C.: Government Printing Office, 1913), 28.

34. Ibid., sec. 186, p. 29.

35. Ibid., secs. 179–82, p. 28.

36. Dr. W. W. Roblee to Conser, 24 April 1922, NA, PSWR, SI, LR.

37. Conser to CIA, 27 October 1913, NA, PSWR, SI, LS.

38. Conser to CIA, 18 March 1912, NA, PSWR, SI, LS, LPB, 456.

39. Numerous letters voice this complaint throughout the research period. For example, see Hall to CIA, 20 October 1904, NA, PSWR, SI, LS, LPB, 299; and Hall to CIA, 5 October 1908, NA, PSWR, SI, LS, LPB, 484.

40. Conser to CIA, 31 March 1915, NA, PSWR, SI, LS.

41. Conser to CIA, 1 April 1915, NA, PSWR, SI, LS.

42. Roblee to Conser, transmitted to CIA, 31 March 1915, NA, PSWR, SI, LS.

43. During the late nineteenth and early twentieth centuries, a number of different medical ideologies existed that influenced the manner in which a physician practiced medicine. A "regular," or "old school," physician practiced traditional medicine, and most Civil Service physicians followed this theoretical inclination. Another type of relatively common doctor during this period was the homeopathic physician. Homeopathic physicians believed that medicines that cured disease produced similar symptoms in the healthy, so the drugs used were given in extremely small doses. A naturopathic physician, on the other hand, did not use any drugs, but employed natural forces such as heat, light, air, water, and massage to treat patients.

44. Indian Service physicians ordered medicines each year from a supply list that contained approximately two hundred items. The supply list was divided into seven categories: acids, solid and fluid extracts, hypodermic tablets, oils, tablets, tinctures, and miscellaneous medicines. The physicians gave their order to the agent or superintendent, who then forwarded it to the Indian Office, where the orders were authorized by the finance department. The Indian Office advertised for medicines and medical supplies in the spring of each year, and pharmaceutical companies submitted bids to the commissioner of Indian affairs, along with a check for 5 percent of the value of the bid. At each Indian Service warehouse, the commissioner opened the bids in the presence of the Board of Indian Commissioners and the bidders, who were required to display samples of the medicines. Pharmaceutical companies generally had a bid accepted only for items in a particular class on the supply list, such as acids or tablets. Once their bid was accepted, the company was required to package the medicines and supplies separately for each agency or school and

to ship them within ninety days. Since the Indian Office received bids based on large quantities, they were able to keep a tight rein on costs. When individual medicines were purchased on the open market, the fiscal benefits disappeared.

45. Hall to CIA, 29 June 1906, NA, PSWR, SI, LS.

46. Circular No. 1170, 16 August 1916, Circulars, 1904–1934, BIA; Circular No. 1214, 27 October 1916, ibid.; Circular No. 1381, 19 December 1917, ibid.

47. Conser to CIA, 18 December 1916, NA, PSWR, SI, LS.

48. Conser to Drs. Taber and Hebert, 19 September 1911, NA, PSWR, RG 75, SI, LS; Conser to CIA, 19 October 1911, NA, PSWR, SI, LS.

49. Conser to CIA, 26 November 1913, NA, PSWR, SI, LS, LPB, 43–47.

50. Ibid.

51. Ibid.

52. *Sherman Bulletin* 15, no. 12 (24 December 1920): 5. The dentist's name was Dr. Lanahan.

53. Conser to CIA, 16 August 1920, NA, PSWR, SI, LS.

54. Putney, "Fighting the Scourge," 171.

55. Ibid., 172.

56. Salaries ranged from $2,000 per year for the superintendent to $300 per year for the assistant cook and the laundress. Nurses' salaries were in the middle, at $600 per year, the same as for some teachers, the seamstress, the baker, the cook, the dairyman, the shoe and harness maker, and one laborer.

57. Irregular nurses were similar to what are now called per diem nurses. They were hired at a rate of $2.00 per day and accrued no benefits. Irregular nurses generally lived locally and were called upon only in emergencies.

58. Hall to CIA, 23 October 1906, NA, PSWR, SI, LS, LPB, 281. This is but one example. Numerous letters throughout the 1902–7 period contain the same plea.

59. *Sherman Bulletin* 1, no. 2 (11 March 1907): 1.

60. Ibid.

61. "The Hospital Course," *Sherman Bulletin* 1, no. 23 (9 October 1907): 1.

62. Some of the sophisticated classes required of nursing students included the following: "Ethics in nursing"; "Administering medicines by hypodermic injection, injunction, inhalation"; "Anesthetics, antipyretics, antispasmodics, and stimulants"; "Amyl nitrate: How made, physiological action, how administered"; "Anatomy: Description of two forms of bony tissue, structure of bones, how bones are classified, and names of bones of the head"; and "Surgical nursing."

63. Hall to CIA, 15 June 1908, NA, PSWR, SI, LS, LPB, 336–37.

64. Ibid.

65. Ibid.

66. *Sherman Bulletin* 16, no. 18 (2 February 1913): 2.

67. Conser to CIA, 19 June 1917, NA, PSWR, SI, LS. The main problem nursing students at Sherman Institute faced in being admitted to "regular" nurses' training programs was that the school did not offer requisite classes in biology and chemistry. Consequently, students had to transfer from Sherman Institute to a Riverside high school in order to take these classes. Nursing students could take the Civil Service examination and apply for jobs within the Indian Service, but in order to be registered nurses in the State of California, they had to have graduated from a regular training school.

68. During the same period, the largest of theses schools—Haskell Institute—had a student population of approximately three hundred less than did Sherman Institute, while those of the other schools had populations averaging 150 and 500, respectively.

CHAPTER FOUR

1. The data sources utilized included the following: *Descriptive Statement of Pupils at Sherman Institute, 1902–1922* (student registers listing all data for each student, including name, age, sex, tribe, blood quantum, band, permanent residence, parents' names and status, and remarks listing activities such as outing, vacation, illness, death); classified student case files; Riverside County death certificates; *Sherman Bulletin;* monthly, semiannual, and annual reports for Sherman Institute; correspondence from parents, teachers, and students; and official correspondence from and to the commissioner of Indian affairs.

2. In this case, illness is differentiated from disease by level of severity, but primarily by whether it appeared as an epidemic. Illness is generally defined as the state of being sick, an ailment; while disease is defined as a pathological condition of the body that presents a group of symptoms peculiar to it and that sets the condition apart as an abnormal entity differing from other normal or pathological body states (*Taber's Cyclopedic Medical Dictionary* [Philadelphia: F. A. Davis Company, 1973], D-47, I-6). For example, pneumonia caused many deaths, but it is classified as an illness instead of a disease because it did not have a consistent set of conditions (that is, it may have been viral pneumonia or bacterial pneumonia, primary or secondary) and it did not reach epidemic proportions.

3. Hall to CIA, 21 October 1904, NA, PSWR, SI, LS, LPB, 305.

4. Hall to CIA, 14 November 1904, NA, PSWR, SI, LS, LPB, 327.

5. Hall to CIA, 11 October 1906, NA, PSWR, SI, LS, LPB, 265.

6. This figure is based on 365 days. Although the school year lasted only nine months, the fiscal year, for which data is compiled, included twelve months. Children remained in residence throughout the year, albeit in considerably smaller numbers during the summer than during the formal school year.

7. Data derived from September 2000 attendance records for Flora Vista Elementary School in Encinitas, California, a coastal city located in north San Diego County. Enrollment at the school is 544, and includes grades K through 6. The school has a modified traditional school year (August 15 to June 15), which is generally the same as that of Sherman Institute. The school was chosen because it is the school my son attends, and I had access to the data.

CHAPTER FIVE

1. Information regarding the etiology, epidemiology, and pathology of epidemic diseases and of illnesses is primarily compiled from: Mark H. Beers and Robert Berkow, eds., *The Merck Manual of Diagnosis and Therapy* (Whitehouse Station, N.J.: Merck Research Laboratories, 1999). This medical reference book was chosen because it has been the most widely used reference by physicians for the past one hundred years.

2. According to the Microsoft Encarta Online Encyclopedia,

> Smallpox is an acute, highly contagious disease that is often fatal. A small brick-shaped virus named *variola* major causes the disease. The virus is usually transmitted through droplets discharged from the nose and mouth of the infected person and inhaled by another person, although fabric recently contaminated by pus or scabs can also serve as a vehicle for the virus. An exposed person has a 50 percent chance of becoming infected and infection confers immunity. Twenty-five percent of smallpox victims die, many within the first few days of the characteristic rash. A person with smallpox is infectious from about the third day through the erupting stage.
>
> The first stage of the disease occurs after a twelve-day incubation period following infection. This initial phase is marked by high fever, chills, nausea, back and muscle pain, prostration, and sometimes vomiting. Convulsions, delirium, and terrifying dreams also may occur during this period. Between the ninth and twelfth days the fever subsides and the victim feels better temporarily, but soon

flat, reddish spots appear on the face, then arms, chest, back, and legs. During the next six to ten days, the flat spots become raised pimples, then pustules. The return of the fever and related symptoms marks the second stage of smallpox. It is during this time that bacteria may secondarily infect the pustules. As recovery commences, the pustules become crusted, often leaving scars, and the related symptoms finally subside. Death is caused either by secondary bacterial infection or by the smallpox virus attacking the throat, heart, and other internal organs, in which case the victim bleeds to death and organs cease to function.

3. Parker to CIA, 8 May 1909, NA, PSWR, SI, LS, LPB, 180.

4. Tonner to Hall, 23 November 1903, NA, PSWR, SI, LR. Tonner chastised Hall for paying the nurses $6.00 per day because, "there has not been a case throughout the service where nurses have been paid higher than $2.50 per day, even for smallpox, and in most cases $1.50 and $2 has been paid." Hall was further scolded for waiting until 3 November to request authorization for the nurses, when they had been hired on 12 October.

5. Ibid.

6. Conser to CIA Leupp, 12 January 1911, NA, PSWR, SI, LS, LPB, 453.

7. Assistant Commissioner of Indian Affairs E. B. Merritt to Conser, 5 June 1916, NA, PSWR, SI, LR.

8. *Nineteenth Biennial Report of the State Board of Health of California* for the fiscal years from 1 July 1904 to 30 June 1906 (Sacramento: California State Printing Office, 1906), 14.

9. *Eighteenth Biennial Report of the State Board of Health of California* for the fiscal years from 1 July 1902 to 30 June 1904 (Sacramento: California State Printing Office, 1904), 18.

10. Beers and Berkow, *The Merck Manual of Diagnosis and Therapy*, 2320–21. Measles is a highly contagious, acute viral infection characterized by fever, cough, head congestion, conjunctivitis, Koplik's spots on the buccal or labial mucosa, and a spreading maculopapular skin rash. It is caused by a paramyxovirus and spread mainly by droplets from the nose, throat, and mouth of the infected person. The communicable period of the disease begins two to four days before the rash appears and lasts until two to five days after onset. Typically, measles begins after a seven- to fourteen-day incubation period with a low fever, cold, hacking cough, and conjunctivitis. Koplik's spots are evident within two to four days, usually in the buccal mucosa near the first and second upper molars. The characteristic rash appears three to five days after onset of symptoms, beginning in front of and below the ears, then spreading down the sides of the neck, to the trunk, and the extremities. At the peak of the illness, the fever may reach

104°F. Before widespread immunization, measles epidemics occurred every two to three years, with small, localized outbreaks in between. Outbreaks have occurred most commonly in previously immunized adolescents and young adults.

11. "Annual Report of Superintendent, Indian Training School at Springfield, South Dakota, July 23, 1903." *ARCIA*, 1903, 435.

12. Data regarding individual measles victims comes from the *Descriptive Statements of Pupils,* general correspondence, and classified Sherman Institute student cases on file at NA, PSWR.

13. The epidemiological consequences of the European invasion on Native Americans have been referred to as "Virgin Soil Epidemics." For a thorough discussion of this topic, see Alfred W. Crosby Jr., *The Columbian Exchange: Biological and Cultural Consequences of 1492* (Westport, Conn.: Greenwood Press, 1972).

14. Hall to Superintendent W. H. Harrison, Navajo Agency, 16 December 1907, NA, PSWR, SI, LS, 92.

15. Conser to Mr. W. W. McConihe, superintendent, Round Valley School, 19 October 1916, NA, PSWR, SI, LS.

16. Conser to McConihe, 20 October 1916, NA, PSWR, SI, LS.

17. Conser to McConihe, 28 October 1916, NA, PSWR, SI, LS.

18. Ibid.

19. Ibid.

20. Beers and Berkow, *The Merck Manual of Diagnosis and Therapy,* 2330–32. Chickenpox is an acute viral infection caused by the varicella-zoster virus, which also causes herpes zoster. It is spread by infected droplets and is extremely contagious. Early symptoms include mild headache, moderate fever, and malaise within eleven to fifteen days after exposure. Within approximately two days a rash erupts, which evolves within a few hours to the characteristic itchy, teardrop vesicles containing clear liquid and standing out from the skin. The acute phase of the disease lasts four to seven days, and treatment is symptomatic. Epidemics occur in winter and early spring in three- to four-year cycles. Infection does not convey permanent immunity, but subsequent bouts are usually so mild as to be without noticeable symptoms. Chickenpox was not recognized as being different than smallpox until the later nineteenth century.

21. Beers and Berkow, *The Merck Manual of Diagnosis and Therapy,* 2303–6. Diphtheria is an acute bacterial disease that usually affects the tonsils, throat, nose, and skin. The disease is transmitted through direct contact with discharge from an infected person's nose, throat, skin, eyes, or lesions. One type of diphtheria involves the throat and nose and another

type involves the skin. Symptoms usually occur within two to four days after infection and include sore throat, low-grade fever, and enlarged neck lymph nodes; skin lesions are painful, red, and swollen. A person with diphtheria remains contagious for up to two weeks, but seldom more than four weeks.

The vaccine for diphtheria is now combined with tetanus and pertussis vaccine to form the DPT vaccination, but during the research period, the diphtheria antitoxin was given alone.

22. Hall to CIA, 25 June 1907, NA, PSWR, SI, LS.

23. Conser to CIA, 7 November 1910, NA, PSWR, SI, LS.

24. Conser to CIA, 19 November 1921, NA, PSWR, SI, LS.

25. Jean A. Keller, "In the Fall of the Year We Were Troubled with Some Sickness," in *Medicine Ways: Disease, Health, and Survival Among Native Americans,* ed. Clifford E. Trafzer and Diane Weiner (Walnut Creek, Calif.: Alta Mira Press, 2001), 32–51.

26. Beers and Berkow, *The Merck Manual of Diagnosis and Therapy,* 1161–63. Typhoid fever is a bacterial infection caused by salmonella typhi. It is spread via contaminated food and water supplies. Following ingestion, the bacteria spread from the gastrointestinal tract to the lymphatic system, liver, and spleen, where they multiply. Salmonella can also directly infect the gallbladder and seed other areas of the body via the bloodstream. Common early symptoms include fever, malaise, and abdominal pain. Diarrhea eventually develops, along with weakness, fatigue, delirium, and obtundation. A rose-colored rash consisting of flattened spots about one-quarter inch across appears on the chest and abdomen. Complications include intestinal hemorrhaging, intestinal perforation, kidney failure, and peritonitis. Treatment includes intravenous hydration and antibiotics, with the illness usually being resolved in two to four weeks. Cases in children are usually milder than in adults. During the nineteenth and early twentieth centuries, the usual mode of transmission was through well water that had been contaminated by "discharges from the bowels" of a carrier—a person with the bacteria already in his or her system. From the privy, fecal material traveled into a cesspool, then into a well through the soil, and infected the drinking water. Milk was a relatively common mode of typhoid transmission during this period because it was often mixed with contaminated water. Flies could also transmit typhoid fever by carrying germs from a carrier's fecal matter to others upon whom they landed.

27. "Report of School at Riverside, California, August 31, 1905," *ARCIA,* 1905 (Washington, D.C.: Government Printing Office, 1906), 416.

Regarding student health, Superintendent Harwood Hall states, "The general health of the pupils has been good, although in the fall of the year we were troubled with some sickness. We have been handicapped, however, owing to the fact of not having our hospital completed. It is now finished and in use." Neither the seven deaths from typhoid fever nor the additional four deaths that had occurred earlier in the year were noted, nor was the fact that at least thirty-five other children had been stricken by typhoid fever.

28. Dr. A. S. Parker to Harwood Hall, 7 December 1904, NA, PSWR, SI, LS, LPB, 358. Transmitted to the commissioner of Indian affairs by Harwood Hall on 8 December 1904, SI, LS, LPB, 359.

29. Ibid.

30. Ibid.

31. Report of Parker summarized in Acting CIA C. F. Larrabee to Conser, 11 April 1905, NA, PSWR, SI, LR.

32. Ibid.

33. Raymond Powett, a twenty-year-old Mission Indian from Cahuilla, California, died of typhoid fever on 2 November 1911. Jose Leonard, a twenty-one-year-old Papago Indian from Indian Oasis, Arizona, died of typhoid fever while at home in 1914. Although Powett's was the only death attributed directly to typhoid fever at Sherman Institute, between 1904 and 1922 four other students developed typhoid fever but died of secondary infections, either pneumonia or tuberculosis.

34. Hall to Mr. John Couts, Valley Center, California, 28 October 1904, NA, PSWR, SI, LS, LPB, 71

35. *Riverside General Hospital Book of Admissions, 1904.* On file at Riverside General Hospital University Medical Center Archives, Moreno Valley, California.

36. According to Sherman Institute's 1904 cash ledger book, during the period of the epidemic, five "irregular nurses" were hired at $3.60 per day to work at the school for varying numbers of days. None of these women were listed in the Riverside City Directory, so it may be that they were hired from out of the area.

37. Hall to CIA, 5 December 1904, NA, PSWR, SI, LS, LPB, 354. No indication was found in any of the correspondence as to why Hall—or Parker—chose to keep the children at Sherman Institute, particularly when so many were critically ill and the regular nursing staff was apparently not trained in dealing with typhoid fever.

38. NA, PSWR, SI, LS, LPB, 299–300. In a transmittal of cash vouchers from Hall to the commissioner of Indian affairs dated 20 October 1904, Hall

states that the supply of various medicines was exhausted and in order to prevent disease and save lives it became necessary to purchase some (Voucher 49: $21.45 to Boyd Keith for medicines and empty barrels) and later, that since there were no medicines on hand as needed for the sick, they were purchased (Voucher 63: $4.10 to Chas. E. Weck). However, records of these purchases were not found in the cash ledger book at Sherman Institute.

39. Alfred W. Crosby, *The Forgotten Pandemic: The Influenza of 1918* (Cambridge: Cambridge University Press, 1989); Wayne Biddle, *A Field Guide to Germs* (New York: Anchor Books, 1995). Spanish Influenza originated in Tibet in 1917, and then spread across Europe via the armies of various nations. It was named Spanish Influenza because the Spanish press was the first to fully document the illness. Influenza is a virus that spreads from one person to another in droplets sprayed from coughs and sneezes or through contamination of the hand through contact with secretions that cause the disease. The first symptoms of the disease are high fever, shivers, coughs, muscular pain, and sore throat. This is followed shortly by fatigue and dizzy spells and a loss of strength to the point of not being able to eat or drink without assistance. The victim then experiences difficulty breathing. Many cases of Spanish Influenza proved fatal. An unusual aspect of Spanish Influenza was that instead of attacking those with weak immune systems, it attacked the young and healthy members of society.

In all, the virus, which killed about 21 million, infected approximately 525 million people throughout the world. That was more than twice the number who had been killed in WWI. Over a quarter of all Americans were infected by the virus, with 33,000 dying in New York City alone. Almost as quickly as Spanish Influenza appeared, it disappeared, briefly reappearing in March 1919.

40. Ibid.

41. "Spanish Influenza at Sherman Institute," *Arlington Times,* 11 October 1918, 1.

42. Kevin Akin, *A Centennial History of Riverside General Hospital* (Riverside, Calif.: Riverside General Hospital, 1993), 53.

43. Conser to CIA, 25 October 1918, NA, PSWR, SI, LS.

44. Ibid.

45. Diane Therese Putney, "Fighting the Scourge: American Indian Morbidity and Federal Indian Policy, 1897–1928" (Ph.D. diss., Marquette University, 1980), 208–9.

46. Hall to CIA, 27 September 1904, NA, PSWR, SI, LS, LPB, 275.

47. *Sherman Bulletin* 1, no. 22 (2 October 1907): 3.

48. *Sherman Bulletin* 1, no. 31 (4 December 1907): 3.

49. Hall to Supt. J. B. Alexander, Sacaton, Arizona, 30 November 1907, NA, PSWR, SI, TS, LPB, 174.

50. Conser to Mr. C. R. Jeffris, supt. Western Navajo School, Tuba, Arizona, 6 December 1911, NA, PSWR, SI, LS, LPB, 489.

51. Conser to Jeffris, 7 December 1911, NA, PSWR, SI, LS, LPB, 8–9.

52. Conser to CIA, 19 May 1915, NA, PSWR, SI, LS.

53. Depositions from Shay Etsitty, Antonio Chico, Mark Blackwater, and Charlie Goode, 19 May 1915, NA, PSWR, SI.

54. Conser to CIA, 12 October 1915, NA, PSWR, SI, LS.

55. Jose Lewis (Pozo Verde, Sasabe, Arizona) to Conser, 8 January 1916, NA, PSWR, SI, LR.

56. Conser to CIA, 2 July 1919, NA, PSWR, SI, LS.

57. Conser to CIA, 28 June 1920, NA, PSWR, SI, LS.

58. Ibid.

59. Conser to CIA, 11 July 1921, NA, PSWR, SI, LS.

60. Beers and Berkow, *The Merck Manual of Diagnosis and Therapy*, 806–7. Scabies is caused by the mite *Sarcoptes scabei*. The infected female mite tunnels into the outer layer of the skin and deposits her eggs along the burrow. The larvae hatch within a few days and create intense itching and secondary infection. Scabies is readily transmitted, often throughout an entire household, usually by skin-to-skin contact with the infected person. It is also spread to a lesser degree by contact with clothing or bedding. A person might have hundreds of itching papules, or as few as ten. Diagnosis requires demonstration of a burrow, which may be difficult, with subsequent microscopic examination of scrapings from its surface. The current preferred treatment is permethrin cream 5 percent, but historically scabies was treated with a 5–10 percent sulfur ointment. Extensive cleaning or fumigating of clothing is unwarranted because the scabies mite does not live long off the human body.

61. Hall to Mr. Oma Bates, farmer, 9 December 1904, NA, PSWR, SI, LS, LPB, 183.

62. Parker to Dr. J. A. Murphy, medical inspector, 8 May 1909, NA, PSWR, SI, LS, LPB, 181.

63. Conser to CIA, 10 September 1909, NA, PSWR, SI, LS, LPB, 349.

64. Beers and Berkow, *The Merck Manual of Diagnosis and Therapy*, 1431–39. Spinal meningitis (meningococcal meningitis) is a severe bacterial infection of the bloodstream and meninges (a thin lining covering the brain and spinal cord). It is a relatively rare disease and usually occurs as a single isolated event. The meningococcal germ is spread by direct contact

with nose or throat discharges from an infected person. Although many people exposed to the germ do not become seriously ill, some may develop fever, headache, vomiting, stiff neck, and a rash. Up to 25 percent of patients who recover have permanent damage to the nervous system. The disease is occasionally fatal. It is now treated with certain antibiotics, but at the time Sherman Institute experienced the disease, there was no effective treatment.

65. M. A. Jamison to Conser, 23 February 1916, NA, PSWR, SI, LR and TR.

66. Jamison family to Conser, 23 February 1916, NA, PSWR, SI, LR.

67. Henry Jamison to Conser, 11 March 1916, NA, PSWR, SI, LR.

68. Ibid.

69. Ibid.

70. Ibid.

71. Beers and Berkow, *The Merck Manual of Diagnosis and Therapy,* 601–16. Pneumonia may be caused by a variety of microorganisms, but infection by the pneumococcus bacteria is most common. Pneumonia may affect an entire lobe, a segment of a lobe, alveoli contiguous to bronchi, or interstitial tissue. The usual mechanism of spread is inhalation of droplets small enough to reach the alveoli and aspirating secretions from the upper airways. Typical symptoms include cough, fever, and sputum production, usually developing over a period of days and accompanied by pleurisy. Diagnosis is based on symptoms combined with X-rays. Current treatment consists of respiratory treatment with oxygen plus antibiotics.

72. Parker to Dr. J. A. Murphy, medical inspector, 8 May 1909, NA, PSWR, SI, LS, LPB, 180–81.

73. Ibid.

74. Beers and Berkow, *The Merck Manual of Diagnosis and Therapy,* 1875–77. Acute nephritis is a syndrome of acute renal failure principally affecting tubules and interstitial tissue with diverse causes. The most common cause is toxicity from hypersensitivity to drug therapy, such as that using semi-synthetic penicillins, sulfonamides, Rifampin, diuretics, Allopurinol, Azathioprine, Antipyrine, anticonvulsants, gold, and Phenylbutazone. Acute nephritis may also be caused by either an acute systemic, bacterial, fungal, or viral infection. Fever occurs in most cases and may be accompanied by an urticarial rash. The kidneys usually become large because of interstitial edema. Renal function usually recovers when the offending drug is withdrawn or when the infection is successfully treated. Biopsy is the only definitive diagnostic method.

75. Mrs. J. T. Mitchell, Wilton, Sacramento, California, to Conser, 8 April 1917, NA, PSWR, SI, LR.

76. Conser to Mrs. J. T. Mitchell, Wilton P.O., Sacramento, California, 10 April 1917, NA, PSWR, SI, LS.

77. Conser to Mr. Russell T. Vaughn, day school teacher, Ukiah, California, 13 April 1917, NA, PSWR, SI, LS.

78. Beers and Berkow, *The Merck Manual of Diagnosis and Therapy*, 1216–17. Blastomycosis is a disease caused by the inhalation of mold spores of the Blastomyces dermatitidis, which convert to yeasts and invade the lungs, occasionally spreading hematogenously to the skin or focal sites in other tissues. The endemic area in the United States for blastomycosis extends into the middle Atlantic and southeastern states, the northern Midwest, upstate New York, and southern Canada. Blastomyces dermatitidis grows as a mold at room temperature, and in its natural site is in soil enriched with animal excreta and moist, decaying organic material. It has rarely been found near beaver dams and where farm animals are kept. In disseminated (systemic) blastomycosis, the hematogenous spread may lead to focal infection in skin, prostate, epididymis, testis, kidneys, vertebrae, ends of long bones, subcutaneous tissues, brain, oral or nasal mucosa, thyroid, lymph nodes, bone marrow, and other tissues.

79. Harriet Sullivan, nurse, to Conser, 4 December 1913, NA, PSWR, SI, LR.

80. Conser to Mr. Loson L. Odle, supt. Yuma School, Yuma, Arizona, 2 February 1914, NA, PSWR, SI, LS.

81. Beers and Berkow, *The Merck Manual of Diagnosis and Therapy*, 1216.

82. Hall to Mr. John Brown, San Bernardino, California, 5 March 1908, NA, PSWR, SI, LS.

83. Conser to CIA, 19 July 1909, NA, PSWR, SI, LS, LPB, 285.

84. Ibid.

85. Aleŝ Hrdliĉka, *Tuberculosis Among Certain Indian Tribes*, Smithsonian Institution Bureau of Ethnology Bulletin 42 (Washington D.C.: Government Printing Office, 1909), 32.

86. Beers and Berkow, *The Merck Manual of Diagnosis and Therapy*, 2422.

CHAPTER SIX

1. Ann F. Ramenofsky, *Vectors of Death: The Archaeology of European Contact* (Albuquerque: University of New Mexico Press, 1987), 142–44.

2. Katherine Ott, *Fevered Lives: Tuberculosis in American Culture since 1870* (Cambridge: Harvard University Press, 1996), 1–8. The introduction to this comprehensive history of tuberculosis in America provides a succinct explanation of the disease.

3. Mark H. Beers and Robert Berkow, eds., *The Merck Manual of Diagnosis and*

Therapy (Whitehouse Station, N.J.: Merck Research Laboratories, 1999), 1193.

4. Ibid., 1194.

5. Other filth diseases include dysentery, typhus, typhoid fever, and cholera.

6. Aleŝ Hrdliĉka, *Tuberculosis among Certain Indian Tribes,* Smithsonian Institution Bureau of Ethnology Bulletin 42 (Washington D.C.: Government Printing Office, 1909), 30.

7. Ibid.

8. Diane Therese Putney, "Fighting the Scourge: American Indian Morbidity and Federal Indian Policy, 1897–1928" (Ph.D. Diss., Marquette University, 1980), 23.

9. Ott, *Fevered Lives,* 101–2.

10. Ibid., 102. Interestingly, the incidence of tuberculosis was actually the lowest among Native American communities, such as Hopi and Navajo, that had the least contact with whites and were therefore considered the least "civilized."

11. Ibid., 102.

12. Putney, "Fighting the Scourge," 5.

13. *Course of Study for the Indian Schools of the United States* (Washington, D.C.: Government Printing Office, 1901), 203.

14. Ibid.

15. Ibid.

16. CIA to secretary of the interior, 12 July 1901, LS, Education, BIA.

17. Putney, "Fighting the Scourge," 41–42.

18. "Brief of Replies to Education Circular No. 99," Briefs of Investigations, 1899–1901, 1:433–37, Records of the Education Division, BIA.

19. During the late nineteenth and early twentieth centuries, expectoration in public was common in both urban and rural settings. This was not a trait exclusive to Native Americans, although as noted by Hrdliĉka in 1908, expectoration inside Indian houses on reservations was a common practice. Anti-spitting ordinances were controversial, despite the fact that most people believed tuberculosis was caused by sputum drying, and then flying into the air, carrying tuberculosis bacilli, which was then inhaled by anyone in the vicinity of the expectorator. At boarding schools in particular, care was taken to keep sputum moist by filling cuspidors with liquid disinfectant, or by covering jars into which students expectorated.

20. Hall to CIA, 17 May 1904, NA, PSWR, SI, LS, LPB, 49.

21. Hall to CIA, 9 April 1904, NA, PSWR, SI, LS, LPB, 436.

22. Hall to Dixie R. Johnson, Con Cow P.O., Butte Co., California, 9 May 1904, NA, PSWR, SI, LS, LPB, 21.

23. Edward Davis, "The Tragedy of the Boarding School," unpublished article, San Diego Historical Society Research Archives. Davis, a white man who lived on the Mesa Grande Reservation for many years and was an honorary elder, wrote this journal entry in response to the deaths of many Mesa Grande children due to tuberculosis after being sent to nonreservation boarding schools. The quotation is from his translation of the story told in Spanish by the girls' father, Francisco Beltrans. While most of Davis's narrative is probably true, his translation of the father's story was undoubtedly colored by the fact that he had been present at the death of Flavia Ruiz a few days before writing the article. Though intended for publication, Davis never completed the article, but instead may have used its writing as an outlet for his grief.

24. Since Davis's intent was that the article be published as a protest against Indian children being sent to nonreservation boarding schools, it may be that he took some dramatic license with the facts in order to more effectively make his point.

25. *Descriptive Statements of Pupils Attending Sherman Institute for the School Year, 1902–03.* SIMA.

26. Hrdlička, *Tuberculosis among Certain Indian Tribes,* 4.

27. Francis E. Leupp, *The Indian and His Problem* (New York: Charles Scribner's Sons, 1910), 356.

28. *ARCIA,* 1908, 26.

29. Putney, "Fighting the Scourge," 106.

30. *ARCIA,* 1912, 23

31. The Sherman Institute students with the highest Tuberculosis Essay contest scores (out of a possible 100 points) are as follows: Elinor Eades, 86; Dorothy Allen, 88; Belle Hildebrand, 86; Luella George, 80; Susan Hildebrand, 93; Enna Ruiz, 92; Edith Leary, 86; Harry Clark, 85; Juana Moro, 83; Perrot Howard, 88; Ima Green, 85; and Rose Montoya, 87. *Sherman Bulletin* 6, no. 18 (1 May 1912): 3.

32. Lewis Meriam, *The Problem of Indian Administration* (Baltimore: Johns Hopkins University Press, 1928), 324.

33. Marie Agnes Castro (Klamath), "Care of Milk," *Sherman Bulletin* 5, no. 11 (15 March 1911): 4.

34. Putney, "Fighting the Scourge," 109.

35. Conser to CIA, 2 December 1916, NA, PSW, SI, LS.

36. Conser to CIA, 23 March 1917, NA, PSWR, SI, TS.

37. Putney, "Fighting the Scourge," 109.

38. Hrdlička, *Tuberculosis among Certain Indian Tribes,* 6–7.

39. Ibid., 4–6.

40. Data supporting this premise have not yet been discovered. However, the same phenomenon was discussed at length, albeit regarding trachoma, in the 1912 Public Health Services report. Students from areas with historically low trachoma morbidity were exposed to the disease upon entering nonreservation boarding schools and coming into contact with children from high-risk populations. When they returned home, they effectively introduced the disease to an area previously free of the disease.

41. Hrdlička, *Tuberculosis among Certain Indian Tribes*, 26.

42. Ott, *Fevered Lives*, 21.

43. Ibid.

44. *Taber's Cyclopedic Medical Dictionary* (Philadelphia, Penn.: F. A. Davis Company, 1973), V-33.

45. The only known case of Von Pirquet tuberculin testing being used on a large scale to diagnose tuberculosis among Indian children was during the 1912 Public Health Services study. The test results revealed that many more students had been exposed to tuberculosis than had developed active cases of the disease. The report concluded, "These very valuable observations support the contention that the Indian is not peculiarly susceptible per se to tuberculosis, but that the great prevalence of this disease among them is due largely to their social habits and unsanitary surroundings." (*Contagious and Infectious Diseases among the Indians*, 40–49, 77).

46. Ott, *Fevered Lives*, 93–94.

47. Beers and Berkow, *The Merck Manual of Diagnosis and Therapy*, 1203–4.

48. Ibid., 1202.

49. Ibid., 1203.

50. While not every medical text was perused to make this conclusion, *The Merck Manual of Diagnosis and Treatment* has been a standard medical reference for over one hundred years, and tuberculous laryngitis is not listed as one of the many types of tuberculosis.

51. Correspondence and records documenting this are contained within the student case file of George Lawrence. NA, PSWR, CSF.

52. It is interesting that Phoenix Indian School and Sherman Institute both had a large number of Navajo students, but they had very different tuberculosis morbidity rates.

53. *ARCIA*, 1912, 17–18.

54. Ibid., 17.

55. *Twenty-first Biennial Report of the State Board of Health of California* for the fiscal years from July 1, 1908 to June 30, 1910 (Sacramento: State Printing Office, 1910), 95. This data represents the only available data regarding white populations that is of a similar temporal period to the Indian data of 1911–12.

CHAPTER SEVEN

1. Gary E. Moulton, ed., *The Journal of the Lewis & Clark Expedition, March 23–June 9, 1806, Volume 7* (Lincoln: University of Nebraska Press, 1991), 85–86 (6 April 1806, Meriwether Lewis).
2. Ibid.
3. Mark H. Beers and Robert Berkow, eds., *The Merck Manual of Diagnosis and Therapy* (Whitehouse Station, N.J.: Merck Research Laboratories, 1999), 715–16.
4. Entropion is the inward curling of the eyelid and lashes, especially the lower lid, resulting in the lid and lashes continuously rubbing against the eye. When lacrimal (tear) ducts become obstructed, they cannot secrete tears, adversely impacting the eyes' cleansing and lubricating capabilities.
5. "Vaccine Treatment of Secondary Infections of Trachoma," *Journal of the American Medical Association* 99, no. 20 (12 November 1932): 1704.
6. *Course of Study for the Indian Schools of the United States* (Washington, D.C.: Government Printing Office, 1901), 201.
7. Ibid.
8. Diane Therese Putney, "Fighting the Scourge: American Indian Morbidity and Federal Indian Policy, 1887–1928" (Ph.D. diss., Marquette University, 1980), 145.
9. Supplemental Circular No. 79, April 10, 1906. Issued by Superintendent of Indian Schools Estelle Reel, approved by Commissioner of Indian Affairs F. E. Leupp. NA, PSWR, SI, LR.
10. Ibid.
11. Hall to Miss Mary A. Israel, 16 February 1907, NA, PSWR, SI, LS, LPB, 129.
12. Ibid.
13. Hall to Mr. Robert Larimer, Sacaton, Arizona, 2 March 1907, NA, PSWR, SI, LS, LPB, 155.
14. Putney, "Fighting the Scourge," 147–48.
15. Conser to CIA, 26 May 1909, NA, PSWR, SI, LS, LPB, 171.
16. Putney, "Fighting the Scourge," 149.
17. U.S. Senate, Subcommittee of the Committee on Indian Affairs, *Hearings, Indian Appropriation Bill, 1913* (Part 1). 62d Cong., 2d sess.,: 32.
18. Conser to CIA, 21 April 1910, NA, PSWR, SI, LS, LPB, 131.
19. Ibid.
20. W. H. Harrison and Daniel W. White, "Management and Treatment of Trachoma among Indians," CF, 21716–1911–734, GS, BIA. In Putney, "Fighting the Scourge," 155.

21. Ibid.

22. L. Webster Fox, *A Practical Treatise on Ophthalmology* (New York: D. Appleton, 1910), 165.

23. For a comprehensive study of the Indian Office's trachoma program after 1924, see Todd Benson, "Blinded with Science: American Indians, the Office of Indian Affairs, and the Federal Campaign against Trachoma, 1924–1927," *American Indian Culture and Research Journal* 23, no. 3 (1999): 119–42.

24. Conser to CIA, 15 September 1910, SIMA.

25. Conser to CIA, 31 March 1915 (Drugs, Ed-Health 22315–15 A J W); Conser to CIA, 1 April 1915; Conser to CIA, 5 June 1915. All NA, PSWR, SI, LS.

26. Harrison and White, "Management and Treatment of Trachoma among Indians," 10–12.

27. Conser to CIA, 1 April 1915, NA, PSWR, SI, LS.

28. Conser to CIA, 31 March 1915 (Drugs, Ed-Health 22315–15 A J W), NA, PSWR, SI, LS.

29. *Regulations of the Indian Office* (Washington, D.C.: Government Printing Office, 1894), 91.

30. Inspection Report, June 30, 1909, CF, 52778–2–09–732, SIMA.

31. Conser to Mrs. Rafeld Valencio, Temecula, California, 3 June 1909, NA, PSWR, SI, CSF.

32. "Contagious and Infectious Diseases among the Indians," *Senate Document No. 1038,* 62d Cong., 3d sess., Serial 6365 (Washington, D.C.: Government Printing Office, 1913).

33. Ibid., 74.

34. Due to the immense geographical extent of the study, the Public Health Service divided the United States into different units, usually delineated by state boundaries, then assigned each to a different research physician, referred to as assistant surgeons (as in assistant surgeon generals). Dr. R. A. Herring was assigned to Southern California, and conducted all of the examinations.

35. "Contagious and Infectious Diseases among the Indians," 32.

36. Ibid., 83–84.

37. The Public Health Service investigations began on 28 September 1912 and were completed by 30 December 1912. Since different physicians conducted examinations there is a distinct possibility that diagnostic techniques and results varied by individual.

38. *ARCIA,* 1916, 4.

39. Though many years' data would have been equally illustrative, the

1911–12 school year was chosen for the following reasons: (1) this year was also used in chapters 4 and 5; (2) it marked the middle of the research period; (3) it was the first full year after the Indian Office began requiring regular trachoma reporting on standardized forms; and (4) it represents the period prior to the reforms of the 1920s.

40. William Campbell Posey, "Trachoma among the Indians of the Southwest," *Journal of the American Medical Association* 88, no. 21 (21 May 1922): 1618–19.

CONCLUSION

1. Circular No. 102, 21 September 1903, NA, PSWR, SI, LR.
2. Lewis Meriam, *The Problem of Indian Administration* (Baltimore: Johns Hopkins University Press, 1928).
3. Hall to Dr. A. S. Parker, 30 January 1903. SIMA, LPB: 313.

   > I am in receipt of communication from Day school teachers, parents, superin-
   > tendents and friends of pupils nearly every day enquiring (*sic*) as to the health
   > of some pupil that is or has been sick. As soon as a child gets sick said child, if
   > able, if not a friend, writes home, and then I am besieged with letters, or if the
   > child lives near enough, parents visit the school immediately. You will see it is
   > necessary that I keep in close touch with the condition of sick ones.

4. Joseph L. Wellington to Conser, 20 May 1912, NA, PSWR, SI, LR.
5. Conser to Mr. V. L. Clardy, clerk and special district agent, Round Valley, 17 June 1909 NA, PSWR, SI, LS, LPB, 388.
6. Sara L. Patton to Conser, 7 September 1911, NA, PSWR, SI, LR.
7. Hall to Mr. Fred Long, Sacaton, Arizona, 8 July 1904, NA, PSWR, SI, LS, LPB, 254.
8. Michael C. Coleman, *American Indian Children at School, 1850–1930* (Jackson: University Press of Mississippi, 1993), 163–64.

Bibliography

GOVERNMENT DOCUMENTS

Annual Report of the Commissioner of Indian Affairs. Washington, D.C.: Government Printing Office, 1891, 1897, 1898, 1899, and 1900–22.

Biennial Reports of the California State Board of Health. Sacramento, Calif.: State Printing Office, 1900–22.

"Contagious and Infectious Diseases among the Indians." Senate Document no. 1038, 62nd cong., 3d sess., serial 6365. Washington D.C.: Government Printing Office, 1913.

County of Riverside Death Certificates. Moreno Valley, Calif.: County of Riverside Office of the Recorder.

Course of Study for the Indian Schools of the United States. Washington, D.C.: Government Printing Office, 1901.

Hailmann, W. N. Circular Letter of Instruction. Washington, D.C.: Government Printing Office, 1895.

Leupp, Francis E. "Fighting Tuberculosis Among the Indians," *Southern Workman,* November 1908: 588. Records of the Board of Commissioners Reference Material, Health, BIA.

Manual of Sherman Institute. Riverside, Calif.: Institute Press, 1912.

Regulations of the Indian Office. Washington, D.C.: Government Printing Office, 1894.

Rules for Indian Service Schools. Washington, D.C.: Government Printing Office, 1913.

U.S. Senate Subcommittee of the Committee on Indian Affairs, Hearings, Indian Appropriation Bill, 1913 (Part I): 62d Cong., 2d sess.

ARCHIVAL COLLECTIONS

Costo Collection. Thomas Rivera Library, University of California, Riverside, Riverside, California.

Local History Collection. Riverside City and County Library, Riverside, California.

Miller-Hutchinson Collection. Riverside Municipal Museum, Riverside, California.

Perris Indian School Collection. Sherman Indian Museum, Riverside, California.

Records of Mission Agency. Record Group 75. National Archives, Pacific Southwest Region, Laguna Niguel, California.

Records of Sherman Institute. Record Group 75. National Archives, Pacific Southwest Region, Laguna Niguel, California.

Records of Soboba Hospital. Record Group 75. National Archives, Pacific Southwest Region, Laguna Niguel, California.

Riverside County Medical Association. Riverside, California.

Riverside General Hospital Archives. Moreno Valley, California.

Sherman Institute Collection. Sherman Indian Museum, Riverside, California.

Dr. Gerald A. Smith Indian Collection. A. K. Smiley Public Library Special Collections, Redlands, California.

BOOKS AND ARTICLES
Primary Sources

Johnston, Basil H. *Indian School Days.* Norman: University of Oklahoma Press, 1989.

Meriam, Lewis, et al. *The Problem of Indian Administration.* Baltimore: Johns Hopkins University Press, 1928.

Moulton, Gary E., *The Journal of the Lewis and Clark Expedition, March 23–June 9, 1806.* Vol. 7. Lincoln: University of Nebraska Press.

Pratt, Richard Henry. *Battlefield and Classroom: Four Decades with the American Indian, 1867–1904.* Edited by Robert M. Utley. New Haven, Conn.: Yale University Press, 1964.

Qoyawayma, Polingaysi. *No Turning Back: A Hopi Indian Woman's Struggle to Live in Both Worlds.* Albuquerque: University of New Mexico Press, 1992.

Talayesva, Don. *Sun Chief: The Autobiography of a Hopi Indian.* Edited by Leo W. Simmons. New Haven, Conn.: Yale University Press, 1942.

Walsdron, Dr. Martha. "The Indian in Relation to Health." *Sanitarian* 37 (1896): 304–5.

Secondary Sources

Adams, David Wallace. *Education for Extinction: American Indians and the Boarding School Experience, 1875–1928.* Lawrence: University Press of Kansas, 1995.

Akin, Kevin. *A Centennial History of Riverside General Hospital.* Riverside, Calif.: Riverside General Hospital, 1993.

"Ashley S. Parker, M.D., President 1901." *The Bulletin.* Riverside County Medical Association, October 1979.

Beers, Mark H., and Robert Berkow, eds. *The Merck Manual of Diagnosis and Therapy.* Whitehouse Station, N.J.: Merck Research Laboratories, 1999.

Benson, Todd. "Blinded with Science: American Indians, the Office of Indian Affairs, and the Federal Campaign against Trachoma, 1924–1927." *American Indian Culture and Research Journal* 23, no. 3 (1999).

Biddle, Wayne. *A Field Guide to Germs.* New York: Anchor Books, 1995.

Carney, Cary Michael. *Native American Higher Education in the United States.* New Brunswick, N.J.: Transaction Publishers, 1999.

Child, Brenda J. *Boarding School Seasons: American Indian Families, 1900–1940.* Lincoln: University of Nebraska Press, 1998.

Coleman, Michael C. *American Indian Children at School, 1850–1930.* Jackson: University Press of Mississippi, 1993.

Costo, Rupert, and Jeanette Henry Costo. *Natives of the Golden State: The California Indians.* San Francisco: Indian Historian Press, 1995.

Crosby, Alfred W. *The Columbian Exchange, Biological and Cultural Consequences of 1492.* Westport, Conn.: Greenwood Press, 1972.

———. *The Forgotten Pandemic: The Influenza of 1918.* Cambridge: Cambridge University Press, 1989.

Ellis, Clyde. *To Change Them Forever: Indian Education at Rainey Mountain Boarding School, 1893–1920.* Norman: University of Oklahoma Press, 1996.

Fox, L. Webster. *A Parctical Treatise on Opthalmology.* New York: D. Appleton, 1910.

Heizer, Robert F., and Albert B. Elsasser. *The Natural World of the California Indians.* Berkeley: University of California Press, 1980.

Hoxie, Frederick E. *A Final Promise: The Campaign to Assimilate the Indians, 1880–1920.* Cambridge: Cambridge University Press, 1984.

Hrdlička, Aleš. "Tuberculosis Among Certain Tribes of the United States." Smithsonian Institution Bureau of Ethnology Bulletin, 42. Washington, D.C.: Government Printing Office, 1909.

Hurtado, Albert L. *Indian Survival on the California Frontier.* New Haven, Conn.: Yale University Press, 1988.

Hyer, Sally. *One House, One Voice, One Heart: Native American Education at the Santa Fe Indian School.* Santa Fe: University of New Mexico Press, 1990.

Journal of the American Medical Association. "Vaccine Treatment of Secondary Infections and Trachoma" 99, no. 20 (12 November 1932).

Keller, Jean A. "In the Fall of the Year We Were Troubled With Some Sickness," in *Medicine Ways: Disease, Health, and Survival among Native Americans,* ed. Clifford E. Trafzer and Diane Weiner, 32–51. Walnut Creek: Alta Mira Press, 2001.

Kvasnicka, Robert M., and Herman J. Viola, eds. *The Commissioners of Indian Affairs, 1824–1977.* Lincoln: University of Nebraska Press, 1994.

Leupp, Francis E. *The Indian and His Problem.* New York: Charles Scribners Sons, 1910.

Lindsey, Donal F. *Indians at Hampton Institute, 1877–1923.* Urbana: University of Illinois Press, 1995.

Lomawaima, K. Tsianina. *They Called It Prairie Light: The Story of Chilocco Indian School.* Lincoln: University of Nebraska Press, 1994.

McBeth, Sally J. *Ethnic Identity and the Boarding School Experience of West-Central Oklahoma American Indians.* Washington, D.C.: University Press of America, 1983.

McDonnell, Janet A. *The Dispossession of the American Indian, 1887–1934.* Bloomington: Indiana University Press, 1991.

McNeill, William H. *Plagues and Peoples.* New York: Doubleday, 1977.

Mihesuah, Devon A. *Cultivating the Rosebuds: The Education of Women at the Cherokee Female Seminary, 1851–1909.* Urbana: University of Illinois Press, 1993.

Murphy, Joseph F. "The Prevention of Tuberculosis in the Indian Schools." *Journal of Proceedings and Addresses of the National Education Association* (1901): 920.

Ott, Katherine. *Fevered Lives—Tuberculosis in American Culture since 1870.* Cambridge, Mass: Harvard University Press, 1996.

Parker, A. S. "Physician and Surgeon." Advertisement in *Riverside City Directory.* Los Angeles: riverside Directory Co., 1905, p. 206.

Posey, William Campbell. "Trachoma among the Indians of the Southwest." *Journal of the American Medical Association* 88, no. 21 (May 1922): 1618–19.

Prucha, Francis Paul. *The Great Father: The United States Government and the American Indians.* Lincoln: University of Nebraska Press, 1984.

Riney, Scott. *The Rapid City Indian School, 1898–1933.* Norman: University of Oklahoma Press, 1999.

Shipek, Florence C. "History of Southern California Mission Indians." In *Handbook of North American Indians: Volume 8, California.* Washington, D.C.: Smithsonian Institution Press, 1978, 610–18.

Szasz, Margaret. *Education and the American Indian: The Road to Self-Determination since 1928.* Albuquerque: University of New Mexico Press, 1977.

Taber's Cyclopedic Medical Dictionary. Philadelphia: F.A. Davis Company, 1973.

Thornton, Russell. *American Indian Holocaust and Survival.* Norman: University of Oklahoma Press, 1987.

Trafzer, Clifford E. *As Long as the Grass Shall Grow and Rivers Flow.* New York: Harcourt College Publishers, 2000.

Trafzer, Clifford E., and Diane Weiner, eds. *Medicine Ways: Disease, Health, and Survival among Native Americans.* Walnut Creek, Calif.: Alta Mira Press, 2001.

Trennert, Robert A., Jr. "Educating Indian Girls at Nonreservation Boarding Schools, 1878–1920." *Western Historical Quarterly* 13, no. 3 (July 1982): 271–90.

———. *The Phoenix Indian School: Forced Assimilation in Arizona, 1891–1935.* Norman: University of Oklahoma Press, 1988.

"William Wallace Roblee, M.D., President 1905," *The Bulletin.* Riverside County Medical Association (November 1979): 25–27.

DISSERTATIONS AND UNPUBLISHED PAPERS

Adams, David Wallace. "The Federal Indian Boarding School: A Study of Environment and Response, 1879–1918." Ed.D diss., Indiana University, 1975.

Davis, Edward. "The Tragedy of the Boarding School." Unpublished article, San Diego Historical Society Research Archives.

Fischbacher, Theodore. "A Study of the Role of the Federal Government in the Education of the American Indian." Ph.D diss., Arizona State University, 1987.

Putney, Diane Therese. "Fighting the Scourge: American Indian Morbidity and Federal Indian Policy, 1897–1928." Ph.D diss., Marquette University, 1980.

Savani, Sister Kathleen. "The Last Song: History of Sherman Institute, Riverside, California." Unpublished manuscript, 1966. Local History Collection, Riverside City and County Library.

NEWSPAPERS AND NEWSLETTERS

Arlington Times (Arlington, California).
Los Angeles Times (Los Angeles, California).
Riverside Enterprise (Riverside, California).
Riverside Press (Riverside, California).
Sherman Bulletin (Riverside, California).

Index